Learning Embedded Android N Programming

Create the perfectly customized system by unleashing the power of Android OS on your embedded device

Ivan Morgillo

Stefano Viola

BIRMINGHAM - MUMBAI

Learning Embedded Android N Programming

First published: July 2016

Production reference: 1260716

Published by Packt Publishing Ltd.
Livery Place
35 Livery Street
Birmingham B3 2PB, UK.

ISBN 978-1-78528-288-1

www.packtpub.com

Credits

Authors
Ivan Morgillo
Stefano Viola

Reviewer
Andrew Reitz

Commissioning Editor
Nadeem Bagban

Acquisition Editor
Kirk D'costa

Content Development Editor
Sanjeet Rao

Technical Editor
Narsimha Pai

Copy Editors
Dipti Mankame
Laxmi Subramanian

Project Coordinator
Judie Jose

Proofreader
Safis Editing

Indexer
Hemangini Bari

Graphics
Kirk D'penha

Production Coordinator
Shantanu N. Zagade

Cover Work
Shantanu N. Zagade

About the Authors

Ivan Morgillo is a computer engineer, a conference speaker, and a community organizer. He is passionate about programming and embedded systems — from DIY domotics to Android devices.

He is cofounder of Alter Ego Solutions, a mobile development consulting company.

He is also the author of *RxJava Essentials*, by *Packt Publishing* and *Grokking Rx*, by *Manning Publications*.

> I want to thank my sister, Selenia, and my mother for their love and support.

Stefano Viola is an embedded software developer with proved experience with Linux embedded devices and microcontrollers. He is an Android platform expert and application developer. He is passionate about programming and embedded systems, from DIY domotics and robots to customized Android devices.

He is currently working at SECO as an embedded software engineer. He is part of AXIOM project, an R&D project by the European Community, and the UDOO team.

> I want to thank my wife, Carolina, my friend, Antonio, and my family for their love and support.

About the Reviewer

Andrew Reitz is an Android developer by day and an outdoor enthusiast by night. He is a maintainer of the Groovy Android plugin and Android Spock. Besides programming, Andrew likes rock climbing, biking, camping, and hanging out with his dog.

www.PacktPub.com

eBooks, discount offers, and more

Did you know that Packt offers eBook versions of every book published, with PDF and ePub files available? You can upgrade to the eBook version at `www.PacktPub.com` and as a print book customer, you are entitled to a discount on the eBook copy. Get in touch with us at `customercare@packtpub.com` for more details.

At `www.PacktPub.com`, you can also read a collection of free technical articles, sign up for a range of free newsletters and receive exclusive discounts and offers on Packt books and eBooks.

https://www2.packtpub.com/books/subscription/packtlib

Do you need instant solutions to your IT questions? PacktLib is Packt's online digital book library. Here, you can search, access, and read Packt's entire library of books.

Why subscribe?

- Fully searchable across every book published by Packt
- Copy and paste, print, and bookmark content
- On demand and accessible via a web browser

Table of Contents

Preface

Android has caused one of the greatest revolutions of our time. Being present on smartphones, TV, tables, watches, embedded boards, it can be considered ubiquitous. Its open source nature gives companies, expert users, and hackers the opportunity to learn from, improve, and customize the system, creating a tailored version of the most popular mobile operating system.

This book is a journey from the origins of the Android project to what's in the future, walking through all the phases needed to build a custom Android system from source and from binary images.

What this book covers

Chapter 1, Understanding the Architecture, explains the Android hardware and software architecture, the Android Compatibility Definition Document, the Android Compatibility Test Suite, and the Android Runtime.

Chapter 2, Obtaining the Source Code – Structure and Philosophy, explains the Android Open Source Project.

Chapter 3, Set up and Build – the Emulator Way, teaches how to set up the build environment and build a system image for the Android Emulator.

Chapter 4, Moving to Real-World Hardware, tells you about how to build a real device and how to flash the system image.

Chapter 5, Customizing Kernel and Boot Sequence, dives into kernel and boot sequence customization, in order to tailor the perfect system.

Chapter 6, "Cooking" Your First ROM, discusses about custom recovery images, root privileges, and Android Kitchen.

Chapter 7, *Tailoring Your Personal Android System*, discusses hacking the Android framework, adding apps, and optimizing the system.

Chapter 8, *Beyond the Smartphone*, discusses what's next, what the Android possibilities are once you step away from the smartphone world.

More about Android N Programming: In this chapter, you will find some more information about Android N Programming at https://www.packtpub.com/ sites/default/files/downloads/MoreaboutAndroidNProgramming.pdf.

What you need for this book

All you need for the journey is a personal computer, Ubuntu Linux or OS X will do, an Internet connection, and your passion!

Who this book is for

If you are a programmer or embedded systems hacker who wants to customize, build, and deploy your own Android version, then this book is definitely for you.

Conventions

In this book, you will find a number of text styles that distinguish between different kinds of information. Here are some examples of these styles and an explanation of their meaning.

Code words in text, database table names, folder names, filenames, file extensions, pathnames, dummy URLs, user input, and Twitter handles are shown as follows: "We can include other contexts through the use of the `include` directive."

A block of code is set as follows:

```
LOCAL_SRC_FILES:=\
        netcat.c \
        atomicio.c
```

Any command-line input or output is written as follows:

```
$ git add art_new_feature
$ git commit -m "Add new awesome feature to ART"
```

New terms and **important words** are shown in bold. Words that you see on the screen, for example, in menus or dialog boxes, appear in the text like this: "Clicking the **Next** button moves you to the next screen."

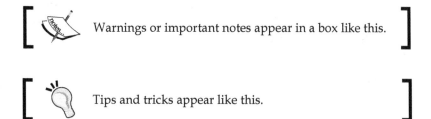

Reader feedback

Feedback from our readers is always welcome. Let us know what you think about this book—what you liked or disliked. Reader feedback is important for us as it helps us develop titles that you will really get the most out of.

To send us general feedback, simply e-mail feedback@packtpub.com, and mention the book's title in the subject of your message.

If there is a topic that you have expertise in and you are interested in either writing or contributing to a book, see our author guide at www.packtpub.com/authors.

Customer support

Now that you are the proud owner of a Packt book, we have a number of things to help you to get the most from your purchase.

Downloading the example code

You can download the example code files for this book from your account at http://www.packtpub.com. If you purchased this book elsewhere, you can visit http://www.packtpub.com/support and register to have the files e-mailed directly to you.

You can download the code files by following these steps:

1. Log in or register to our website using your e-mail address and password.
2. Hover the mouse pointer on the **SUPPORT** tab at the top.
3. Click on **Code Downloads & Errata**.
4. Enter the name of the book in the **Search** box.
5. Select the book for which you're looking to download the code files.
6. Choose from the drop-down menu where you purchased this book from.
7. Click on **Code Download**.

You can also download the code files by clicking on the **Code Files** button on the book's webpage at the Packt Publishing website. This page can be accessed by entering the book's name in the **Search** box. Please note that you need to be logged in to your Packt account.

Once the file is downloaded, please make sure that you unzip or extract the folder using the latest version of:

- WinRAR / 7-Zip for Windows
- Zipeg / iZip / UnRarX for Mac
- 7-Zip / PeaZip for Linux

The code bundle for the book is also hosted on GitHub at `https://github.com/PacktPublishing/Learning-Embedded-Android-N-Programming`. We also have other code bundles from our rich catalog of books and videos available at `https://github.com/PacktPublishing/`. Check them out!

Errata

Although we have taken every care to ensure the accuracy of our content, mistakes do happen. If you find a mistake in one of our books—maybe a mistake in the text or the code—we would be grateful if you could report this to us. By doing so, you can save other readers from frustration and help us improve subsequent versions of this book. If you find any errata, please report them by visiting `http://www.packtpub.com/submit-errata`, selecting your book, clicking on the **Errata Submission Form** link, and entering the details of your errata. Once your errata are verified, your submission will be accepted and the errata will be uploaded to our website or added to any list of existing errata under the Errata section of that title.

To view the previously submitted errata, go to `https://www.packtpub.com/books/content/support` and enter the name of the book in the search field. The required information will appear under the **Errata** section.

Piracy

Piracy of copyrighted material on the Internet is an ongoing problem across all media. At Packt, we take the protection of our copyright and licenses very seriously. If you come across any illegal copies of our works in any form on the Internet, please provide us with the location address or website name immediately so that we can pursue a remedy.

Please contact us at copyright@packtpub.com with a link to the suspected pirated material.

We appreciate your help in protecting our authors and our ability to bring you valuable content.

Questions

If you have a problem with any aspect of this book, you can contact us at questions@packtpub.com, and we will do our best to address the problem.

1
Understanding the Architecture

In this chapter, the user will learn about Android hardware and software architecture. We will provide an overview on the *Android Compatibility Definition Document* to properly understand what we need in order to create a fully compliant and certified device.

The user will learn about the **Android Application Framework (AAF)**, the two different Android runtime systems—Dalvik, and ART, and a collection on Google-provided system libraries.

The user will have a first hands-on moment, setting up and running Android Compatibility Test Suite. We will test together an existing certified device and we will take the first step on the path towards the creation of a certified device.

An overview of the Android system

Android, as with every other operating system, has a layer-based structure. The next image shows a properly abstracted overview of the whole system architecture:

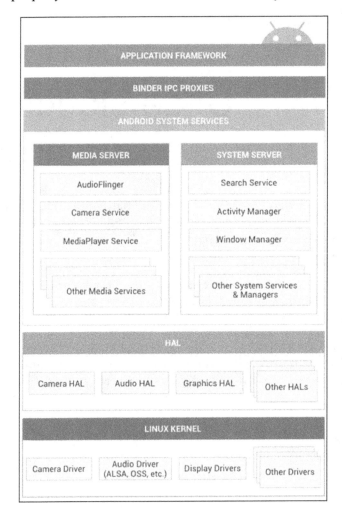

We can divide the system into the following main layers:

- Linux kernel
- Hardware abstraction layer
- Core libraries and runtime environment

- Application framework
- Binder IPC
- Applications

The software layer closest to the hardware architecture is the *Linux kernel*. This layer is in charge of communicating with the hardware components and provides an easy-to-use interface for the layer above.

Moving up on the architecture path, we have Android runtime and core libraries. This layer provides the basics tools for the application framework. The application framework is a collection of **ready-to-use** components that the system provides to the Applications layer via the Android SDK. The top layer contains all those applications we use everyday — games, productivity apps, multimedia, and so on.

Linux kernel

Android is based on the Linux kernel, but it's not a classic Linux-based desktop system: it's not Ubuntu. However, Android architecture designers and developers rely on the Linux kernel, because it's open source, it's extensively tested worldwide, and it can be easily tailored to fit Android-specific hardware needs, on any kind of device.

From a very pragmatic point of view, choosing to base the system on an open source heart reinforced the Android philosophy of being an open system, supported by its community and trusted by enterprise companies, thanks to its transparency. Besides, this approach saved a lot of development time — they didn't have to start from scratch and they could focus on the rest of the architecture, taking advantage of a popular and well-documented core.

The vanilla Linux kernel needed some love to properly fit all the Android requirements. Most of the contributions by Google were focused on:

- Fixing bugs
- Enabling new hardware
- Improving power management
- Improving error reporting
- Improving performance
- Improving security

From a hardware point of view, the Android team made a great effort to add new goodies to the Linux kernel. Lots of fixes and hacks were released to improve Bluetooth support and management, lots of **General Purpose Input/Output (GPIO)** drivers were added, ARM compatibility was enhanced, as ARM was the primary Android-supported architecture and also MMC management received lots of contributions. The new ADB gadget driver was added to help developers to communicate via USB with external devices.

From a memory point of view, the Android team introduced PMEM, the process memory allocator. This gave the ability to manage large physically contiguous memory regions between user space and kernel space. Working in a specific low-resource hardware domain, the Android team released Ashmem, Android Shared Memory, which targeted low-memory devices and provided an easy-to-use file-based API to manage shared memory, especially under memory pressure.

From a power management point of view, the Android team introduced an improved suspend system, wakelocks, and Android Alarm Timers, the kernel implementation to support Android Alarm Manager.

The other interesting contributions were the kernel support for Android logcat command, that provides logs of system messages, application debug messages, and exceptions, and Android Binder, an Android-specific interprocess communication system, used for remote method invocation too.

Hardware abstraction layer – HAL

To overcome the increasing hardware fragmentation, Android engineers created an abstraction layer that allows the system to interact with the hardware just being aware of a specific intercommunication interface. The system completely ignores the low-level implementation of hardware and drivers. This approach enforces the idea of developing software *against an interface* instead of *against an implementation*. With this approach, the Android system does not know and does not need to know how hardware is accessed or managed.

As a mid-level layer between the hardware and the system, Android HAL is commonly developed using native technology – C/C++ and shared libraries. There is no constraint from Google about how we need to implement our HAL and our device drivers: it's up to us to design it as we think best for our scenario. There is only one simple rule:

> *Our implementation must provide the same interface that the system is expecting.*

Libraries and the application framework

Going up on the architecture ladder, we find the two most important software layers. The Android application framework and Android system libraries are the middleware between the bare hardware, managed by the Linux kernel, and all those fancy, shiny apps we have on our smartphones.

Libraries

Android system libraries are a set of libraries, specifically created to work on Android, to allow and help with system components and app development. The most important are:

- **SQLite**: SQLite is the entry point to the SQL world. It's a tiny SQL implementation for embedded systems and it provides a standard way to access data published by content providers or SQL DB created by the user.

- **SSL**: SSL provides the standard security environment for network communication.

- **OpenGL**: OpenGL libraries are the link between the Java (and C/C++ JNI) world and the OpenGL/ES 3D graphics rendering API.

- **SGL**: SGL provides a way to access 2D rendering engine.

- **Media framework**: Media framework provides codecs for rendering, recording, and playback for the most common media formats.

- **WebKit**: WebKit is the popular HTML rendering engine.

- **libc**: The libc library is a BSD-derived implementation of the standard C library, specifically tuned to best perform on embedded Linux-based devices.

- **Surface manager**: Surface manager manages access to the display subsystem.

The application framework

This is the core of the Android software ecosystem. It provides a plethora of managers that facilitate the most common tasks of Android developers and the Android system itself. The most important components of the Application Framework are:

- **Activity manager**: This provides the *navigation backstack* and manages the Android activity lifecycle

- **Resource manager**: This provides access to noncode resources contained in the apps: graphics, localized string, styles, and colors

- **Location manager:** This is in charge of providing the most accurate position information, using data collected by the GPS sensor, from cell towers and Wi-Fi networks nearby

- **Notification manager**: This enables apps to display notification alerts in the status bar, according to Google Design Guidelines, to provide a common and familiar user experience

- **Content providers**: This provides a common approach to share data between different apps, for instance, accessing contacts data or sharing a common data set between two apps

- **Views and widgets**: These comprise the UI core of the Android experience. Buttons, text fields, and layouts are the building blocks of every Android system component and user app

Everything on Android is achieved using the official Android SDK that provides a consistent and documented way to use all these system managers, views, and logic components to let you create the next big hit of the Google Play Store.

Binder IPC

From an Application Framework point of view, the Binder Inter-Process Communication (IPC) is a hidden layer. It takes care of creating a transparent communication channel between the high-level Android API, accessible via the Android SDK, and the actual Android system.

The application layer

All the applications created by third-party entities, such as smartphone manufacturers or Android programmers will be installed on the application layer.

Usually, this relies on a read/write area of the handset solid memory, but for software provided by manufacturers, typically, it uses a read-only memory area to be sure that these applications will always be installed no matter what. Apps such as Google Maps, YouTube, Samsung TouchWiz Nature, and HTC Sense are examples of apps in this very group: they are shipped with the device's operating system, they are installed on a read-only memory area of the device, and they are meant to be uninstallable as a core component of the system.

As we will see, this is not 100% true—once you have the proper skill set, you will be able to manipulate the whole system. In the following chapters, you will acquire these skills and you will learn how to heavily modify an already existing Android version and get rid of those apps, if necessary.

Android compatibility

Every successful Android device on the market, before being launched, has been certified. Manufacturers have designed, developed, and tested their device according to precise guidelines, rules, and constraints.

To make the task as easy as possible, Google has created the Android Compatibility Program that defines details and tools that help OEMs to create a device that will properly support the OS, the SDK, and the developers' expectations:

> *"To run Android apps on a variety of Android devices."*

As a manufacturer, creating and distributing a certified device has critical importance. Our goal is to create a device with a unique, but at the same time familiar, user experience: we have to be cool, but not weird! Users want to customize their Android device and they want to be sure that their favorite apps will run smoothly, without problems of any sort. Developers want to be sure that they won't waste time fixing bugs on every different smartphone, tablet, or TV — they want a common ecosystem on which they can rely.

A well-defined and well-supported ecosystem brings more certified devices that bring more and more developers that bring more and more happy users. The following diagram shows exactly how the Android ecosystem lives thanks to the constant creation of well-designed, well-produced, certified devices:

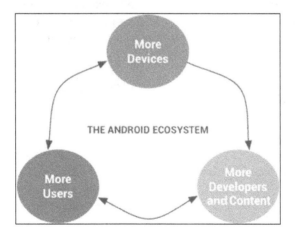

The Android Compatibility Definition Document

The **Android Compatibility Definition Document (CDD)** is Google's way to specify guidelines, rules, and constraints to be considered for an Android-compatible device. Every device designer and manufacturer has to refer to the CDD to be able to easily port Android onto its own hardware platform.

For each release of the Android platform, Google provides a detailed CDD. The CDD represents the *policy* aspect of Android compatibility and its role is to codify and clarify all the requirements and eliminate any ambiguity. The main goal is to provide rules for manufacturers to let them create complex hardware devices, compatible with Android SDK and Android apps.

Designing and developing a new device is no easy task. Even the smallest detail matters. Think about OpenGL support. There is no possible way to be sure that the graphical experience will be great for the user. The only thing that's possible is working according to the guidelines and then "test, test, and test". That's why providing as many details and guidelines as possible is the only way to help the manufactures to achieve their goal.

However, the CDD does not attempt to be comprehensive—it couldn't be. It just serves as guidance to approach as easily as possible the final goal—a compatible device. Further help comes from the source code itself and from the Android SDK API that can be considered a compatibility-proof test bench. Think about CDD as an overview of the minimum set of constraints to be compliant with: it's the very first step of the journey.

Device types

In the beginning, Android was born to run on digital cameras. Luckily for us, a lot has happened since then: smartphones invaded our world! Then we had tablets and MP3 players. Nowadays, we have TVs, watches, media centers, glasses, and even cars, running Android and Android apps. Every device on the market will probably land in one specific category, according to its features. CDD gives a few pointers about which category your new device would be placed in:

- Every device with an embedded touchscreen, a power source that allows mobility, and that can be held in hand can be considered an **Android Handset**.

- An **Android Television device** is a device designed for media content: video, music, TV, games, with users sitting about three meters or ten feet away. This kind of device must have an embedded screen or an output video interface—HDMI, VGA, DVI, or a wireless display port.

- A device designed to be worn on a wrist, with a touchscreen display with a diagonal between 2.79 cm and 6.35 cm is considered an **Android Watch**.

- Having a car with an infotainment system, based on Android, gives us an **Android Automotive implementation**.

Software compatibility

From a software execution point of view, the basic requirement is being capable of executing the Android Dalvik bytecode. Our device must support the *Android Application Programming Interface* and must provide complete implementations of any documented behaviors of any documented API exposed by the Android SDK or annotated with the @SystemAp annotation.

Hardware compatibility is a tricky task, because even if our device is lacking some specific hardware, for instance GPS or accelerometers, our implementation must contain GPS-related code and should be capable of handling inappropriate requests in a reasonable way to avoid crashes or misbehaviors.

One of the main players of software compatibility is the ability of our device to support intents. Every device properly implementing Android API must support Android loose-coupling intent system. Intents allow Android apps to easily request functionality from other Android components and avoid the effort to implement everything from scratch. The Android system has a set of core applications that implement the intent pattern:

- Desk clock
- Browser
- Calendar
- Contacts
- Gallery
- Global Search
- Launcher
- Music
- Settings

As a vendor, we could integrate the default Android components or implement our own component, according to the public API. Those components will have special system permissions to act as system apps and they will be the first proposed choice for the matching intent filter.

For instance, when a developer ask to open a web page, the system will suggest "our browser component" as the first chosen app to perform the task. Of course, being a good citizen means that we must provide a proper settings menu to give the user the possibility to override our default choice and let the final user pick a different app for the task.

Beyond Java

Android applications development is mostly based on Java programming. The SDK is based on Java, the runtime system is fully compliant with Java6, partially with Java7, and Google is already experimenting with Java8. Most developers will easily approach the platform if they already know Java programming language. However, Android offers a lot more to those developers that are dealing with heavy-duty, performance-oriented scenarios: Android Native API.

Native API

Native API gives the developers the opportunity to call native C, and partially C++, code from an Android Java application. Native code is compiled as standard ELF .so files and stored in the app APK file. Being native code, it has to be compiled for every architecture we are going to support, because, contrary to the bytecode, it can't be built once and run on every architecture.

As integrators, we must embrace one or more **Android Application Binary Interfaces** (**ABIs**) and aim for having full compatibility with the Android NDK. Of course, Google provides guidelines and constraints to easily reach this goal. These are the basic rules for proper compatibility:

- Our implementation must include support for code running in the managed environment, that is Java code, to call into native code, using the standard **Java Native Interface** (**JNI**) semantics

- If our implementation supports the 64-bit ABI, we must support its relative 32-bit version, too, because we must provide compatibility to non-64 bit potential devices

- Google suggests that we build our implementation using the source code and header files available in the Android Open Source Project—just don't reinvent the wheel

From a libraries point of view, our implementation must be source-compatible (that is, header compatible) and binary-compatible (for the ABI) with all the following libraries:

- libc (C library)
- libm (math library)
- liblog (Android logging)
- libz (Zlib compression)
- libdl (dynamic linker)
- libGLESv1_CM.so (OpenGL ES 1.x)
- libGLESv2.so (OpenGL ES 2.0)
- libGLESv3.so (OpenGL ES 3.x)
- libEGL.so (native OpenGL surface management)
- libjnigraphics.so, libOpenSLES.so (OpenSL ES 1.0.1 audio support)
- libOpenMAXAL.so (OpenMAX AL 1.0.1 support)
- libandroid.so (native Android activity support)
- libmediandk.so (native media APIs support)

These libraries also provide minimal support for the C++ JNI interface as well as support for OpenGL.

An implementation of each one of these libraries must be present in our system to be compatible with Android NDK. This is a dynamic list and we cannot treat it as a definitive set of libraries: future versions of Android could add new libraries and increase development possibilities and scenarios. That's why native code compatibility is challenging. For this reason, Google strongly suggests to use the implementations of the libraries listed earlier from the Android Open Source Project, taking advantage of the Open Source philosophy of Android and to enjoy well-supported and well-tested source code.

Maintaining 32-bit support

Nowadays, all major manufactures are switching to 64-bit architecture and new ARMv8 architecture deprecates lots of old CPU operations. Unfortunately, the market is still full of 32-bit compatible software and even on 64-bit architecture we must still support these deprecated operations, to avoid scaring developers and losing precious market share. Fortunately, we can choose to make them available via real hardware support or software emulation, at the expense of performance.

Supporting 32-bit architecture can be very tricky. We can just think about one simple scenario, for example, accessing the /proc/cpuinfo file. Legacy versions of the Android NDK used /proc/cpuinfo to discover CPU features. For compatibility with applications built using 32-bit NDK, we must specifically include the following things in /proc/cpuinfo when it is read by 32-bit ARM applications:

- **Features**: This is followed by a list of any optional ARMv7 CPU features supported by the device
- **CPU architecture**: This is followed by an integer describing the device's highest supported ARM architecture (for example, 8 for ARMv8 devices)

The tricky part is that these requirements only apply when /proc/cpuinfo is read by 32-bit ARM applications. The file must be not altered when read by 64-bit ARM or non-ARM applications.

From Dalvik to ART runtime

The original Android runtime implementation was Dalvik. Dalvik was a virtual machine, specifically created for Android, due to the necessity to target low-memory devices. It was an integral part of the system until Android KitKat.

As we already said, Android applications are mostly written in Java. When Dalvik was the in-use runtime system, the Java code was compiled into bytecode. This bytecode was then translated to Dalvik bytecode and finally stored into a .dex (Dalvik Executable). After this procedure, Dalvik was able to run the Android app.

Although Dalvik had been designed for slow devices, with low memory, its performance has never been astonishing, not even when the **Just-In-Time** compilation was introduced, back with Android 2.2 Froyo. Dalvik JIT was supposed to bring a huge performance boost to Android apps and, from some points of view, it did, but with limitations, such as the infamous *maximum methods number*, and the pressure from alternative solutions forced Google to look forward to a new runtime:

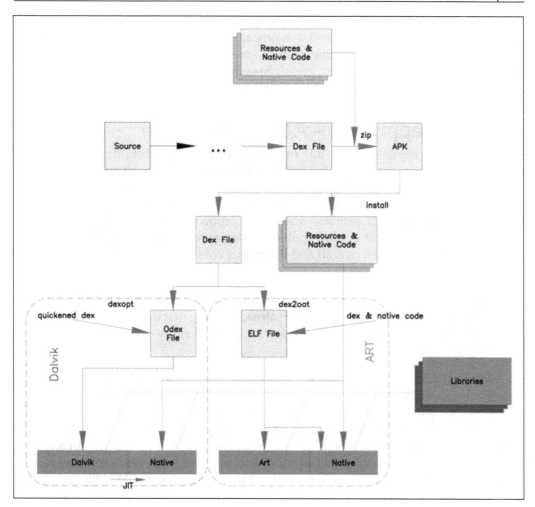

The Android runtime

When Android 4.4 *KitKat* was released, users could select a new experimental runtime environment in the **Settings** menu: ART. Android RunTime or, shortened, ART, is the current default runtime solution that replaced Dalvik from Android 5 *Lollipop*. The previous diagram shows a comparison between Dalvik and ART architecture.

The idea behind Dalvik's JIT (just-in-time) execution was to profile the applications while they were being executed and dynamically compile the most-used segments of the bytecode into native machine code. Native execution of these most-used segments called **traces** would then greatly speed-up the execution of the application even though most of the code would still be interpreted.

A new old approach – AOT compilation

Art re-introduces the concept of AOT (ahead-of-time) compilation. It works as most compilers do, that is, it compiles the whole application code into the native machine code, without interpreting bytecode at all. This takes some time, but it is done only once when the user downloads the app, so considering the time and amount of resources needed for JIT profiling and optimization that are needed on every application start, it is an acceptable trade-off. Also, since the whole application is now compiled, it is quicker overall and the power consumption is reduced, which improves the device autonomy.

ART is the default runtime since Android 5, but Android needs to ensure compatibility with all those apps that are already on the market and all those devices that are running a previous version of Android and won't receive any operating system updates.

For backward compatibility reasons, the input bytecode is the same for ART and Dalvik. The application APK file still contains standard .dex files, but replaces the .odex files (Optimized Dalvik Executables) with the standard Unix ELF files (Executable and Linkable Format). During the installation, ART uses dex2oat utility to compile the bytecode into native code stored in the ELF file. As already mentioned, this step is performed only once and requires fewer resources and less overhead than Dalvik's JIT compilation. The downside is that the APK files are larger because they effectively contain double the code (uncompiled bytecode and compiled executable). After this compilation, the system will run just the ELF executable.

The bottom line is faster apps, but a bit less free space on your smartphone memory.

Garbage collection and other improvements

AOT compilation is not the only improvement that ART brought in. One of the most important features is the improved garbage collection. **Garbage Collection (GC)** is a form of automatic memory management, completely different from the old idea where the developer was the one in charge of allocating memory when needed and freeing it when it was not needed anymore.

The whole philosophy is based on the concept of **Garbage Collector**, an entity that tries to reclaim memory occupied by objects that are not used anymore in the program. It's a well-known tool in the Java world and Android has always suffered from its downside—GC is very slow and blocking.

Android 2.3 introduced the concurrent garbage collector—GC is not blocking the app anymore when it occurs, but there will always be an overall slowdown when it occurs. Finally, ART introduced a few more performance improvements:

- Just one pause for garbage collection instead of Dalvik's two pauses
- GC processing is now parallelized, reducing the duration of the GC pause
- New Rosalloc memory allocator that uses thread-local region allocations for smaller objects and separate locks for bigger objects, instead of a single global lock
- Full garbage collection is run only when the phone is locked so that the user doesn't notice when the GC is run
- There is a compacting GC that reduces memory fragmentation and so diminishes the need to kill other applications just because bigger contiguous memory chunks are needed

From a development and debugging point of view, ART brought in the support for sampling profiler, support for more debugging features, and improved diagnostic details in exceptions and crash reports.

Waiting for Android Nougat

The upcoming version of Android will bring some enhancement to the current ART runtime. Google will introduce a so-called Profile-guided JIT/AOT compilation. JIT stands for Just In Time and looks similar to the old Dalvik approach: a compiler with code profiling capabilities. This JIT compiler will work together with ART and will provide constant performance improvement as it will continuously be profiling code and resource usage.

To improve performance during the installation phase, ART won't pre-compile Ahead-Of-Time the whole app. Instead, thanks to the profiling approach, it will detect hot methods in the app and will only pre-compile them, leaving unused parts of the app uncompiled. This precompilation process is smartly performed when the device is idle and charging, to have the smallest negative impact on the user experience and allow the user to install in instants apps that in Android 6 would take several seconds to be installed.

This whole new approach aims to improve applications and system performance on low end devices, reducing RAM memory footprint, battery draining and increasing runtime performance, for a satisfying Android experience on a wide range of devices.

Meeting the Compatibility Test Suite

We are aware of the CDD and we did our best to create a compatible device. A lot of aspects could still have glitches and we surely want to get rid of them. To make sure that everything works as expected, our Android implementation must be tested with Android Compatibility Test Suite. Android CTS will accompany us throughout the journey to our certified device. We will constantly use it to keep an eye on what is working and what is not working yet.

Every new version of Android platform comes with a new **Compatibility Test Suite (CTS)**. This automated testing suite has two main components:

- Tradefed, that manages text execution from the desktop.
- Test cases executed on the **Device Under Test (DUT)**. These cases are regular JUnit tests written in Java and packaged as Android .apk files so that they can be executed on the target device.

There is also the CTS Verifier, a tool for manual testing that consists of the verifier app that is executed on the device and collects the test results; and other executables or scripts that are executed on the desktop machine in order to provide further data or control for some test cases in the Verifier app.

The following diagram shows the CTS workflow:

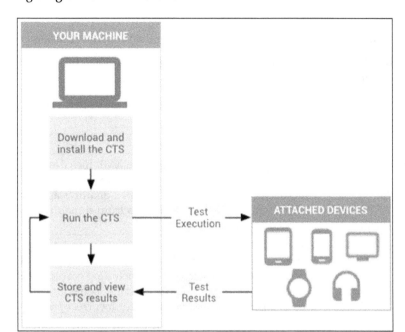

The test suite on your computer will install the test on the device and will launch it. The device will test that particular subset of features and will give the results back to the test suite on your computer. The test suite will store these results, install the next test, and will start the cycle again, until every test is executed.

Currently, the CTS provides two main types of test cases:

- Unit tests
- Functional tests

Unit tests test the smallest logical units of code within the Android platform, for example, a single class, such as `java.util.HashMap`.

Functional tests are used to test a specific function that can consist of numerous API method calls.

Google is planning to provide more tests in the future versions of the test case. A couple of ideas are:

- **Robustness tests**: This tests the system's durability under stress conditions

- **Performance tests**: This tests the system's performance, such as frames per second

The following table shows the areas covered by the Compatibility Test Suite:

Area	Description
Signature tests	For each Android release, there are XML files describing the signatures of all public APIs contained in the release. The CTS contains a utility to check those API signatures against the APIs available on the device. The results from signature checking are recorded in the test result XML file.
Platform API Tests	These tests test the platform (core libraries and Android Application Framework) APIs as documented in the SDK Class Index to ensure API correctness, including correct class, attribute and method signatures, correct method behavior, and negative tests to ensure expected behavior for incorrect parameter handling.
Dalvik Tests	These tests focus on testing the Dalvik Executable Format.
Platform Data Model	The CTS tests the core platform data model as exposed to application developers through Content Providers, as documented in the SDK `android.provider` package: contacts, browser, settings, and so on.
Platform Intents	The CTS tests the core platform intents as documented in the SDK Available Intents.
Platform Permissions	The CTS tests the core platform permissions as documented in the SDK Available Permissions.
Platform Resources	The CTS tests for correct handling of the core platform resource types, as documented in the SDK Available Resource Types. This includes tests for: simple values, drawables, nine-patch, animations, layouts, styles and themes, and loading alternate resources.

CTS setup

Our journey will be very practical and hands-on, that's why in this section we are going to set up Android Compatibility Test Suite to test an existing device. We can't start working on our own Android implementation without knowing what we are going to support and test. To be able to run Android CTS, we will need:

- A computer running Linux or OS X
- *Android SDK*:
  `http://developer.android.com/sdk/installing/index.html`
- *Java SDK 6 or 7*: `http://www.oracle.com/technetwork/java/javase/downloads/index.html`
- *Android CTS*:
  `http://source.android.com/compatibility/downloads.html`
- *Android CTS Media*: `https://dl.google.com/dl/android/cts/android-cts-media-1.1.zip`

There are a lot of files to download. In the meantime, we will set up our device.

Device setup

We are testing an existing device, a smartphone, so we are already satisfying needs such as having a screen and we can move to device software configuration.

Tests should be executed on a *clean* device, so we should run a **Factory Restore** to erase all the data on the smartphone. Be sure of having a backup of your data if you are not using a development device. On Android 4.4 KitKat, you can reach the specific menu by navigating to **Settings | Backup & reset | Factory data reset**.

This will take a while—the device will shut down and the erasing process will start. The procedure will remove every single byte that is not part of the original Android system provided with your device, restoring all the settings and bringing the device to its original setup.

When the device restarts, we need to select `English US` language by navigating to **Settings | Language & input | Language**.

Now we need to turn on the **Location**: We need Wi-Fi and GPS and we need to provide some Internet connectivity. We need to disable any **Screen Lock** by navigating to **Settings | Security | Screen Lock = 'None'**.

We need a few settings from the **Developer options** menu. On a brand new installation of a vanilla Android system this menu is hidden. We can enable using the following steps:

1. Navigate to **Settings | About phone**.
2. Scroll to the bottom.
3. Tap continuously on build number item.
4. You are now a developer!

> If you are working with an HTC, Samsung, or Sony device and its custom version of Android, the previous steps could be a bit different. We leave it as an exercise to find the right navigation path for your non-vanilla Android version.

Once the **Developer options** menu has been enabled, navigate back to the **Settings** screen. In the **Developer options** menu, we need to enable the following:

- USB debugging
- Stay awake
- Allow mock locations

Before running any tests, it's important that the device is on a steady support to avoid triggering accelerometers and the gyroscope. The camera should be pointing to a focusable object. Don't press any buttons or keys during the tests—this could invalidate test results.

Media files setup

To properly run all the tests, we will need a few multimedia files on the device—Android CTS media files. First of all, let's connect the device to the USB. If this is the first time that you connect this device to this host PC, the device will display a dialog to authorize the connection—allow the connection:

Any Android device can communicate with a host PC using Android ADB. This key tool is covered in great detail in the next chapters, so, for now, we can start downloading the latest Android SDK from `https://developer.android.com/studio/index.html#downloads`, according to your platform. Once the download is completed, decompress the file and you will be provided with an `android-sdk` folder, containing a `platform-tools` folder, containing adb executable.

Back to our media files setup now:

1. Open a terminal.

2. Navigate to the downloaded file, for instance:

   ```
   $ cd ~/Downloads
   ```

3. Unzip the file:

   ```
   $ unzip android-cts-media-1.1.zip
   ```

4. Enter the brand new `android-cts-media` folder with:

   ```
   $ cd android-cts-media
   ```

5. This folder contains a file that we must make executable:

   ```
   $ chmod u+x copy_media.sh
   ```

6. Now we are ready to copy all the media files we need onto the device:

   ```
   $ ./copy_media.sh all
   ```

The next screenshot shows the output of the whole procedure:

Run!

Everything is in place now and we can use `cts-tradefed` to run some test plans. Move to the Android CTS folder and run the following command to enter the `cts` console:

```
$ ./tools/cts-tradefed
```

```
● ● ●                          3. bash
[hamen:~/bin/android-cts] $ ./tools/cts-tradefed
Android CTS 4.4_r3
07-25 17:47:09 I/: Detected new device TA9290D3VX
cts-tf > ▮
```

The previous screenshot shows how `cts-tradefed` automatically identifies our connected device and gets ready to test.

CTS console provides a few useful commands:

- `list plans`: This will list all the available test plans in the repository
- `list packages`: This will list all the available test packages in the repository
- `run`: This will allow us to run all the tests we want

Typically, the following test plans are available:

- All CTS tests required for compatibility
- Signature tests the signature verification of all public APIs
- Android tests for the Android APIs
- Java tests for the Java core library
- VM tests for ART or Dalvik
- Performance tests for your implementation

As our first approach to CTS, we are going to run *CTS* plan:

```
cts-tf > run cts --plan CTS --disable-reboot
```

The testing will start immediately and the console will be full of log messages in the blink of an eye, as shown in the following screenshot:

```
                                    3. bash
cts-tf > [hamen:~/bin/android-cts] 7s $ ./tools/cts-tradefed
Android CTS 4.4_r3
07-25 17:55:05 I/: Detected new device TA9290D3VX
cts-tf > run cts --plan CTS --disable-reboot
07-25 17:55:20 I/TestInvocation: Starting invocation for 'cts' on build '4.4_r3' on device TA9290D3VX
07-25 17:55:20 I/TA9290D3VX: Created result dir 2015.07.25_17.55.20
07-25 17:55:53 I/TA9290D3VX: Collecting device info
07-25 17:55:54 I/TA9290D3VX: ------------------------------------------------
07-25 17:55:54 I/TA9290D3VX: Test package android.aadb started
07-25 17:55:54 I/TA9290D3VX: ------------------------------------------------
07-25 17:56:43 I/TA9290D3VX: com.android.cts.aadb.TestDeviceFuncTest#testBugreport PASS
07-25 17:56:43 I/TA9290D3VX: com.android.cts.aadb.TestDeviceFuncTest#testExecuteShellCommand PASS
07-25 17:56:47 I/TA9290D3VX: com.android.cts.aadb.TestDeviceFuncTest#testGetLogcat_size PASS
07-25 17:56:49 I/TA9290D3VX: com.android.cts.aadb.TestDeviceFuncTest#testGetScreenshot PASS
07-25 17:56:49 I/TA9290D3VX: com.android.cts.aadb.TestDeviceFuncTest#testPull_noexist PASS
07-25 17:56:49 I/TA9290D3VX: com.android.cts.aadb.TestDeviceFuncTest#testPushDir PASS
07-25 17:56:49 I/TA9290D3VX: com.android.cts.aadb.TestDeviceFuncTest#testPushPull_extStorageVariable PASS
07-25 17:56:49 I/TA9290D3VX: com.android.cts.aadb.TestDeviceFuncTest#testPushPull_normal PASS
```

Now, grab some coffee or make some good tea: this will take a while. `cts-tradefed` will test everything that is possible to test with an automatic test. Luckily for us, there is a lot that can be tested in this way.

Analyzing the test results

Time has passed, the tea has gone, and the tests are over. On a quad-core smartphone, such as a Motorola Moto G or Nexus 4, this could take up to 10 hours. Eventually, we have got some nice results to check out. According to the folder's path we are working in, we will have results in a `.zip` file in the `cts` folder:

```
$ unzip ~/bin/android-cts/repository/results/START_TIME.zip
```

Unzipping the file, we will find a `testResult.xml` file. Opening this file with a recent web browser (Firefox is working fine here) will show plenty of meaningful tables, with all kind of test and results. The next screenshot shows the initial Test Summary. We have information about the test duration, how many tests were executed, how many tests passed, and how many tests failed:

Test Summary	
CTS version	4.4_r3
Test timeout	600000 ms
Host Info	Error-retrieving-name.local (Mac OS X - 10.10.4)
Plan name	CTS
Start time	Sat Jul 25 17:55:20 CEST 2015
End time	Sun Jul 26 02:53:21 CEST 2015
Tests Passed	24868
Tests Failed	29
Tests Timed out	0
Tests Not Executed	0

As you can see, even testing a certified smartphone, currently on the market, will produce some failed tests. This gives you an idea about the complexity of producing the perfect Android device.

The next screenshot shows Test Summary by Package, specifying the test results one test after the other. For brevity, we are showing just a subset of the results:

Test Summary by Package					
Test Package	Passed	Failed	Timed Out	Not Executed	Total Tests
PairingSetup	0	1	0	0	1
android.aadb	11	0	0	0	11
android.acceleration	6	0	0	0	6
android.accessibility	27	0	0	0	27
android.accessibilityservice	54	0	0	0	54
android.accounts	28	0	0	0	28
android.admin	18	0	0	0	18
android.animation	79	0	0	0	79
android.app	294	0	0	0	294
android.bionic	540	0	0	0	540
android.bluetooth	9	0	0	0	9

The previous Test Summary screenshot shows that 29 tests have failed. If we dig into the test result file, we see that detailed reports are also available. This further information is hugely useful to precisely spot the failed test, like the one in the following screenshot, and investigate the issue:

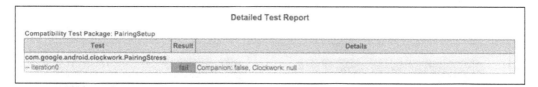

The test result file tries to play polite and, for brevity, does not show the full stacktrace of the failed test. To reach the stack trace of the failure, we must inspect the source code of `testResult.xml`. For every executed test, there is a corresponding `<Test>` tag. For those tests that failed, we will have a `<StackTrace>` tag too. That's what we are looking for!

As a final note, `testResult.xml` contains a huge section with all the information about the device it has been able to retrieve. It's a very large amount of data that, for brevity, we are not reporting here, not even as an example.

Diving deeper with CTS Verifier

We already know that there are lots of APIs and functions that we can automatically test with `cts-tradefed`, but what about all the other APIs and functions that cannot be tested within an automated environment?

CTS Verifier comes in every time an API or a function cannot be tested on a device without manual input. These are scenarios involving audio quality, touchscreen effectiveness, accelerometer precision and reactivity, camera quality, and features that are meant so specifically for human interaction that they are impossible to test without human interaction.

Setup

All we need to run CTS Verifier is an Android certified device and the appropriate CTS Verifier APK file. As we are testing an Android 4.4 device, we need to pay attention to downloading the proper CTS Verifier version. You can download the APK for your Android version and device architecture here: `http://source.android.com/compatibility/downloads.html`.

You just need to unzip the downloaded file and you will find a folder hierarchy and two .apk files. You can install CtsVerifier.apk using ADB:

```
$ adb install -r CtsVerifier.apk
```

The following screenshot shows the properly installed CTS Verified app and the initial screen:

Manual testing

As we know, CTS Verifier contains tests that need manual input to execute, evaluate, pass, or fail. Every test has its own **Info** screen that helps the tester to perform the test. As an example, we will run the **Accelerometer Test**, in the **Sensors** section.

Launching the test, we are welcomed by the info screen, as shown in the following screenshot:

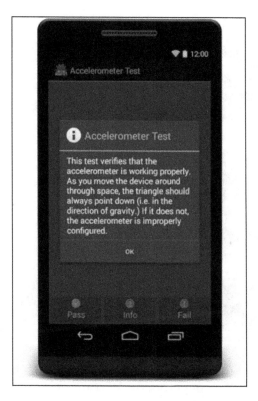

The **Info** button explains how to perform the test and what to evaluate. As we move into the testing, we can evaluate if the accelerometer is working as expected. The following screenshot shows three different moments of the test:

- The smartphone lays on the desk
- The smartphone is held in hand, in portrait mode
- The smartphone is held in hand, in landscape mode

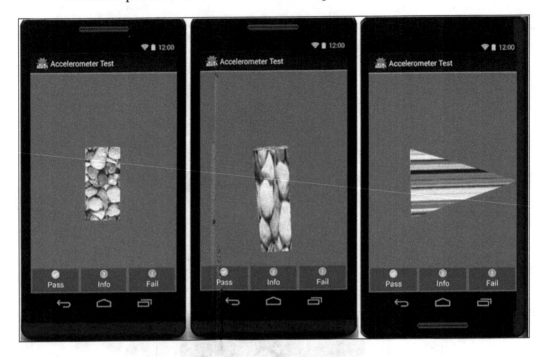

As specified in the **Info** button, the arrow is always pointing in the same direction as the gravity: the sensor is working properly. We can consider that we have passed the test and click on the **Pass** button.

We have passed our first test. CTS Verifier provides dozens of tests and, one by one, we are going to run, verify, and pass them, in the long journey towards our first Android Certified Device.

Retrieving the results

When every test has been executed, we can save the result using the Save icon in the top-right corner of the initial screen, as shown in previous screenshot. The results will be saved on the device and a dialog box will show the precise path, as shown in the following screenshot:

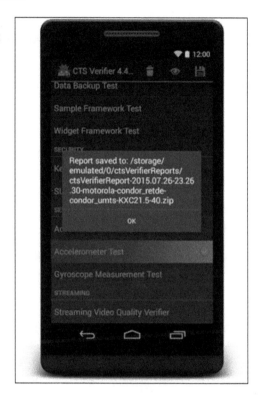

Now, let's open a terminal and copy all the results from the phone to our computer:

```
$ adb pull /mnt/sdcard/ctsVerifierReports/ .
$ unzip *.zip
```

At this point, we have a ctsVerifierReport-[...].xml with all the info about our manually executed tests.

Congratulations! You have fully tested an Android device. Step 0 of our journey is complete.

Summary

In this chapter, we learned what we are going to need to create a certified Android device. We saw the Android Compatibility Definition Document and we learned how to design a system to match the Android architecture. We had an overview of the two different runtime systems: Dalvik and ART and their main differences.

We had a full immersion into Android device testing, we learned how to run CTS automated tests and CTS manual tests on a already certified device.

The next chapter will be very *hands-on*. We will learn how to retrieve Android source code and we will understand the code structure and organization.

2
Obtaining the Source Code – Structure and Philosophy

In the previous chapter, we had an overview about the system layer-based architecture and we had our first hands-on experience, testing a real-world device using CTS tools suite.

In this chapter, the user will learn about the philosophy behind the Android and Google development model. We will show how the source code is organized, which are the main branches, and what the workflow is. We will create a step-by-step journey to retrieve the **Android Open Source Project** (**AOSP**) source code and prepare the environment by installing all the required tools.

The user will learn how to contribute to the Android Open Source Project, how to use tools such as git, the version-control system, and, repo, the repository manager.

To complete the chapter, we will dig into the AOSP folder structure, analyzing the most important components that create the most popular mobile operating systems of the world.

The Android philosophy

Android is an open source platform created to be compatible with a huge number of different devices, from a hardware point of view to a purpose point of view. The main goal is to provide a freely available software platform for both large enterprise companies and small independent makers or even single developers. Android aims to provide an easy way to create innovative solutions and bring them to market with no effort.

Everything started in 2005, when Google acquired Android Inc., a small company that was developing an operating system for mobile devices. A couple of years later, the Open Handset Alliance was born. In 2007, 84 companies, including mobile operators, handset manufacturers, and semiconductor and software companies, publicly announced their brand new, upcoming mobile operating system.

For one more whole year the project was kept a secret. Google worked hard to bring the project to version 1.0 and in 2008 Android was shown to the world. In the following seven years, four major versions of the system have been released. The following table tells the chronological history of all the Android versions. Every single version was released as open source software to the world. Every version, but `Honeycomb`, that was an ugly PR slip for Google, which spent a lot of energy to bring it down and replace it with `Ice Cream Sandwich` as soon as possible:

Version	Codename	API level	Open source	Date
1.0	Unknown	1 - 2	Yes	September 2008
1.5	Cupcake	3	Yes	April 27, 2009
1.6	Donut	4	Yes	September 15, 2009
2.0	Eclair	5 - 6 -7	Yes	October 26, 2009
2.2	Froyo	8	Yes	May 20, 2010
2.3	Gingerbread	9 - 10	Yes	December 6, 2010
3.0	Honeycomb	11 - 12 - 13	No	February 22, 2011
4.0	Ice Cream Sandwich	14 - 15	Yes	October 18, 2011
4.1	Jelly Bean	16 - 17 - 18	Yes	June 9, 2012
4.4	KitKat	19 - 20	Yes	October 31, 2013
5.0	Lollipop	21 - 22	Yes	November 12, 2014

The license

Creating an open source platform brings in a few concerns about which license gives the perfect balance between protection and freedom. The goal is to give manufacturers enough freedom to adapt the system to their own hardware without being scared of dark licenses, trying to steal their intellectual property. To reach this goal, Google picked one of the most famous open source licenses available at the time and applied it to most parts of the operative system.

The license that Google uses to protect the Android Open Source Project (AOSP) is the Apache Software License, Version 2.0, also known as Apache 2.0, and it covers almost every line of code published to AOSP. The Apache 2 license doesn't apply to one big system component—the kernel. Linux Kernel is protected by GNU Public License, V2, and it comes with a *system exception* to be able to be shipped with Android.

Being open source and being easily adaptable to popular hardware, it launched Android to the top of the mobile market at rocket speed, reaching one billion active devices all over the world with over one million apps available on the Google Play Store. One billion active devices is the result of a winning strategy—providing manufacturers with a software solution for their hardware, easy to integrate and customize, coming free of charge and community supported, in a market that was dominated by Apple.

Open source, closed doors

A closer look at the project shows how Android is slightly different from other open source projects: Android is developed by Google behind closed doors. Lots of people in the community don't agree about considering Android as *open* as Linux is. In fact, the two approaches are completely different. Yes, both of them have an open source license, but Linux is a community-developed project, Android, instead, is completely developed by Google.

Every technical discussion, every decision, every roadmap step is decided by Google. When the development life cycle completes, Google releases a new version of the operative system, updates the public source code repository and everybody is able to download the latest version of the OS.

Of course, there are e-mailing lists for discussion and support and there are a few ways to contribute to the project, but everything is decided by the Android development team.

The Android development model

To assure the stability of the Android current release, Google keeps the source code in *code lines*. This approach provides a proper mechanism to keep separated the current stable version, available on all latest devices, from the currently under development, unstable version. As you may easily notice, Google is using a different naming convention for Android compared to the usual nomenclature of open source projects—`code line` is used instead of `branch`, because a single `code line` can be based on multiple git `branches`.

The following diagram shows how the source code history evolves over time, through different branches and releases:

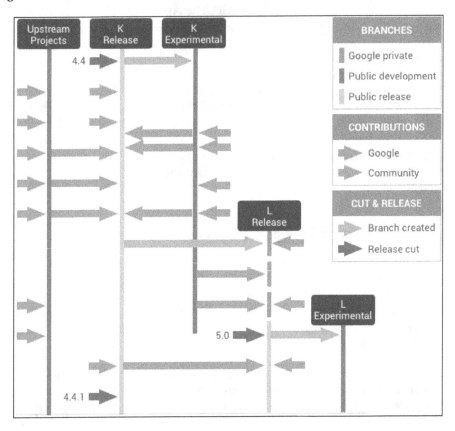

The previous diagram shows the main `public branch`, Upstream, on the left. This branch is the main public development branch where all the critical bug fixes are released constantly, and where all the main experimentation with new devices and new technology is performed. Every developer or manufacturer can obtain this set of source code and start to create their own Android device.

On the right side of the diagram, we can see Google's private branch. This branch contains the Android `next version`. Generally, all the development is done by Google itself, with the support of a hardware partner that provides a reference device. Typically, this device is a high-end, top-class device that Google appoints as Google's next reference device, also known as Nexus. Every new Nexus has been chosen keeping in mind Google Android's development roadmap—every technical hardware specification supports or discourages particular software development, to create the perfect symbiosis between the device and the operating system.

When the internal development reaches the desired stable point, the new version is released, every branch is updated accordingly and a new public/private development cycle begins, once again.

Source code tags and builds

To effectively refer to a specific Android version, every public release, since Android 1.5, comes with a fancy pop codename, a version number, and a more developer-oriented API level.

The following table shows how the correspondence between codename/version/API level is not always a one-to-one relationship. Most of the time, the code name has a longer life cycle than the version number:

Code name	Version	API level
Lollipop	5.1	API level 22
Lollipop	5.0	API level 21
KitKat	4.4 - 4.4.4	API level 19
Jelly Bean	4.3.x	API level 18
Jelly Bean	4.2.x	API level 17
Jelly Bean	4.1.x	API level 16
Ice Cream Sandwich	4.0.3 - 4.0.4	API level 15, NDK 8
Ice Cream Sandwich	4.0.1 - 4.0.2	API level 14, NDK 7
Honeycomb	3.2.x	API level 13
Honeycomb	3.1	API level 12, NDK 6
Honeycomb	3.0	API level 11
Gingerbread	2.3.3 - 2.3.7	API level 10
Gingerbread	2.3 - 2.3.2	API level 9, NDK 5
Froyo	2.2.x	API level 8, NDK 4
Eclair	2.1	API level 7, NDK 3
Eclair	2.0.1	API level 6
Eclair	2.0	API level 5
Donut	1.6	API level 4, NDK 2
Cupcake	1.5	API level 3, NDK 1
(no code name)	1.1	API level 2
(no code name)	1.0	API level 1

Nexus

The Nexus family contains all those Android devices that Google designs, produces, and sells, with the help of its hardware manufacture partners.

One of the peculiarities of the Nexus family is the bare Android system it equips the device—there is no customization of any sort, neither from the manufacturer nor from the telephone carrier. The system is based on pure Android source code, providing the user with the purest Android experience. As an advanced note, the device bootloader can be easily and legally unlocked, to allow every sort of modification any expert user could desire. Security-wise, the Nexus devices are the first ones that receive security fixes and system updates—stay updated, stay safe!

The Nexus family is continuously growing in numbers and quality and it now contains smartphones, tablets, and even digital players. The upcoming tables show an overview on all the currently available models.

Phones

Here is a list of all stock Nexus phones:

Name	Android version	Release date	Vendor
Nexus One	2.1 updated at 2.3	January 2010	HTC
Nexus S	2.3 updated up to 4.1.2	December 2010	Samsung
Galaxy Nexus	4.0 updated up to 4.3	November 2011	Samsung
Nexus 4	4.2 updated up to 5.1	November 2012	LG
Nexus 5	4.4 updated up to 5.1	October 2013	LG
Nexus 6	5.0 updated up to 5.1	October 2014	Motorola

Tablets

Here is a list of all stock Nexus tablets:

Name	Android version	Release date	Vendor
Nexus 7	4.1 updated at 5.0	June 2012	Asus
Nexus 7	4.3 updated up to 5.0	November 2013	Asus
Galaxy 9	5.0 updated up to 5.1	October 2014	HTC
Nexus 10	4.2 updated up to 5.1	November 2012	LG

Digital media players

Here is a list of all stock Nexus digital media players:

Name	Android version	Release date	Vendor
Nexus Q	4.0	June 2012	Google
Nexus Player	5.1	November 2014	Google and Asus

Every single device in these tables has its own Android build, specifically tailored for its hardware and purpose. The following table is an example of builds code names and versions that Google provides for all the expert Android users who want to manually replace the operative system and want to retrieve the official build by Google:

Build	Branch	Version	Supported devices
LVY48C	android-5.1.1_r8	Lollipop	Nexus 6 (For Project Fi ONLY)
LMY48G	android-5.1.1_r6	Lollipop	Nexus 7 (flo)
LYZ28E	android-5.1.1_r5	Lollipop	Nexus 6 (For T-Mobile ONLY)
LMY47Z	android-5.1.1_r4	Lollipop	Nexus 6 (For Sprint, USC ONLY)
LMY48B	android-5.1.1_r3	Lollipop	Nexus 5
LMY47X	android-5.1.1_r2	Lollipop	Nexus 9 (volantis)
LMY47V	android-5.1.1_r1	Lollipop	Nexus 7 (flo/grouper), Nexus 10, Nexus Player
LMY47O	android-5.1.0_r5	Lollipop	Nexus 4, Nexus 7 (flo/deb)
...	...	...	...

Every build is identified by a `build-code`, for instance, LMY47O. The first letter is the initial letter of the code name, for instance, Lollipop; the second letter identifies the branch used to produce this build; the following two letters identify the release date, based on quarters notation—A is Q1 2009, F is Q2 2010, and so on. The two numbers following the quarter letter specify the release day. The last letter identifies the build number. This notation is not critically precise. Google often reuses the same build code for more than one build. We need to consider it as a rough estimation of the release date.

Source code tools

Android is a huge project, with an astonishing amount of source code. Google itself manages the source code and stores it on its servers which are publicly accessible to the developers and advanced users.

Considering the complexity of the project, we will need only two tools to retrieve the source code:

- git
- repo

Let's have a quick overview on these powerful tools that will accompany us during our journey.

Git

Git is currently the most popular source code version control system, openly available in the world. It's an impressive tool created by Linus Torvalds (yes, the same Linus Torvalds who created the Linux kernel contained in Android).

In 2005, Torvalds was struggling to find a proper way to manage the amount of code and contributions from the developers who were working on its Linux kernel. No tool available at that time was enough and, in a few days, he created the first working version of his new distributed revision control system that was able to manage a huge project with speed and flexibility.

Git provides effective and easy-to-achieve solutions for modular systems and Google takes full advantage of this opportunity. Every contribution to the Android code base is provided using git features — commits, branches, and patches.

The system is kept as modular as possible to allow developers and OEM to extract and replace components that need to be customized. Knowing this, it's easy to guess how many git repositories Android contains — dozens of interconnected repositories of different sizes and structures.

Repo

To overcome the difficulty of managing a plethora of different repositories, Google created `git-repo`, a tool written in Python that acts like a coordinator upon git and allows automation of some common parts of the workflow.

Repo comes in handy in a lot of scenarios. Most of all, all those network operations that involve the source code: retrieving, updating, and pushing the code to the remote servers. Repo is a pivot tool and we will learn a lot about it in the next sections.

Gerrit

Worth mentioning, Gerrit is the code review tool used to evaluate and approve every contribution made to AOSP. It provides a graphical user interface to monitor the evolution of the code base and represent the central point where all the contributions end before being accepted and merged into the main code base, or rejected if the review resolves in a *no, thanks*.

Setting up the environment

The Android build system is officially supported by Ubuntu Linux. Google assures that the system setup, the environment setup, and all the requirements are easily reproducible on this particular Linux distribution. The truth is, nowadays, every Linux distribution can be prepared to perform a proper Android build with little effort.

To be closest to the guidelines and because we think that Ubuntu is the easiest system to set up for the job, in this book we are going to use Ubuntu Linux 15.04 to perform all our building procedures.

If you are working on OS X or Windows and you prefer to stick to these operating systems, we are going to show you how to achieve our goal even using a virtual machine.

Free space

The amount of free space on the hard drive needed by the build system is massive. The Android source code by itself can reach 100 gigabytes of occupied space. When we move to more advanced scenarios, such as building using a caching system, such as `ccache`, to speed up multiple system builds, we can easily reach 200 gigabytes of occupied space. It's very important to be sure that this kind of free space is available on your machine, because filling up the hard disk during the building process could bring the system into an unstable state.

Another note is about your connection speed—considering the amount of data needed to get ready to build, be sure to have a fast Internet connection, or an appropriate amount of patience.

Installing the required tools

Even if officially the supported Linux distribution is Ubuntu, the following procedures and commands are equally correct on every Debian-based distribution, if it is actually installed on your computer or is running as a virtual machine.

To be able to acquire the source code, retrieving it from Google *git repository*, we need to install git. Let's open a Terminal and run:

```
~$ sudo apt-get install git
```

Apt will ask for our super user password and will take care of installing git in the system. Once we have git, we need its trusted companion tool — repo. Repo does not need a real installation. It's a Python script, so we just need to download it and place it in a handy folder.

Let's create a `bin` folder in our home folder and add it to the system path:

```
~$ mkdir ~/bin
```
```
~$ export PATH=~/bin:$PATH
```

Now that we have a folder, we can download `repo` using `curl`:

```
~$ curl https://storage.googleapis.com/git-repo-downloads/repo >
~/bin/repo
```
```
~$ chmod a+x ~/bin/repo
```

 If `curl` is not available in your system, you can install it using `apt-get` as shown in the following command:
```
~$ sudo apt-get install curl
```

The following is the output:

```
x  -  □  esteban@dronix: ~/WORKING_DIRECTORY

                                         esteban@dronix: ~/WORKING_DIRECTORY 121x11

esteban@dronix:~/WORKING_DIRECTORY$ curl https://storage.googleapis.com/git-repo-downloads/repo > ~/bin/repo
  % Total    % Received % Xferd  Average Speed   Time    Time     Time  Current
                                 Dload  Upload   Total   Spent    Left  Speed
100 24081  100 24081    0     0   144k      0 --:--:-- --:--:-- --:--:--  145k
esteban@dronix:~/WORKING_DIRECTORY$ chmod a+x ~/bin/repo
esteban@dronix:~/WORKING_DIRECTORY$
```

The previous screenshot shows the download and our `chmod` command, to make `repo` properly executable. The `repo` tool comes with a collection of help commands accessible like this:

```
$ repo help
```

This command lists all the available commands, as shown in the next screenshot:

```
esteban@dronix:~/WORKING_DIRECTORY$ repo help
usage: repo COMMAND [ARGS]
The most commonly used repo commands are:
  abandon        Permanently abandon a development branch
  branch         View current topic branches
  branches       View current topic branches
  checkout       Checkout a branch for development
  cherry-pick    Cherry-pick a change.
  diff           Show changes between commit and working tree
  diffmanifests  Manifest diff utility
  download       Download and checkout a change
  grep           Print lines matching a pattern
  info           Get info on the manifest branch, current branch or unmerged bra
  init           Initialize repo in the current directory
  list           List projects and their associated directories
  overview       Display overview of unmerged project branches
  prune          Prune (delete) already merged topics
  rebase         Rebase local branches on upstream branch
  smartsync      Update working tree to the latest known good revision
  stage          Stage file(s) for commit
  start          Start a new branch for development
  status         Show the working tree status
  sync           Update working tree to the latest revision
  upload         Upload changes for code review
See 'repo help <command>' for more information on a specific command.
See 'repo help --all' for a complete list of recognized commands.
esteban@dronix:~/WORKING_DIRECTORY$
```

For further help, every command, for instance `info`, has its own help screen accessible like this:

```
$ repo help command
```

The following screenshot shows the help screen for the `info` command:

```
×  –  □   esteban@dronix: ~/WORKING_DIRECTORY

                        esteban@dronix: ~/WORKING_DIRECTORY 80x21

esteban@dronix:~/WORKING_DIRECTORY$ repo help info

Summary
-------
Get info on the manifest branch, current branch or unmerged branches

Usage: repo info [-dl] [-o [-b]] [<project>...]

Options:
  -h, --help             show this help message and exit
  -d, --diff             show full info and commit diff including remote
                         branches
  -o, --overview         show overview of all local commits
  -b, --current-branch   consider only checked out branches
  -l, --local-only       Disable all remote operations
esteban@dronix:~/WORKING_DIRECTORY$ ▮
```

Getting ready

As we already know, Google is the official manager of the entire hardware infrastructure supporting Android—everything is hosted and maintained by Google. The source code repository also provides a web UI to graphically navigate the source code. This source code browser is available at `https://android.googlesource.com/`.

The following screenshot shows an example of what the page looks like:

Every single item of the list shown in the previous screenshot is a `git` repository. This can give you a perfect idea of the importance of Google's `repo` tool—manually managing this many repositories would be pure madness! Using `repo`, retrieving, downloading, and creating the proper folder structure is a few-lines' task. Let's do it!

First things first—create a working folder. Open a Terminal and create a folder like this:

```
~$ mkdir WORKING_DIRECTORY
~$ cd WORKING_DIRECTORY
```

Once in the folder, run:

```
~/WORKING_DIRECTORY$ repo init -u
https://android.googlesource.com/platform/manifest
```

The URL specifies the project manifest file. The manifest specifies which repositories are necessary for the download and what the folder structure is that must be expected to run.

During this phase, `repo` will ask for your full name and e-mail. This sort of registration is needed to enable the system to receive your contributions. Gerrit will use this information to communicate with you with notifications and news. Obviously, your name will be associated to every contribution, fix, or feature you will submit in the future. Making sure that the provided e-mail address is a valid Google account is a wise choice.

A successful initialization ends with:

```
repo has been initialized
```

Congrats! We now have an initialized repo in the current folder and a configuration folder, named `.repo`, containing, for instance, the downloaded manifest file.

Run `ls -la` in your Terminal to spot the `.repo` folder.

Currently, our folder contains the `master` branch of the whole Android project. It has to be considered a development branch, so we have no guarantee that the system will work on a device or even build on our system. We can use this branch to submit some contribution, but this is a task for another step of our journey. Our current goal is to try to build a working system, so the smart move is to switch to a branch or a TAG that officially supports a specific device.

To switch to a specific branch, we will use `repo`, which will take care of configuring every single repository involved, to bring us to a stable and guaranteed environment:

```
:~/WORKING_DIRECTORY$ repo init -u
https://android.googlesource.com/platform/manifest -b android-
5.1.1_r3
```

The previously shown table contains every possible branch we could switch to.

To retrieve the whole list of available branches, we are going to use a trick — cloning one specific repository that provides this very information: `manifest.git`. Let's open a Terminal and clone it:

```
$ git clone
http://https://android.googlesource.com/platform/manifest.git
manifest
```

Enter the folder we have just created and get the list:

```
$ cd manifest
```

```
$ git branch -a
```

The following screenshot shows part of the huge list of available branches:

```
x  -  □   esteban@dronix: ~/tags_branches/manifest
                        esteban@dronix: ~/tags_branches/manifest 80x35
esteban@dronix:~/tags_branches/manifest$ git branch -a
* master
  remotes/origin/HEAD -> origin/master
  remotes/origin/adt_23.0.3
  remotes/origin/android-1.6_r1
  remotes/origin/android-1.6_r1.1
  remotes/origin/android-1.6_r1.2
  remotes/origin/android-1.6_r1.3
  remotes/origin/android-1.6_r1.4
  remotes/origin/android-1.6_r1.5
  remotes/origin/android-1.6_r2
  remotes/origin/android-2.0.1_r1
  remotes/origin/android-2.0_r1
  remotes/origin/android-2.1_r1
  remotes/origin/android-2.1_r2
  remotes/origin/android-2.1_r2.1p
  remotes/origin/android-2.1_r2.1p2
  remotes/origin/android-2.1_r2.1s
  remotes/origin/android-2.2.1_r1
  remotes/origin/android-2.2.1_r2
  remotes/origin/android-2.2.2_r1
  remotes/origin/android-2.2.3_r1
  remotes/origin/android-2.2.3_r2
  remotes/origin/android-2.2.3_r2.1
  remotes/origin/android-2.2_r1
  remotes/origin/android-2.2_r1.1
  remotes/origin/android-2.2_r1.2
  remotes/origin/android-2.2_r1.3
  remotes/origin/android-2.3.1_r1
  remotes/origin/android-2.3.2_r1
  remotes/origin/android-2.3.3_r1
  remotes/origin/android-2.3.3_r1.1
  remotes/origin/android-2.3.4_r0.9
  remotes/origin/android-2.3.4_r1
  remotes/origin/android-2.3.5_r1
```

Downloading the code

Everything is in place: folders are ready, repo is properly configured, we have tons
of free hard disk space and a fast Internet connection. Let's sync!

Open a Terminal and run:

```
$ repo sync
```

Make yourself a tasty coffee as this will take some time! The `repo` tool is going to download every single file of every single repository specified in the manifest file, for more than 50 gigabytes.

Hands on the code

Knowing that we will adapt Android to our hardware, it's important to have a clear understanding about the workflow to create and submit contributions. To achieve this goal, we will use both `repo` and `git`.

The contribution workflow is based on five steps:

1. We create a new topic branch:

   ```
   $ repo branch
   ```

2. We develop all the edits, fixes, and features we want. We add these contributions to the next commit:

   ```
   $ git add our_files
   ```

3. We save our staged file to the git repo:

   ```
   $ git commit -m "Add awesome new feature"
   ```

4. We submit our new commits to the code review server:

   ```
   $ repo uploads
   ```

Our code has been submitted and it's waiting to be reviewed—fingers crossed!

If you don't want to download the whole code base and you know already which specific module you are going to customize, you can sync just this module:

```
$ repo sync art
```

When our module has been synced, we need to create a new branch to keep our environment organized, with a clear structure and an easy way to compare our edits with the original content. To create our new `topic branch`, we need to enter the module folder and run a `repo` command:

```
$ cd art/
$ repo start my_branch .
```

If everything is in place, we run this command:

```
$ repo status .
```

This command will be a bit comforting:

```
:$ […] /art$ repo status .

project art/                          branch my_branch
```

During our work, we can create as many branches as we need and we can list them as follows:

```
$ git branch
```

The following screenshot shows the list of all the branches in the current module:

```
X  —  □   esteban@dronix: ~/WORKING_DIRECTORY/art
                         esteban@dronix ~/WORKING_DIRECTORY/art 80x10
esteban@dronix:~/WORKING_DIRECTORY$ cd art/
esteban@dronix:~/WORKING_DIRECTORY/art$ git branch
* (detached from android-5.1.1_r3)
  master
  my_branch
esteban@dronix:~/WORKING_DIRECTORY/art$
```

The current branch is the one with the star symbol (asterisk). Now that we know which are the available branches, we can switch from branch to branch using:

```
$ git checkout branch_name
```

For every fix or feature we add, a new Git commit will land in our branch:

```
$ git add art_new_feature
$ git commit -m "Add new awesome feature to ART"
```

Once all our edits are complete, we need to get ready to submit our contribution to the Gerrit system and to the developers in charge of reviewing every code proposal.

Before being able to submit our patches, we need to generate a new password to access the source code repository. Google provides a quick service to generate a password at the URL https://android-review.googlesource.com/new-password.

Choose your Google account that you want to connect to the Android source code repository and you will land at the git cookie configuration page. Google has everything already set up for you. Just copy and paste the configuration in one of your Terminals and you are ready to go.

To submit our branch, we update the module to be sure it is aligned with `upstream` and then we update:

```
$ repo sync
```

```
$ repo upload
```

Once we ask for uploading, `repo` will ask for confirmation, showing all the contributions we are submitting, as shown in the following screenshot:

```
x  —  □   esteban@dronix: ~/WORKING_DIRECTORY
                        esteban@dronix: ~/WORKING_DIRECTORY 80x9

esteban@dronix:~/WORKING_DIRECTORY$ repo upload art
Upload project art/ to remote branch refs/tags/android-5.1.1_r3:
  branch my_branch ( 1 commit, Fri Aug 14 04:44:17 2015 +0200):
        8a9047f4 TEST
to None (y/N)?
```

After the confirmation, `repo` will establish a secure connection with the repository server and your contribution will be stored online. You are now an Android developer or at least you are getting there!

A look inside AOSP

At this point, we have our copy of AOSP so we can start looking inside to see what the project consists of.

Before delving inside, we must warn you that, when generating a new build image from scratch, you won't find any of the Google applications that you can find on most of the Android devices. That is because the Google applications are not licensed under Apache 2.0 license, so they are not provided with the public project. We are talking about applications such as Play Store, Gmail, YouTube, Maps, and all other official Google apps.

These applications are provided only to the compatible devices, that is, the devices that pass the `Compatibility Test Suite` we met in the first chapter.

Being able to distribute an Android device with all Google's app on-board is no easy trip. After confirming that the device is compatible using CTS, it is also necessary to obtain a particular **Google Mobile Services (GMS)** license by contacting Google directly.

Obviously, you can find those applications in their binary form on the Internet and add it like that to your build. It's not the official way to achieve the goal and we support a cleaner conduct to distribute our awesome device, but is worth mentioning that there are blurry shortcuts.

Going back to our source code, let's take a look inside our WORKING_DIRECTORY and see where we can find the basic Android components that AOSP is composed of.

The next screenshot shows a clear overview of all the folders contained in the root directory:

```
x  –  □   esteban@dronix: ~/WORKING_DIRECTORY
                  esteban@dronix: ~/WORKING_DIRECTORY 71x32

esteban@dronix:~/WORKING_DIRECTORY$ ls -l
total 100
drwxrwxr-x    3 esteban esteban 4096 Aug  6 16:01 abi
drwxrwxr-x   14 esteban esteban 4096 Aug 14 04:43 art
drwxrwxr-x   10 esteban esteban 4096 Aug 11 04:22 bionic
drwxrwxr-x    4 esteban esteban 4096 Aug 11 04:43 bootable
drwxrwxr-x    7 esteban esteban 4096 Aug 14 14:20 build
drwxrwxr-x   12 esteban esteban 4096 Aug 11 04:26 cts
drwxrwxr-x   13 esteban esteban 4096 Aug 11 04:22 dalvik
drwxrwxr-x    6 esteban esteban 4096 Aug  6 16:01 developers
drwxrwxr-x   20 esteban esteban 4096 Aug  6 16:02 development
drwxrwxr-x   11 esteban esteban 4096 Aug  6 16:02 device
drwxrwxr-x    3 esteban esteban 4096 Aug  6 16:02 docs
drwxrwxr-x  192 esteban esteban 4096 Aug 11 04:52 external
drwxrwxr-x   17 esteban esteban 4096 Aug  6 16:09 frameworks
drwxrwxr-x   13 esteban esteban 4096 Aug  6 16:09 hardware
drwxrwxr-x   16 esteban esteban 4096 Aug 11 04:54 libcore
drwxrwxr-x    5 esteban esteban 4096 Aug 11 04:54 libnativehelper
-r--r--r--    1 esteban esteban   87 Aug  6 16:01 Makefile
drwxrwxr-x    8 esteban esteban 4096 Aug 14 15:42 ndk
drwxrwxr-x    4 esteban esteban 4096 Aug  6 18:14 out
drwxrwxr-x    9 esteban esteban 4096 Aug  6 16:10 packages
drwxrwxr-x    6 esteban esteban 4096 Aug 14 15:43 pdk
drwxrwxr-x   16 esteban esteban 4096 Aug 11 04:55 prebuilts
drwxrwxr-x   27 esteban esteban 4096 Aug 11 05:02 sdk
drwxrwxr-x    9 esteban esteban 4096 Aug 11 04:20 system
drwxrwxr-x    3 esteban esteban 4096 Aug  6 16:16 tools
esteban@dronix:~/WORKING_DIRECTORY$
```

The ART directory

One of the most important folders is surely `art/`. It contains the source code for the new `Runtime Environment`, designed and devolved by Google.

ART is an acronym of Android RunTime and it has been introduced in the Android 4.4 Kitkat as an alternative to the Dalvik Virtual Machine. It has completely replaced Dalvik in Android 5.0 Lollipop. The old Dalvik VM was based on a **Just-In-Time (JIT)** compiler technology, that is, it interprets and compiles an application source code into machine code in real time. This implementation has its advantages, but also disadvantages since runtime compilation certainly impacts system performance.

ART is based on an AOT (Ahead-of-time) technology, which compiles all the application code at the time of application installation, that is, before the execution. That obviously requires more time to install the application, but that time is usually imperceptible seeing the hardware performance of the latest Android devices.

The bionic directory

Bionic is the C-runtime for Android. Unlike most Linux distributions, Android doesn't use the GNU C library (`glibc`). The main differences between the GNU C library and `bionic` is the license— `glibc` is distributed under the GPL license while bionic has the BSD license. A more permissive license is crucial in a world so commercially oriented.

Other very important features are the lightness and the size. Bionic is much smaller than glibc, which makes it more usable for embedded systems such as cell phones. Also, it has been made having in mind low-performance processors, so it performs better.

A big part of the bionic source code comes from the OpenBSD project, but there are also some parts, such as `pthread` and the dynamic linker, that have been written from scratch, to be sure to meet the performance, lightness, and flexibility requirements.

The build directory

This directory contains the whole Android build system. It contains all the `makefile` core templates.

Besides that, it contains `envsetup.sh`, a script that allows the developer to work with Android sources without struggling with environment management. We will explain it in more detail later in the book, but in short, launching this script gives you various utilities that enable you to perform various operations on the source code, for example, compile specific modules or perform searches on specific files such as on all `.java` files, and so on.

The external directory

All the packages regarding open source projects used by Android can be found in this directory. It contains various libraries as well as very important utilities such as `zlib`, `SQLite`, and `webkit`.

The device directory

Here you can find all the configurations and definitions for specific devices. The following screenshot gives an overview of the content. As you can see, it's full of folders with names of well-known manufacturers:

```
esteban@dronix: ~/WORKING_DIRECTORY/device
           esteban@dronix: ~/WORKING_DIRECTORY/device 80x17

esteban@dronix:~/WORKING_DIRECTORY/device$ ls -l
totale 36
drwxrwxr-x   9 esteban esteban 4096 ago  6 16:02 asus
drwxrwxr-x   4 esteban esteban 4096 ago 14 14:45 common
drwxrwxr-x  15 esteban esteban 4096 ago  6 16:02 generic
drwxrwxr-x   4 esteban esteban 4096 ago 11 04:20 google
drwxrwxr-x   4 esteban esteban 4096 ago  6 16:02 htc
drwxrwxr-x   6 esteban esteban 4096 ago  6 16:02 lge
drwxrwxr-x   4 esteban esteban 4096 ago  6 16:02 moto
drwxrwxr-x  10 esteban esteban 4096 ago 14 15:04 sample
drwxrwxr-x   3 esteban esteban 4096 ago  6 16:02 samsung
esteban@dronix:~/WORKING_DIRECTORY/device$
```

There are all the definitions for the official Google devices, that is for all the Nexus devices, but there are also other directories such as:

- `common`: This directory contains certain information about the GPS and a script that allows you to extract the binary parts regarding a specific device so that they can be included in the image build.

- `generic`: This directory contains the configuration for the generic device called "goldfish" and is used to build the emulator image.

- `google`: This directory contains the code for the **Accessory Development Kit (ADK)**. It also contains a DEMOKIT Android app that allows you to control the ADK board. ADK is a reference implementation for hardware manufacturers and hobbyists that can be used as a starting point for making Android accessories;

- `sample`: This directory contains a complete example of how to write your own shared library for Android, without modifying the Android framework. It also shows how to write JNI code to be included in the library, and a client application that uses such a library.

The frameworks directory

This folder is very important because it contains the source code for the Android framework. It is here that you can find all the main components of Android such as Activity, Services, and so on. Here you can also find the mapping used between the native code in C/C++ and the code in Java.

The out directory

As intuitive as it can sound, when the build is done, the result of the compilations is in this directory. Here we will find images that are ready to be flashed on our device or emulator, under named subdirectories, such as `out/product/generic/` for the emulator image. In one of its subfolders, in the `out/host/linux-x86/`, you can also find all the tools that are needed from the host side, such as `fastboot`, `zipalign`, `dexdump`, and so on.

The packages directory

As the folder name says, here you can find all the standard Android application packages, for example, `Camera`, `Calculator`, `Dialer`, `Launcher`, `Settings`, and so on. Once again, these are not Google apps such as `YouTube` or `Maps`, but just the system apps that are common to every Android installation.

The system directory

The `system/` directory contains the source code of the Android `system core`, that is a minimal Linux system that takes care of the initialization of the device before the ART virtual machine starts any Java-based service.

Inside this folder, you can find the source code for the `init` process and the relative `init.rc` default script that initializes and dynamically configures the platform, as well as applications such as `Toolbox` (the Android alternative to `BusyBox`) and the source codes for the `adb` and `fastboot` utilities that we will explain in more detail in the coming chapters.

The rest of the directory structure

Here are the remaining folders that are part of the AOSP:

- `abi`: This is the source file for `libgabi++`.

- `bootable`: This includes the boot and startup related code. Some of it is legacy, the fastboot protocol info could be interesting since it is implemented by boot loaders in a number of devices such as the Nexus ones.

- `cts`: This directory contains the code for the compatibility test suite.

- `dalvik`: This directory contains the code for the Dalvik virtual machine.

- `development`: This directory contains development tools — the source code of the SDK and the NDK.

- `docs`: This directory contains the documentation relative to the Android Open Source Project. It contains a subfolder called `source.android.com`, which contains all the required files to generate the static HTML. You can see the result of the build at `http://source.android.com/`.

- `Note`: This directory is the online version that often doesn't coincide with the one present in the AOSP.

- `hardware`: This folder contains HAL (Hardware Abstraction Layer), libraries that enable interfacing with the device hardware.

- `libcore`: This directory contains Apache Harmony.

- `ndk`: This directory contains the script to generate the Native Development Kit, that allows the use of the native code written in C/C++ from Android applications.

- `pdk`: This is the Platform Development Kit, a set of utilities that Google sends to various OEMs so that they can update their own frameworks before important system updates.

- `prebuilts`: This directory contains precompiled files, including various toolchain versions.

- `sdk`: This is the Software Development Kit.

- `tools`: These are some external IDE tools.

Summary

In this chapter, we have learned lots of very important things that represent the basis of Android.

We started with the Android philosophy regarding the licenses and the development model touching on different versions of Android that followed. We have learned to install and use the tools necessary to contribute to the AOSP project, and also how to download a copy of the AOSP source code, selecting the right TAG to get the wanted version of Android.

In the next chapter, we will make the first build, generating an image for the emulator, but first we will explain how the Android build system works and what tools we need to install.

3
Set up and Build – the Emulator Way

In the previous chapter, we learned how to retrieve the source code and we had an overview of the folder's structure. We now know how the branching model works and how to contribute to the project. This is an important topic, because Android is an open source prot, but it's managed in a very different way compared to other popular open source projects.

In this chapter, we will set up the whole environment to get ready to build our first Android system and flash it to a real target. Our efforts will be focused to create a fully-working version for the official Android emulator.

The user will learn how to use tools such as `adb` and `fastboot`, two of the most important tools that Google provides.

Preparing the host system

To build a complex system such as Android, we need to satisfy a few hardware and software requirements. First of all the host system.

The official Linux distribution supporting the Android build environment is `Ubuntu Linux`. Google periodically releases new Android builds for its devices and all of them are created using Ubuntu. Currently, Google is using Ubuntu 14.04 even if this is not the latest version available.

Every example in this book will be developed and executed on a common notebook, with an Intel i5 CPU and 4 GB of RAM, running Ubuntu Linux 15.05, that's the latest available version. Using a different Linux version proves that if all the requirements are satisfied, you could build Android with any Linux distribution or even Mac OS X – if you can't set up Ubuntu, trying with a different version will be challenging, but will be worth trying, as a learning experience.

If you are a Microsoft Windows user, it is sad to say, you won't be able to build Android using the native operative system. A possible solution is using a virtual machine running Ubuntu, for instance.

Hardware requirements

Digging into hardware requirements, you will just need a recent personal computer. As anticipated in the previous section, we are going to use a middle-end notebook for our examples. It's a Lenovo x220, with Intel i5 CPU and 4GB of RAM: it's enough to do the job and it's affordable, but the build time won't be small.

To speed up the build time, using a high-end PC is advisable. A faster CPU, with more cores, and more RAM will take advantage of multithreading and parallel building and will significantly reduce the build time, allowing you to experiment more during the journey.

A critical point of the environment setup is the necessary hard disk free space. The required amount is considerable – the source code alone needs approximately 100 GB to be stored. The whole build process will require approximately 150GB. If we are trying to build as fast as possible, probably we will enable the building system caching option, ccache. The caching system will require even more free space.

The following table will give you a rough estimation about minimum and recommended hardware:

	Minimum	Recommended
Processor	4 core processor at 2 GHz	8 core processor at 2.5 GHz
RAM	8 GB	16 GB
Disk Space	200 GB	500 GB

Software requirements

In this book, we are going to build the system using Ubuntu Linux 15.04. If you cannot obtain this version, you can successfully use an older version, like the guys at Google, a totally different distribution or even a Virtual Machine.

One of the basic requirements, when it comes to the operating system, is the architecture: if we are planning to build Android 2.3 or greater, we will need a 64-bit system. Older versions of Android will do fine with a 32-bit system, but that's an improbable scenario.

Installing Java JDK

Oracle's *Java Development Kit* is a crucial requirement, essential to be able to build Android. Every Android version needs a specific JDK version. According to what version we want to build, we are going to install:

- JDK 5 for Cupcake to Froyo
- JDK 6 for Gingerbread to KitKat
- JDK 7 for KitKat, Lollipop, and Marshmallow

We are going to build Android Lollipop 5.1.1 and we are going to need at least JDK 7. Installing JDK on Ubuntu is quite straightforward. Let's start by opening a Terminal and firing the following command:

```
~$ sudo apt-get install openjdk-7-jdk
```

The apt-get command will resolve all the dependencies, download all the required packages and install them. If you are a *Mouse and icons* user, you can achieve the same goal using **Ubuntu Software Center**, as shown in the following screenshot:

If you are a Java developer or you plan to build different Android versions for specific reasons, Ice Cream Sandwich and Lollipop, for instance, you could end up having more than just one version of the Java Development Kit. This multipurpose scenario brings a few more steps of configuration. We need to specify which JDK version will be used as the default one in the system. Using our trusted Terminal, let's run these commands:

```
~$ sudo update-alternative –config javac
```

The following screenshot shows the output. As you can see, it lists all the available JDK versions and lets you pick the one to set as default. In our scenario, we are using JDK 7 because we are planning to build Android 5 or greater.

```
×  –  □   esteban@dronix: ~

                              esteban@dronix: ~ 83x16

esteban@dronix:~$ sudo update-alternatives --config javac
There are 3 choices for the alternative javac (providing /usr/bin/javac).

  Selection    Path                                        Priority   Status
------------------------------------------------------------------------------
    0            /usr/lib/jvm/java-8-oracle/bin/javac         1079      auto mode
*   1            /usr/lib/jvm/java-7-openjdk-amd64/bin/javac  1071      manual mode
    2            /usr/lib/jvm/java-7-oracle/bin/javac         1078      manual mode
    3            /usr/lib/jvm/java-8-oracle/bin/javac         1079      manual mode

Press enter to keep the current choice[*], or type selection number: 1
esteban@dronix:~$
```

Installing system dependencies

Even if Java is a key player in the Android world, we also need a few *low-level* tools to satisfy all the Android build system requirements. Some of them are common tools and there is a chance that they are already installed, but our goal is to set up a whole system from scratch: we can't risk missing a dependency.

Using your Terminal, run the following `apt-get` command:

```
~$ sudo apt-get install bison g++-multilib git gperf libxml2-utils \
     make python-networkx zlib1g-dev:i386 zip
```

As usual, `apt-get` will resolve all the dependencies and install all the required packages. The following screenshot shows the output of the command in the scenario in which you already have all the required packages, lucky you:

```
x  -  □   esteban@dronix: ~
                              esteban@dronix: ~ 80x19
esteban@dronix:~$
esteban@dronix:~$ sudo apt-get install bison g++-multilib git gperf libxml2-util
s make python-networkx zlib1g-dev:i386 zip
Reading package lists... Done
Building dependency tree
Reading state information... Done
bison is already the newest version.
g++-multilib is already the newest version.
git is already the newest version.
gperf is already the newest version.
libxml2-utils is already the newest version.
make is already the newest version.
python-networkx is already the newest version.
zip is already the newest version.
zlib1g-dev:i386 is already the newest version.
0 upgraded, 0 newly installed, 0 to remove and 111 not upgraded.
esteban@dronix:~$
```

At this point, your Ubuntu contains all the required packages and applications to build the world's most popular mobile operating system.

Setting up a Mac OS X environment

One of the most important requirements to build Android is a case-sensitive filesystem. If you are planning to build Android using OS X, the most practical way to satisfy this requirement is to create a partition or a disk image containing a case-sensitive filesystem.

Creating a case-sensitive disk image

OS X provides a handy graphical utility to create a new disk image. Fire up `Spotlight` and launch `Disk Utility`. The upper toolbar contains a **New Image** button that takes you to the disk image creation screen, as shown in the following screenshot:

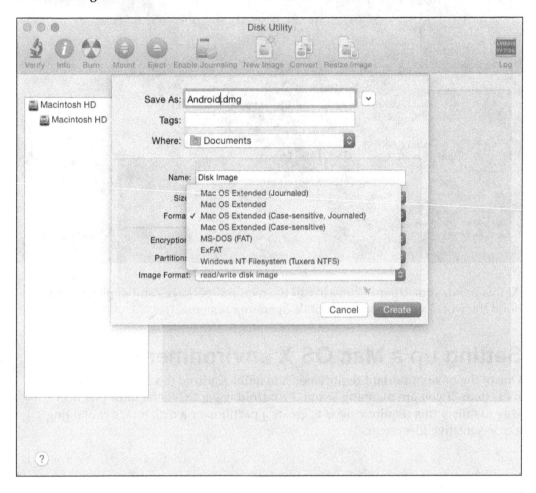

As you can see from the preceding screenshot, the crucial setting is the **Format**: it has to be `Case-sensitive, Journaled`. For the **Size** setting, the larger the better, keeping in mind that an Android build could use hundreds of gigabytes in no time. As minimal size, we suggest at least 50 GB.

If you are more a *command line* type, it's possible to create this disk image using the Terminal and `hdiutil`, as shown in the following command:

```
~$ hdiutil create -type SPARSE -fs 'Case-sensitive Journaled HFS+' \
-size 50g ~/android.dmg
```

If the disk image creation succeeded, we now have a `.dmg` or `.dmg.sparsefile` file on our disk. Once we have mounted it, we can use it as a normal hark disk—downloading Android source code and proceeding with the building procedure.

The two following commands will give you the ability to mount and unmount the disk image:

```
~$ hdiutil attach ~/android.dmg -mountpoint /Volumes/android-disk;
~$ hdiutil detach /Volumes/android-disk;
```

If you run out of space, the following command will give you the opportunity to resize the disk image and allow you to continue working on your desired Android build:

```
~$ hdiutil resize -size <new-size-you-want>g
~/android.dmg.sparseimage
```

Installing the required software

Once we have our installation disk image, the same as for Linux, we need to install all those software requirements we need to properly build the system.

Installing the Java Development Kit is very straightforward: just download the proper `.dmg` file from `http://www.oracle.com` and install it. The same rules about Android target version and required Java version apply here too.

Further, we will need:

- **Xcode**: The installation is well documented at `https://developer.apple.com` as Xcode is the main player of iOS development.
- **MacPorts**: It's an open source project that will help us to install lots of useful tools. You can install it following the installation info at `http://www.macports.org/install.php`.

Once we have these two main pieces of the puzzle in place, we need to install make, git, bison, and GPG packages, using MacPorts, with the following command on your Terminal:

```
~$ POSIXLY_CORRECT=1 sudo port install gmake bison libsdl git gnupg
```

Last but not least, we need to increase the maximum number of possible file descriptors. OS X comes with a tiny value—the average user does not need all those file descriptors, but we are going to need a bigger amount due to the hundreds of files involved in the Android build procedure. To increase this value, we will need to launch our Terminal and run the following command:

```
~$ ulimit -S -n 1024
```

Now, the limit is up to 1,024 files. We can make this value persistent by adding this to the ~/.bash_profile file, in your home folder.

The Android build system

Before digging into configuring and building your first Android system, we will have an overview of the build system itself, the tools involved, and the unique approach to the whole process Google has.

There is very little official documentation available about creating new modules and about the build system itself. Most of your knowledge at the end of this journey will come from your own hands-on experience and from our experience that we put in these pages.

An overview

As with lots of projects out there, open source or closed source, Android uses the powerful tool make to build the whole system, but compared to all other projects, Android uses it in a completely different way.

The common approach of using make would be to use a hierarchy of Makefiles: one single root Makefile retrieves and runs every other Makefile, contained in some of the subfolders of the project. Usually, every subfolder represents a submodule of the main project and it can be built alone or could depend upon other modules. Unlike other projects, Android has no menuconfig or any other graphical configuration utility to customize the build system, enable or disable modules. Every sort of build configuration is done using environment variables that we will show in the next sections.

Moreover, the whole module building is unconventional. Taking the Linux kernel as an example, usually, when a module is built, in the same folder with the source code, we have the compiled files. Module after module, the build system compiles everything and, at the very end, it retrieves the required files, links them together, and generates the final output. Android works in a different way. As you will notice approaching the build completion, Android tries to keep every module folder as clean as possible—every compiled file ends up in the /out folder, so that it's easier to clean everything, just delete this folder and have everything perfectly in order in a blink of an eye.

As you could guess at this point, the build system is completely custom made by Google. Everything has been designed and developed from scratch, using existent tools, but approaching the problem in an unusual way. Android developers created a single huge Makefile, containing all the needed information to build every single module and to assemble the final system image.

The whole build system is contained in the build/ folder. This folder contains:

- Utility shell scripts
- Utility Python scripts
- A set of .mk files containing all the necessary information to create all the system modules

Every single module has its own folder. This folder contains the most important file to build the module Android.mk. This file contains all the information needed to perform a smooth compilation of the module source code and generate a binary file.

Module Android.mk files are the first step of the building procedure—the build system scans every folder looking for these files and includes them into the single huge Makefile that it will use for further steps.

The source code root folder contains a Makefile with the following content:

```
### DO NOT EDIT THIS FILE ###
include build/core/main.mk
### DO NOT EDIT THIS FILE ###
```

The file looks pretty empty, but it contains the most important .mk file of all — main. mk. This file, located in build/core, contains a sequence of checks and all the needed operations to retrieve all the Android.mk files to build all the modules.

 Without special configuration, the Android build system only creates the Android system image. To generate CTS, NDK, and SDK, we will need a bit more setup effort as we will see later.

Bootstrap

The whole build system is fired up, thanks to a single shell script — build/envsetup. sh. As you can see in the following screenshot, this script is in charge of preparing the building environment. It sets up a few configurations and provides useful tools that make our work much easier: it's the Swiss Army knife of the Android build system.

Fire up your Terminal and run the script as follows:

```
~$ . build/envsetup.sh
```

Here is the output:

```
x – □   esteban@dronix: ~/WORKING_DIRECTORY
                    esteban@dronix: ~/WORKING_DIRECTORY 80x24

esteban@dronix:~/WORKING_DIRECTORY$ . build/envsetup.sh
including device/samsung/manta/vendorsetup.sh
including device/htc/flounder/vendorsetup.sh
including device/generic/mini-emulator-x86_64/vendorsetup.sh
including device/generic/mini-emulator-mips/vendorsetup.sh
including device/generic/mini-emulator-x86/vendorsetup.sh
including device/generic/mini-emulator-arm64/vendorsetup.sh
including device/generic/mini-emulator-armv7-a-neon/vendorsetup.sh
including device/lge/mako/vendorsetup.sh
including device/lge/hammerhead/vendorsetup.sh
including device/moto/shamu/vendorsetup.sh
including device/asus/fugu/vendorsetup.sh
including device/asus/deb/vendorsetup.sh
including device/asus/tilapia/vendorsetup.sh
including device/asus/flo/vendorsetup.sh
including device/asus/grouper/vendorsetup.sh
including sdk/bash_completion/adb.bash
esteban@dronix:~/WORKING_DIRECTORY$ 
```

The previous screenshot shows the output of `envsetup.sh`, that brings the system to be fully operational and ready to build. To have a list of all the commands that we now have available, on your Terminal, run:

`:~$ hmm`

```
 x  -  □   esteban@dronix: ~/WORKING_DIRECTORY
                          esteban@dronix: ~/WORKING_DIRECTORY 98x30
esteban@dronix:~/WORKING_DIRECTORY$
esteban@dronix:~/WORKING_DIRECTORY$ hmm
Invoke ". build/envsetup.sh" from your shell to add the following functions to your environment:
- lunch:   lunch <product_name>-<build_variant>
- tapas:   tapas [<App1> <App2> ...] [arm|x86|mips|armv5|arm64|x86_64|mips64] [eng|userdebug|user]
- croot:   Changes directory to the top of the tree.
- m:       Makes from the top of the tree.
- mm:      Builds all of the modules in the current directory, but not their dependencies.
- mmm:     Builds all of the modules in the supplied directories, but not their dependencies.
           To limit the modules being built use the syntax: mmm dir/:target1,target2.
- mma:     Builds all of the modules in the current directory, and their dependencies.
- mmma:    Builds all of the modules in the supplied directories, and their dependencies.
- cgrep:   Greps on all local C/C++ files.
- ggrep:   Greps on all local Gradle files.
- jgrep:   Greps on all local Java files.
- resgrep: Greps on all local res/*.xml files.
- sgrep:   Greps on all local source files.
- godir:   Go to the directory containing a file.

Look at the source to view more functions. The complete list is:
adb_get_product_device adb_get_traced_by addcompletions add_lunch_combo cgrep check_product check_
variant choosecombo chooseproduct choosetype choosevariant core coredump_enable coredump_setup cpr
oj croot findmakefile gdbclient gdbclient_old gdbwrapper get_abs_build_var getbugreports get_build
_var getdriver getlastscreenshot get_make_command getprebuilt getscreenshotpath getsdcardpath get_
symbols_directory gettargetarch gettop ggrep godir hmm is isviewserverstarted jgrep key_back key_h
ome key_menu lunch _lunch m make mangrep mgrep mm mma mmm mmma pez pid printconfig print_lunch_men
u qpid resgrep runhat runtest sepgrep set_java_home setpaths set_sequence_number set_stuff_for_env
ironment settitle sgrep smoketest stacks startviewserver stopviewserver systemstack tapas tracedmp
ump treegrep
esteban@dronix:~/WORKING_DIRECTORY$ ▮
```

The previous screenshot shows the output of the `hmm` command. We will have a look at lots of them later, but as a yummy anticipation:

- `lunch`: This command helps you configure everything we need for a specific target with one single command

- `mm`: This command lets you compile just the module contained in your current folder

Setup

A proper configuration environment is one of the most important things for a build system. Every build system provides a clear way to specify, for instance, which module to build of which platform we are targeting. Having the Linux kernel as a great example, we can say that it provides a handy graphical menu to perform all the necessary configurations:

```
$ make menuconfig
```

Menuconfig lets you enable or disable modules to be built, select the desired platform, and tons of other different possible configurations. Every single configuration bit is saved in a `.config` file that can be easily read or edited and reused for the build procedure.

As we anticipated, Android is based on something completely different. There is no graphical interface to perform the configuration. The only sort of interactive or automatic configuration system is `envsetup.sh`, which we already learned about. So why does Android not have any cool tools to configure the build system? Simply, because it does not need one! We are not supposed to disable all the modules we don't want to build, so Android just does not provide an easy way.

Let's say that we are building Android for a new device we have just created and it does not have a camera on-board. We might want to remove that part of the system that manages the camera. There is no official way to do it. If we want to do it, we need to get our hands dirty and with time and pages we will be able to do it.

We can safely say that the whole Android build system configuration can be stripped down to setting a few environment variables. The build system will use these variables to figure out which device we are targeting or which toolchain it is supposed to use.

The most important variables are:

- TARGET_PRODUCT
- TARGET_BUILD_VARIANT
- TARGET_BUILD_TYPE
- TARGET_TOOLS_PREFIX
- TARGET_PREBUILT_KERNEL
- OUT_DIR

In the upcoming sections, we are going to learn all about these variables we can manipulate to perfect our build.

The TARGET_PRODUCT variable

This variable contains the information to specify the device we are preparing the system for. We are currently targeting the official emulator, so we are going to set the variable as `aosp_arm`. If we want to build the system for Google's Nexus 6, we will set the variable to `aosp_shamu`, or to `aosp_hummerhead` for Google's Nexus 5.

For quick access to all the values, specific for all the supported devices, we have provided a handy table as follows:

Device	Code Name	TARGET_PRODUCT
Nexus 6	shamu	aosp_shamu
Nexus Player	fugu	aosp_fugu
Nexus 9	volantis (flounder)	aosp_flounder
Nexus 5 (GSM/LTE)	hammerhead	aosp_hammerhead
Nexus 7 (Wi-Fi)	razor (flo)	aosp_flo
Nexus 7 (Mobile)	razorg (deb)	aosp_deb
Nexus 10	mantaray (manta)	full_manta
Nexus 4	occam (mako)	full_mako
Nexus 7 (Wi-Fi)	nakasi (grouper)	full_grouper
Nexus 7 (Mobile)	nakasig (tilapia)	full_tilapia
Galaxy Nexus (GSM/HSPA+)	Yakju (maguro)	full_maguro
Galaxy Nexus (Verizon)	mysid (toro)	aosp_toro
Galaxy Nexus (Experimental)	mysidspr (toroplus)	aosp_toroplus
Panda Board (Archived)	panda	aosp_panda
Motorola Xoom (US Wi-Fi)	wingray	full_wingray
Nexus S	soju (crespo)	full_crespo
Nexus S 4G	sojus (crespo4g)	full_crespo4g

As you can imagine, every device supports a specific version of the system. For instance, with our current downloaded source base, tag android-5.1.1:

- aosp_arm
- aosp_arm64
- aosp_mips
- aosp_mips64
- aosp_x86

- aosp_x86_64
- aosp_manta
- aosp_flounder
- mini_emulator_x86_64
- mini_emulator_mips
- mini_emulator_x86
- mini_emulator_arm64
- m_e_arm
- aosp_mako
- aosp_hammerhead
- aosp_shamu
- full_fugu
- aosp_fugu
- aosp_deb
- aosp_tilapia
- aosp_flo
- aosp_grouper

Once we have decided on the target device, fire up a Terminal and run:

```
$ export TARGET_PRODUCT=aosp_arm
```

The TARGET_BUILD_VARIANT variable

Every Android.mk file refers to this variable to enable and disable the sections of its codebase to be compiled or not. This variable has three possible values and it specifies the build variant. We can set it to:

- eng: Here, every module tagged with user, debug, and eng is enabled
- userdebug: Here, every module tagged with the user and debug is enabled
- user: Here, every module tagged with the user is enabled

We can use the variable as follows:

```
$ export TARGET_BUILD_VARIANT=eng
```

The TARGET_BUILD_TYPE variable

This variable specifies which type of build we are going to perform for every module. If we are going to create a development system, we are going to need more logging information, for instance. For this scenario, we are going to set this variable as debug, build, and test our system. After this phase, we will rebuild the system with this variable set to release, to disable the verbose logging and all the development perks.

The TARGET_TOOLS_PREFIX variable

This variable specifies the path for a custom toolchain to be used during the build process. Usually, it stays empty, but, gaining experience, you should try different toolchains, freely available on the Internet. One of the most famous and optimized custom toolchains is developed and distributed by the Linaro team.

The OUT_DIR variable

If for some specific reason we want to override the default path of the out/ folder, we can use this variable to specify a custom path. This variable is extremely useful in all the scenarios that have multiple hard drives or network shares. For instance, we could run the build process on a fast SSD disk and store the output on a standard old-fashioned disk or even a network disk, to share it with our teammates.

The TARGET_PREBUILT_KERNEL variable

This is a quite advanced variable. It allows us to provide the system with a kernel different from the default one. Every target device comes with a precompiled default kernel because the Android build system is not going to build it—it's already there.

Injecting a custom kernel is a very interesting topic that opens lots of interesting scenarios. In *Chapter 5, Customizing Kernel and Boot Sequence*, we are going to build a custom kernel and inject it into our Android system, to create a fully customized Android experience: this variable will be one of the most important pieces of the puzzle.

The buildspec.mk file

If we want to persist these variables, we can add them to a buildspec.mk file. Every time we will run make, the system will check this file, evaluate all the variables, and move forward accordingly. The buildspec.mk file comes in a handy template version in the build/ folder as buildspec.mk.default. This template file contains every available variable. Every variable is commented, disabled by default, and comes with a small note about its purpose and how to use it.

We could consider this file the equivalent of the Linux kernel .config file, even if we have a smaller amount of possible configurations.

The lunch command

A few sections ago, we had a first bite at lunch already. If we don't want to manually set all those environment variables or we don't want to use buildspec.mk, we can use lunch. We can find it available in the system, after we have executed envsetup.sh.

Let's have a look at the command. Open a Terminal and reach your WORKING_DIRECTORY. Be sure to have launched envsetup.sh and then run:

```
$ lunch
```

```
x  —  □    esteban@dronix: ~/WORKING_DIRECTORY
                    esteban@dronix: ~/WORKING_DIRECTORY 80x34

esteban@dronix:~/WORKING_DIRECTORY$ lunch

You're building on Linux

Lunch menu... pick a combo:
      1.  aosp_arm-eng
      2.  aosp_arm64-eng
      3.  aosp_mips-eng
      4.  aosp_mips64-eng
      5.  aosp_x86-eng
      6.  aosp_x86_64-eng
      7.  aosp_manta-userdebug
      8.  aosp_flounder-userdebug
      9.  mini_emulator_x86_64-userdebug
     10.  mini_emulator_mips-userdebug
     11.  mini_emulator_x86-userdebug
     12.  mini_emulator_arm64-userdebug
     13.  m_e_arm-userdebug
     14.  aosp_mako-userdebug
     15.  aosp_hammerhead-userdebug
     16.  aosp_shamu-userdebug
     17.  full_fugu-userdebug
     18.  aosp_fugu-userdebug
     19.  aosp_deb-userdebug
     20.  aosp_tilapia-userdebug
     21.  aosp_flo-userdebug
     22.  aosp_grouper-userdebug

Which would you like? [aosp_arm-eng] ▊
```

The preceding screenshot shows the output of the command and, as you can easily see, it helps us to pick the exact combination on the variable we want. Every specific Android version has its own `lunch` command and every lunch command version has its output. The preceding screenshot shows the output for tag android-5.1.1.

Once you have picked the desired configuration, `lunch` will show a summary of every variable it's going to set up and goes back to the Terminal, as shown in the following screenshot:

```
x  -  □   esteban@dronix: ~/WORKING_DIRECTORY
                 esteban@dronix: ~/WORKING_DIRECTORY 80x23


============================================
PLATFORM_VERSION_CODENAME=REL
PLATFORM_VERSION=5.1.1
TARGET_PRODUCT=aosp_shamu
TARGET_BUILD_VARIANT=userdebug
TARGET_BUILD_TYPE=release
TARGET_BUILD_APPS=
TARGET_ARCH=arm
TARGET_ARCH_VARIANT=armv7-a-neon
TARGET_CPU_VARIANT=krait
TARGET_2ND_ARCH=
TARGET_2ND_ARCH_VARIANT=
TARGET_2ND_CPU_VARIANT=
HOST_ARCH=x86_64
HOST_OS=linux
HOST_OS_EXTRA=Linux-3.19.0-26-generic-x86_64-with-Ubuntu-15.04-vivid
HOST_BUILD_TYPE=release
BUILD_ID=LMY48I
OUT_DIR=out
============================================

esteban@dronix:~/WORKING_DIRECTORY$ 
```

We are now ready to fire out the `make` command and build our first Android version!

Building the system

You have downloaded the source code, initialized the whole environment using `envsetup.sh` and configured every system variable with `lunch`. You are now ready to build the system. Open a Terminal and run:

```
:~$ make -j8
```

The building system will fire up, looking for all those modules and `Android.mk` files to include into the build process and perform the compilation.

If you want to enjoy a more verbose compilation output, you can run:

```
:~$ make -j8 showcommands
```

With this extra parameter, the build system will print all *GCC* compilation logs and all `javac` compilation logs, to give you as much information as possible during the building process.

More about make

The `make` command offers a few interesting options that come handy in specific scenarios.

Building a module

For instance, if you want to build just one single module, you can run:

```
~$ make art
```

In this example, we are building only `art`. The module name is contained in the `Android.mk` file of the `module` folder. Just scroll the file and you will find a variable `LOCAL_MODULE` that represents the exact module name to use with `make`.

We can retrieve the module name also using the `mm` command. With a Terminal, just reach the module folder and run:

```
$ mm
```

Cleaning a module

If we are not satisfied after the module building is completed, we can clean all the compilation files and have a fresh start. Open a Terminal, reach the module folder, and run:

```
~$ make clean-<module>
```

Cleaning everything

If you want to clean the whole project and prepare the system for a new from-scratch build, open a Terminal, reach the `WORKING_DIRECTORY`, and run:

```
~$ make clean
```

This command removes every compilation file from the folder we have specified in the `OUT_DIR` variable.

Listing modules

```
$ make modules
```

This command shows the list of every module available in the AOSP architecture. The amount of available modules is massive: we will have to wait for a few seconds to see any output from this command.

Recreating an image

This command recreates the system images, based on the current status of the source base, using an incremental building approach, as shown here:

```
$ make snod
```

This is a crucial command during development. Think about developing a single module. When you reach a development milestone, you build the module with:

```
$ make module_name
```

If everything is working, you might like to inject your brand new module into your Android system image. You can achieve this with:

```
:$ make module_name snod
```

Building tools

The following command will create and provide us with two of the most important tools for an Android expert — adb and `fastboot`:

```
:$ make tools
```

We will have plenty of time to learn about them in the next pages.

Beyond the system image

We are currently building a system image ready to be flashed to a device. Unfortunately, this procedure keeps out a few useful tools that we want to build as well: NDK, SDK, and CTS.

Android SDK

Google provides the official Android SDK via the Android Developers website. It's already compiled for every platform and ready to be downloaded. In a more advanced scenario, you might need to extend the SDK and redistribute it as your own. Building a custom SDK is a three command job, with those we already learned about in the previous sections:

```
~$ . build/envsetup.sh
~$ lunch sdk-eng
~$ make
```

The output of this procedure will be a brand new custom Android SDK in out/ host/linux-x86/sdk/.

Android NDK

Android NDK is the native equivalent, based on C/C++, of the Android SDK, based on Java. To build the NDK, open a Terminal, reach WORKING_DIRECTORY, and run:

```
~$ cd ndk/build/tools
~$ export ANDROID_NDK_ROOT=path/to/WORKING_DIRECTORY/ndk
~$ ./make-release
```

The system will alert you about the possible long duration of the process. Just accept the message and prepare some coffee in the meantime.

Android CTS

CTS is a well-known tool. We learned everything about it in the previous chapters. To build our own version, we need only one command:

```
~$ make cts
```

Inside an AOSP module

The AOSP project is incredibly huge. The amount of modules contained in the source base is massive. Android 5 Lollipop contains about 4,000 different modules. They go from native modules, written in C/C++, to providing system components: daemons, libraries, and Java modules, to provide everything that is needed from APKs to JAR files.

Every module contains an Android.mk file. This file contains every single piece of information needed to build the module. The Android build system does not use a recursive-make approach, but merges every Android.mk file to create one single huge Makefile to build the system: every Android.mk file is a piece of the puzzle.

In addition to Android.mk, the module folder also contains CleanSpeck.mk. This file helps the system to properly clean every compiled file when we execute a module clean command.

Diving into Android.mk

The quickest path to knowledge is getting your hands dirty. We are going to analyze a real Android.mk file from the Android source code to understand structure and purpose. In the previous chapter, we learned that the external/ folder contains lots of third-party tools that enrich the Android system. One of these tools is netcat. Let's see its Android.mk file:

```
LOCAL_PATH:= $(call my-dir)
include $(CLEAR_VARS)

LOCAL_SRC_FILES:=\
        netcat.c \
        atomicio.c

LOCAL_CFLAGS:=-O2 -g

LOCAL_MODULE_TAGS := eng

LOCAL_MODULE_PATH := $(TARGET_OUT_OPTIONAL_EXECUTABLES)

LOCAL_MODULE:=nc

# gold in binutils 2.22 will warn about the usage of mktemp
LOCAL_LDFLAGS += -Wl,--no-fatal-warnings

include $(BUILD_EXECUTABLE)
```

A few cryptic lines that need more detailed study:

```
LOCAL_PATH:= $(call my-dir)
```

This line specifies the LOCAL_PATH variable and sets it to the current module path. As you can guess, the $(call my-dir) function returns the current module path.

This function is part of a collection of useful functions that the system provides to be used during the development of new modules. The whole list is contained in `build/core/definitions.mk`. Every function comes with code, obviously, and a tiny, but effective description of its purpose, as shown in the next screenshot:

```
×  —  □    esteban@dronix: ~/WORKING_DIRECTORY/build/core

                    esteban@dronix: ~/WORKING_DIRECTORY/build/core 80x32
#################################################################
## Retrieve the directory of the current makefile
## Must be called before including any other makefile!!
#################################################################

# Figure out where we are.
define my-dir
$(strip \
  $(eval LOCAL_MODULE_MAKEFILE := $$(lastword $$(MAKEFILE_LIST))) \
  $(if $(filter $(BUILD_SYSTEM)/% $(OUT_DIR)/%,$(LOCAL_MODULE_MAKEFILE)), \
    $(error my-dir must be called before including any other makefile.) \
    , \
    $(patsubst %/,%,$(dir $(LOCAL_MODULE_MAKEFILE))) \
  ) \
)
endef

#################################################################
## Retrieve a list of all makefiles immediately below some directory
#################################################################

define all-makefiles-under
$(wildcard $(1)/*/Android.mk)
endef

#################################################################
## Look under a directory for makefiles that don't have parent
## makefiles
#################################################################

# $(1): directory to search under
                                                    150,8        5%
```

```
include $(CLEAR_VARS)
```

This line solves one big issue due to the nature of the Android build system—having all the Android.mk files merged into one single Makefile creates a dangerous scenario in which LOCAL_ variables from module A could be improperly used by module B. The $(CLEAR_VARS) function resets all the previously set variables and allows the current module to safely access its local variables, using this code:

```
LOCAL_SRC_FILES:=\
        netcat.c \
        atomicio.c
```

The following line specifies the source files contained in the current module:

```
LOCAL_CFLAGS:=-O2 -g
```

The following line specifies which argument we are going to pass to the compiler:

```
LOCAL_MODULE_TAGS := eng
```

This line specifies which variant this module belongs to. This is closely related to the environment variable TARGET_BUILD_VARIANT we learned about in the previous sections. Specifying eng here will make this module available when we will build the eng build variant of the system:

```
LOCAL_MODULE_PATH := $(TARGET_OUT_OPTIONAL_EXECUTABLES)
```

This line specifies where to install the compiled executable file when the build process succeeds. In this specific case, the final file will be placed in the xbin/ folder of the system image. This variable is optional. The system will act based on default values, already specified in the global configuration. We can use this variable to specify a *different* destination folder:

```
LOCAL_MODULE:=nc
```

This line has been anticipated a few sections ago. This specifies the module name. It has to be unique and it will also be the executable file's final name. In this case, our netcat utility will become the nc exectutable, as commonly seen on *nix systems:

```
LOCAL_LDFLAGS += -Wl,--no-fatal-warnings
```

As for the compiler also, the linker will have its set of specific arguments. This line specifies which options the linker will operate according to:

```
include $(BUILD_EXECUTABLE)
```

This line specifies which type of module we are trying to build. Our current module is an executable utility, so we are going to specify $(BUILD_EXECUTABLE) and the system will properly produce an executable file from all the module source code.

Android.mk variables ecosystem

In the previous section, we analyzed a real-world Android.mk. This gave us a bit of confidence about creating our own Android module. In this section, we will continue our journey with an overview about all the variables we can use in our Android.mk.

LOCAL_ variables are all those variables necessary to achieve the proper module configuration and compilation. These kinds of variables get canceled by $(CLEAN_VARS) and are by far the most common kind in all Android.mk files.

The INTERNAL_, HOST_, and TARGET_ variables should not be used for custom purposes because they are commonly used by the build system itself.

The BUILD_ variables specify the build type, as we already saw in a previous example where we used BUILD_EXECUTABLE.

Technically speaking, we could use any kind of variable, but that's a dangerous game. It is hard to predict how the build system will manipulate our Android.mk files to create its Makefile: order might be not respected, names could be overridden, and scopes could be invalidated. To play safely and rely on the build system architecture, let's focus on using only LOCAL_ variables for our tasks.

There is no official documentation about these variables. The upcoming list is the result of hard work, taking risks, guessing, and scavenging bits of information from all around the build system.

The LOCAL_ variables

When it comes to LOCAL_ variables, we can customize our module according to this list:

- LOCAL_PATH: This specifies the path of the module. Usually, the value is retrieved using the $(call my-dir) function.

- LOCAL_MODULE: This specifies the name of the module and, if we are dealing with an executable module, the name of the executable.

- LOCAL_MODULE_CLASS: This specifies the class the module belongs to. Based on its class, every result of the module building process will be placed in the proper folder. The examples of possible classes are EXECUTABLE, ETC, SHARED_LIBRARY, STATIC_LIBRARY, and APPS.

- LOCAL_SRC_FILES: This specifies the list of all source files contained in the module, separated by whitespace.

- LOCAL_PACKAGE_NAME: This specifies the name of the app, for instance: Contacts, Phone, Calculator, and so on.

- LOCAL_SHARED_LIBRARIES: This specifies the shared libraries that may be required.

- LOCAL_MODULE_TAGS: This specifies a tag, such as eng, and the system will include this module in every build that will target the eng type as TARGET_BUILD_VARIANT.

- LOCAL_MODULE_PATH: This specifies a custom installation path to override the one specified in the BUILD_ template.

- LOCAL_CC: This specifies a different C compiler to be used.

- LOCAL_CXX: This specifies a different C++ compiler to be used.

- `LOCAL_CFLAGS`: This helps to add mode flags to the C compiler command line.
- `LOCAL_CPPFLAGS`: This helps to add mode flags to the C++ compiler command line.
- `LOCAL_CPP_EXTENSION`: This specifies a custom extension for C++ files, if for some reason the actual extension is not `.cpp`.
- `LOCAL_C_INCLUDE`: This specifies the path for custom C header files needed to build the module.
- `LOCAL_LDFLAGS`: This helps to add mode flags to the linker command line.
- `LOCAL_PREBUILT_EXECUTABLES`: During the creation of a `BUILD_PREBUILD` kind of module, this variable will contain every binary executable that will be part of the final system image. We are going to learn more about this in the next chapters.
- `LOCAL_PREBUILT_LIBS`: During the creation of a `BUILD_PREBUILD` kind of module, this variable will contain every library that will be part of the final system image.
- `LOCAL_PREBUILT_PACKAGE`: During the creation of a `BUILD_PREBUILD` kind of module, this variable will contain every prebuild APK that will be part of the final system image.

The BUILD_ variables

The following list contains the most common `BUILD_` variables available during the development of a custom module:

- `BUILD_EXECUTABLE`: When necessary to build using native C/C++ code, we can add this line to our configuration:

```
include $(BUILD_EXECUTABLE)
```

- `BUILD_PREBUILT`: This allows us to add binary components to our final image.
- `BUILD_MULTI_PREBUILT`: This allows us to create modules that inject the final image with binarie components of the same category. It's usually used with `LOCAL_MODULE_CLASS` to specify the class and the position to place the binary files.
- `BUILD_PACKAGE`: This allows us to create modules that generate APK files.
- `BUILD_SHARED_LIBRARY`: This allows us to create modules that generate shared library files.

- `BUILD_STATIC_LIBRARY`: This allows us to create modules that generate static library files.

- `BUILD_JAVA_LIBRARY`: This allows us to create modules that generate Java library files.

Module template examples

In this section, we are going to analyze real-world module template snippets, to have a clear idea about what a fully operational module template looks like.

The native executable template

If you are going to work on a generic native single-file executable application, for example, `your_executable.c`, you can use the following snippet to build it:

```
LOCAL_PATH:= $(call my-dir)
include $(CLEAR_VARS)

LOCAL_SRC_FILES:= your_executable.c
LOCAL_MODULE:= your_executable

include $(BUILD_EXECUTABLE)
```

The shared library template

This snippet comes in handy if you are working with a so-called shared library: your library would be composed of a set of files, that is, `foo.c` and `bar.c`, and would be built accordingly:

```
LOCAL_PATH:= $(call my-dir)
include $(CLEAR_VARS)

LOCAL_SRC_FILES:= foo.c bar.c
LOCAL_MODULE:= libmysharedlib
LOCAL_PRELINK_MODULE := false    # Prevent from prelink error

include $(BUILD_SHARED_LIBRARY)
```

The application template

If you are going to work on a whole application, you could use the following snippet:

```
LOCAL_PATH:= $(call my-dir)
include $(CLEAR_VARS)
LOCAL_MODULE_TAGS:= eng
```

```
LOCAL_SRC_FILES:= $(call all-java-files-under src)
LOCAL_PACKAGE_NAME:= MyApplication

include $(BUILD_PACKAGE)
```

This snippet will build every .java file in the specified path and package everything as MyApplication.

Creating a custom device

During our journey, you learned how to retrieve the source code and how to set up the build system. In this section, you are going to learn how to create a new target device and add it to the build system. The device we are going to create now has specific hardware features. It's a proof-of-concept device, with the only purpose of showing you how easily and quickly you can create a brand new device and then customize it.

Every device definition is contained in the device/ folder. First level folders contains all the manufacturer's folders. Every manufacturer folder contains its own devices. Let's create our own manufacturer and device folders: our brand is Irarref and our model is an F488. Open a Terminal, reach the WORKING_DIRECTORY folder, and run:

~$ mkdir -p device/irarref/f488

Once we have the folder structure in place, we need to create all those files that will allow the build system to detect our device and make it available as a target for the build system. We are going to create the following files:

- Android.mk: Describes in a generic way how to compile the source files. Essentially, it represents a snippet of the global Makefile that will be later incorporated by the build system at the appropriate time.

- AndroidProducts.mk: This file contains a PRODUCS_MAKEFILEs variable, with a list of all the available products. In our scenario, we only have one device and it's represented by these files.

- full_f488.mk: This file specifies any relevant information about the device.

- BoardConfig.mk: This file specifies any relevant information about the device board.

- vendorsetup.sh: This script makes the device available to envsetup.sh and lunch.

Diving into device configuration

As we know, our first device is quite simple, but very instructive. Let's see how our device specification is spread inside all our configuration files:

- `Android.mk`:

  ```
  LOCAL_PATH:= $(call my-dir)
  Include $(CLEAN_VARS)

  Ifneq ($(filter f488, $(TARGET_DEVICE)),)
  Include $(call all-makefile-unter, $(LOCAL_PATH))
  Endif
  ```

- `AndroidProducts.mk`:

  ```
  PRODUCT_MAKEFILES:= $(LOCAL_DIR)/full_f488.mk
  ```

- `full_f488.mk`:

  ```
  $(call inherit-product,
  $(SRC_TARGET_DIR)/product/aosp_base.mk
  #
  DEVICE_PACKAGE_OVERLAY:=

  PRODUCT_PACKAGE+=
  PRODUCT_COPY_FILES+=
  PRODUCT_NAME:= full_f488
  PRODUCT_DEVICE:= f488
  PRODUCT_MODEL:= Android for Irarref F488
  ```

- `BoardConfig.mk`:

  ```
  TARGET_NO_BOOTLOADER := true
  TARGET_NO_KERNEL := true
  TARGET_CPU_ABI := armeabi
  HAVE_HTC_AUDIO_DRIVER := true
  BOARD_USES_GENERIC_AUDIO := true

  # no hardware camera
  USE_CAMERA_STUB := true

  # CPU
  TARGET_ARCH_VARIANT := armv7-a-neon
  ARCH_ARM_HAVE_TLS_REGISTER := true
  ```

- `vendorsetup.sh`:

  `add_lunch_combo full_f488-eng`

Our `Android.mk` is pretty standard and completely based on what we have learned in the previous sections. `AndroidProducts.mk` just includes `full_f488.mk`, as expected.

The `full_f488.mk` file contains a few interesting lines. First of all, it includes `aosp_base.mk`, a configuration file provided by the system, common to lots of real devices.

Moving on, we found a few interesting variables:

- `DEVICE_PACKAGE_OVERLAY:=`: This variable allows us to create a custom overlay, customizing, for instance, some settings of specific modules in the AOSP system. If you check, for instance, this variable in the equivalent file for the `shamu` device, you can notice that they are using it to customize a few settings in the launcher application.

- `PRODUCT_PACKAGE+=`: This variable allows us to add packages to the compilation process.

- `PRODUCT_COPY_FILES+=`: This variable performs a file copy operation. The syntax is pretty straight forward: `source_file:dest_file`

- `PRODUCT_NAME:= full_f488`: This variable specifies the product name. This is the exact same value that `lunch` will print as `TARGET_PRODUCT`.

- `PRODUCT_DEVICE:= f488`: This variable specifies the device name.

- `PRODUCT_MODEL:=`: Android for Irarref F488: This variable specifies the device model label that we will find in our Android system under **Settings | About phone | Model Number**.

With all these files in place, you can now relaunch `envsetup.sh` and our brand new proof-of-concept device will be in the list of the available devices.

From zero to the screenlock

So far we have gathered an incredible amount of information about the architecture, about how to configure the build system, and our PoC device. It's time to create our first image for a real device and use it! We want to keep away all the possible hardware-related issues, so we will target the simplest nonhardware Android device: the Android emulator.

We are going to build the latest available Android Lollipop source code. As we learned, we are going to download it, configure it to target the emulator, build it, and try it on the device.

Setup

Let's set up our WORKING_DIRECTORY and download our precious source code. Open a Terminal and run the following commands:

```
:$ mkdir WORKING_DIRECTORY
```

```
:$ cd WORKING_DIRECTORY
```

```
:$ repo init -u https://android.googlesource.com/platform/manifest -b \
android-5.1.1_r9
```

```
:$ repo sync
```

After the download is completed, we can configure the environment. Let's run:

```
:$ build/envsetup.sh
```

This will create all those handy tools we will need during the work. We now have lunch, for instance, and running it we can keep on configuring the environment:

```
:$ lunch
```

Let's choose a target device:

```
aosp_arm-eng
```

The lunch command will set up everything and show us a configuration report, as shown in the next screenshot:

```
 ×  —  ☐   esteban@dronix: /media/esteban/NAS500/embedded_android/WORKING_DIRECTOR
        esteban@dronix: /media/esteban/NAS500/embedded_android/WORKING_DIRECTORY_E 80x24

Which would you like? [aosp_arm-eng]

============================================
PLATFORM_VERSION_CODENAME=REL
PLATFORM_VERSION=5.1.1
TARGET_PRODUCT=aosp_arm
TARGET_BUILD_VARIANT=eng
TARGET_BUILD_TYPE=release
TARGET_BUILD_APPS=
TARGET_ARCH=arm
TARGET_ARCH_VARIANT=armv7-a
TARGET_CPU_VARIANT=generic
TARGET_2ND_ARCH=
TARGET_2ND_ARCH_VARIANT=
TARGET_2ND_CPU_VARIANT=
HOST_ARCH=x86_64
HOST_OS=linux
HOST_OS_EXTRA=Linux-3.19.0-26-generic-x86_64-with-Ubuntu-15.04-vivid
HOST_BUILD_TYPE=release
BUILD_ID=LMY48I
OUT_DIR=out
============================================
```

Build

Everything is in place. We need only one command to launch the build procedure:

```
:$ make -j8
```

Once the build process is over, head to out/target/product/generic/. This folder will contain our built images. The following screenshot shows the result of the build process: a folder full of .img files, ready to be flashed into the device:

```
× — □   esteban@dronix: /media/esteban/NAS500/embedded_android/WORKING_DIRECTOR
⊞   esteban@dronix: /media/esteban/NAS500/embedded_android/WORKING_DIRECTORY_E 80x19
total 1143808
-rw-rw-r--  1 esteban esteban        7 Aug 17 02:27 android-info.txt
drwxrwxr-x  2 esteban esteban     4096 Aug 17 04:44 cache
-rw-r--r--  1 esteban esteban 69206016 Aug 17 16:42 cache.img
-rw-rw-r--  1 esteban esteban    62468 Aug 25 22:17 clean_steps.mk
drwxrwxr-x  4 esteban esteban     4096 Aug 17 06:24 data
drwxrwxr-x  3 esteban esteban     4096 Aug 17 04:57 dex_bootjars
drwxrwxr-x  5 esteban esteban     4096 Aug 17 03:48 gen
-rw-rw-r--  1 esteban esteban     1660 Aug 17 16:40 hardware-qemu.ini
-rw-rw-r--  1 esteban esteban    62995 Aug 17 14:38 installed-files.txt
drwxrwxr-x 14 esteban esteban     4096 Aug 17 14:38 obj
-rw-r--r--  1 esteban esteban      736 Aug 25 22:17 previous_build_config.mk
-rw-rw-r--  1 esteban esteban   801869 Aug 17 05:42 ramdisk.img
drwxrwxr-x  8 esteban esteban     4096 Aug 17 05:02 root
drwxrwxr-x  6 esteban esteban     4096 Aug 17 05:01 symbols
drwxrwxr-x 14 esteban esteban     4096 Aug 17 13:02 system
-rw-r--r--  1 esteban esteban 576716800 Aug 17 14:39 system.img
-rw-r--r--  1 esteban esteban 576716800 Aug 17 06:24 userdata.img
-rw-------  1 esteban esteban 576716800 Aug 17 20:00 userdata-qemu.img
```

Run

To launch the emulator, Android provides the emulator command. This command will be available the moment the compilation ends. Using the .img files, we have in the out/ folder, we can run it like this:

```
$ emulator -system out/target/product/generic/system.img -ramdisk
out/target/product/generic/ramdisk.img -data
out/target/product/generic/userdata-qemu.img
```

After a few moments, the emulator window will pop up and you will see something like the following screenshot:

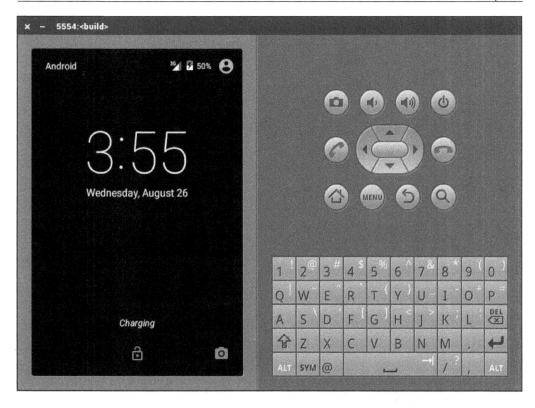

You can use the emulator with mouse and keyboard, performing the same operations you would do on a real device. Android emulator is a powerful tool and the amount of possibilities is almost endless. If you would like to dig into the topic, the Android Developers website provides a specific page for it: `http://developer.android.com/tools/help/emulator.html`.

Summary

This chapter was a great run! You prepared your system to build your first Android system. You learned how to configure and customize the build system. You learned the basic skills to create a custom module and include it into your system image. You created a system image from scratch and tested it on the Android emulator.

In the next chapter, we will raise the bar. We are going to move our efforts to a real hardware device. We will work with a smartphone, the Nexus 5, and a development board, the UDOO. We will manipulate the bootloader and the recovery partition to take complete control of the system.

4
Moving to Real-World Hardware

In the previous chapter, you learned how to set up the necessary environment configurations and how to build your first vanilla system, targeting the emulator. In this chapter, we will have a quick overview of the fundamental tools of every expert Android user and we will complete our first system for a real device—configure, build, flash, and test.

Debugging tools

Debugging tools are some of the tools that no developer can live without. With embedded systems such as Android systems they are even more important. Android provides lots of debugging tools to facilitate complex or boring tasks. The two most important tools are definitely `adb` and `fastboot`.

Introducing ADB

ADB stands for Android Debug Bridge and it's a toolkit made of two crucial parts:

- Adb server running on the device
- Adb client running on the PC

Usually, `adb` is considered a command-line tool, but you can find a few graphical frontends online if you prefer to use it in a more graphical way. Android Studio, the official IDE by Google for Android development, uses `adb` to communicate with every device and provide cool tools such as `Android Device Monitor`. Using the graphical interface, we can analyze logs coming from the device or even take a screenshot for debugging purposes.

The following screenshot shows how the **Android Device Monitor** can be used to retrieve huge amounts of information from devices and apps running on the devices:

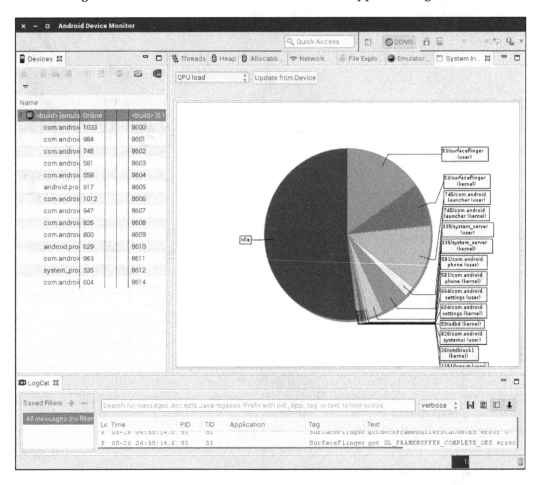

During our journey, we will use `adb` mostly on the command line, due to the embedded nature of our work. As we know, the emulator behaves like a hardware device, so we can easily use `adb` to communicate with it. Let's see a couple of useful commands to interact with our running emulator.

First of all, we need a handy list of all the available commands. That's easily achievable with the following command:

```
$ adb --help
```

Now, we need to detect the connected devices. On our trusty Terminal, run the following command:

```
$ adb devices
```

```
×  −  □   esteban@dronix: ~/WORKING_DIRECTORY
▟ |                    esteban@dronix: ~/WORKING_DIRECTORY 80x7

esteban@dronix:~/WORKING_DIRECTORY$ adb devices
List of devices attached
emulator-5554   device

esteban@dronix:~/WORKING_DIRECTORY$ ▉
```

The previous command will scan for every attached device and will list them. The previous screenshot shows that our emulator is attached and ready to communicate. In a multidevice scenario, we could have some issue when properly detecting our devices. Adb gives us a further option, -l:

```
[hamen:~/WORKING_DIRECTORY] $ adb devices -l
List of devices attached
ZX1B226467              device usb:341065728X product:condor_retde model:XT1021 device:condor_umts
TA9290D3VX              device usb:340983808X product:falcon_reteu model:XT1032 device:falcon_umts

[hamen:~/WORKING_DIRECTORY] $ ▉
```

Using the -l option, adb will show more details about the devices, and this will help us to identify them properly, as shown in the previous screenshot.

Once we have detected the device, we can communicate with it in a few ways. One of the most common way is connecting it to the device's internal shell. Every Android device comes with a system shell: it's a common tool for embedded or remote systems. To connect the the internal shell, we simply need to run the following command:

```
$ adb shell
```

If we have more then one device, we will need to specify which device we want to connect to, like this:

```
$ adb -s ZX1B226467 shell
```

Once we are connected to the internal shell, we can treat the system like a common *nix system. We can run an ls command:

```
$ ls -l
```

As shown in the next screenshot, we obtain the directory listing:

```
 x  —  □    esteban@dronix: ~/WORKING_DIRECTORY
                      esteban@dronix: ~/WORKING_DIRECTORY 80x37
esteban@dronix:~/WORKING_DIRECTORY$ adb shell
root@generic:/ # ls -l
drwxr-xr-x root      root                 2015-08-26 03:52 acct
drwxrwx--- system    cache                2015-08-26 03:53 cache
lrwxrwxrwx root      root                 1970-01-01 01:00 charger -> /sbin/healthd
dr-x------ root      root                 2015-08-26 03:52 config
lrwxrwxrwx root      root                 2015-08-26 03:52 d -> /sys/kernel/debug
drwxrwx--x system    system               2015-08-26 03:54 data
-rw-r--r-- root      root             281 1970-01-01 01:00 default.prop
drwxr-xr-x root      root                 2015-08-26 03:52 dev
lrwxrwxrwx root      root                 2015-08-26 03:52 etc -> /system/etc
-rw-r--r-- root      root           11166 1970-01-01 01:00 file_contexts
-rw-r----- root      root             922 1970-01-01 01:00 fstab.goldfish
-rwxr-x--- root      root          375308 1970-01-01 01:00 init
-rwxr-x--- root      root             944 1970-01-01 01:00 init.environ.rc
-rwxr-x--- root      root            2836 1970-01-01 01:00 init.goldfish.rc
-rwxr-x--- root      root           21728 1970-01-01 01:00 init.rc
-rwxr-x--- root      root            1927 1970-01-01 01:00 init.trace.rc
-rwxr-x--- root      root            3885 1970-01-01 01:00 init.usb.rc
-rwxr-x--- root      root             301 1970-01-01 01:00 init.zygote32.rc
drwxrwxr-x root      system               2015-08-26 03:52 mnt
dr-xr-xr-x root      root                 1970-01-01 01:00 proc
-rw-r--r-- root      root            2771 1970-01-01 01:00 property_contexts
drwx------ root      root                 2014-09-16 19:33 root
drwxr-x--- root      root                 1970-01-01 01:00 sbin
lrwxrwxrwx root      root                 2015-08-26 03:52 sdcard -> /storage/sdcard
-rw-r--r-- root      root             471 1970-01-01 01:00 seapp_contexts
-rw-r--r-- root      root              62 1970-01-01 01:00 selinux_version
-rw-r--r-- root      root          118317 1970-01-01 01:00 sepolicy
-rw-r--r-- root      root            9438 1970-01-01 01:00 service_contexts
drwxr-x--x root      sdcard_r             2015-08-26 03:52 storage
dr-xr-xr-x root      root                 2015-08-26 03:52 sys
drwxr-xr-x root      root                 1970-01-01 01:00 system
-rw-r--r-- root      root             323 1970-01-01 01:00 ueventd.goldfish.rc
-rw-r--r-- root      root            4464 1970-01-01 01:00 ueventd.rc
lrwxrwxrwx root      root                 2015-08-26 03:52 vendor -> /system/vendor
root@generic:/ # ▊
```

We suggest you explore the filesystem and play around. You will find that you can do almost whatever you want, from manipulating files to manipulating applications.

Pushing files to devices

Adb gives us dozens of useful commands to manage our devices:

```
$ adb push
```

The `adb push` command is certainly one of the most useful. It allows us to copy files from our computer to our Android device. The next screenshot shows how to upload a single file to our device:

```
X  —  ☐   esteban@dronix: ~

                              esteban@dronix: ~ 80x7

esteban@dronix:~$ echo "hello pippo" > pippo.txt
esteban@dronix:~$ adb push pippo.txt /sdcard/
0 KB/s (12 bytes in 0.041s)
esteban@dronix:~$ █
```

We have created a new file, `pippo.txt`, containing a single line, `hello pippo`, then we uploaded this file to our connected device, into the `/sdcard/` folder. As you can see, the first argument is the filename and the second one is the destination we want to copy the file to.

The next screenshot shows `pippo.txt` successfully uploaded to the device's `/sdcard/` folder:

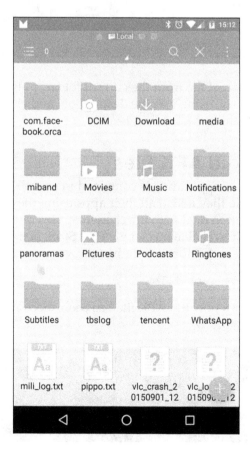

Pulling files from devices

During development, we could need to retrieve a file from the device. To achieve this, `adb` gives us the opposite of `push`, which is `pull`:

```
$ adb pull
```

The preceding command is able to retrieve a file from a connected device and copy it to our computer. The syntax is fairly similar to `push`, simply with an inverse outcome. The next screenshot shows how to `pull` our `pippo.txt` from the device and copy it to the current directory:

```
✕  ─  ☐    esteban@dronix: ~
                              esteban@dronix: ~ 80x8
esteban@dronix:~$ rm pippo.txt
esteban@dronix:~$ adb pull /sdcard/pippo.txt .
0 KB/s (12 bytes in 0.082s)
esteban@dronix:~$ cat pippo.txt
hello pippo
esteban@dronix:~$
```

We have deleted our original file from the current folder, pulled the one on the device to the current folder, using . as the destination, and checked that the copied `pippo.txt` file contains the expected line, `hello pippo`.

Installing Android APK files

As we know, any Android application is contained in an APK file. Usually, users don't see this file, because they install all their apps using the Google Play Store. As advanced users, we often deal with unreleased applications, for debugging and testing. These apps aren't available on Google Play Store yet, so `adb` gives us the opportunity to manually install them with the following command:

```
~$ adb install <path to .apk file>
```

The next screenshot shows how the APK file has been successfully installed on our device number ZX1B226467:

```
1& [hamen:~/embedded_android_programming] $ l
embedded_android_programming.apk
1& [hamen:~/embedded_android_programming] $ adb -s ZX1B226467 install embedded_android_programming.apk
5898 KB/s (1843802 bytes in 0.305s)
        pkg: /data/local/tmp/embedded_android_programming.apk
Success
1& [hamen:~/embedded_android_programming] 11s $
```

Logcat

Every complex system such as Android needs a logging system. Android provides logging capabilities via `logcat` to help users with development and monitoring. Using the following command:

```
~$ adb logcat
```

We can instruct `adb` to connect to the Android logging system, select the default buffer, and start printing every single system logging message, in real-time, to our terminal. Android provides other two logging buffers for advanced use:

- `radio`: This contains all the relevant logging messages related to the radio communication system
- `events`: This contains messages related to the system events

We can select a buffer different from the default using the `-b` option. For instance, if we want all the logs related to events, we can use the following command:

```
:~$ adb logcat -b events
```

Adb `logcat` comes with a few interesting output modes. We can select them using the `-v` option and the mode name:

- brief
- color
- long
- printable
- process
- raw
- tag
- thread
- threadtime
- time
- usec

The next screenshot shows `logcat` output when we choose the `color` mode:

As you can see, `logcat` will use a different color for every different logging level. We can even filter according to the logging level itself, using the following command:

```
~$ adb logcat *:E
```

In this case, we are only displaying error messages. The next screenshot shows every available filtering argument we can use:

For a complete list of all the possible options available with `logcat`, you can access the `logcat` command help using the following command:

```
~$ adb logcat -h
```

The following screenshot shows the full list of all the available options with their description:

```
x  –  □   esteban@dronix: ~
▦ |                                          esteban@dronix: ~ 110x63
esteban@dronix:~$
esteban@dronix:~$ adb logcat -h
Unrecognized Option h
Usage: logcat [options] [filterspecs]
options include:
  -s              Set default filter to silent.
                  Like specifying filterspec '*:S'
  -f <filename>   Log to file. Default is stdout
  -r <kbytes>     Rotate log every kbytes. Requires -f
  -n <count>      Sets max number of rotated logs to <count>, default 4
  -v <format>     Sets the log print format, where <format> is:

                     brief color long printable process raw tag thread
                     threadtime time usec

  -D              print dividers between each log buffer
  -c              clear (flush) the entire log and exit
  -d              dump the log and then exit (don't block)
  -t <count>      print only the most recent <count> lines (implies -d)
  -t '<time>'     print most recent lines since specified time (implies -d)
  -T <count>      print only the most recent <count> lines (does not imply -d)
  -T '<time>'     print most recent lines since specified time (not imply -d)
                  count is pure numerical, time is 'MM-DD hh:mm:ss.mmm'
  -g              get the size of the log's ring buffer and exit
  -L              dump logs from prior to last reboot
  -b <buffer>     Request alternate ring buffer, 'main', 'system', 'radio',
                  'events', 'crash' or 'all'. Multiple -b parameters are
                  allowed and results are interleaved. The default is
                  -b main -b system -b crash.
  -B              output the log in binary.
  -S              output statistics.
  -G <size>       set size of log ring buffer, may suffix with K or M.
  -p              print prune white and ~black list. Service is specified as
                  UID, UID/PID or /PID. Weighed for quicker pruning if prefix
                  with ~, otherwise weighed for longevity if unadorned. All
                  other pruning activity is oldest first. Special case ~!
                  represents an automatic quicker pruning for the noisiest
                  UID as determined by the current statistics.
  -P '<list> ...' set prune white and ~black list, using same format as
                  printed above. Must be quoted.

filterspecs are a series of
  <tag>[:priority]

where <tag> is a log component tag (or * for all) and priority is:
  V    Verbose (default for <tag>)
  D    Debug (default for '*')
  I    Info
  W    Warn
  E    Error
  F    Fatal
  S    Silent (suppress all output)

'*' by itself means '*:D' and <tag> by itself means <tag>:V.
If no '*' filterspec or -s on command line, all filter defaults to '*:V'.
eg: '*:S <tag>' prints only <tag>, '<tag>:S' suppresses all <tag> log messages.

If not specified on the command line, filterspec is set from ANDROID_LOG_TAGS.

If not specified with -v on command line, format is set from ANDROID_PRINTF_LOG
or defaults to "threadtime"

esteban@dronix:~$ ▊
```

Fastboot

Fastboot is the tool that Android gives us to manipulate the device Flash Memory and its partitions, using a computer and an USB connection. Fastboot does not communicate with the Android system. It communicates with a specific firmware able to interact in a minimal system environment: `bootloader` mode.

In the bootloader mode, the system initializes only the minimal amount of hardware and software to accomplish the most critical operations of all:

- `flash`: This option is used to deploy a new binary system image from the host computer to the device partitions
- `erase`: This option is used to delete a specific partition
- `reboot`: This option is used to reboot the device in one of the available booting modes: recovery, bootloader, or standard
- `format`: This option is used to format a specific partition

The next screenshot shows the output of the following command, the full list of all the available options of `fastboot`:

```
~$ fastboot --help
```

As you can easily imagine, `fastboot` will be a big player in the future, when we will start building and testing our custom Android system:

```
 x  —  □   esteban@dronix: ~/WORKING_DIRECTORY
                        esteban@dronix: ~/WORKING_DIRECTORY 83x41

esteban@dronix:~/WORKING_DIRECTORY$ fastboot
usage: fastboot [ <option> ] <command>

commands:
  update <filename>                         reflash device from update.zip
  flashall                                  flash boot, system, vendor and if found,
                                            recovery
  flash <partition> [ <filename> ]          write a file to a flash partition
  erase <partition>                         erase a flash partition
  format[:[<fs type>][:[<size>]] <partition> format a flash partition.
                                            Can override the fs type and/or
                                            size the bootloader reports.
  getvar <variable>                         display a bootloader variable
  boot <kernel> [ <ramdisk> [ <second> ] ]  download and boot kernel
  flash:raw boot <kernel> [ <ramdisk> [ <second> ] ] create bootimage and
                                            flash it
  devices                                   list all connected devices
  continue                                  continue with autoboot
  reboot                                    reboot device normally
  reboot-bootloader                         reboot device into bootloader
  help                                      show this help message

options:
  -w                                        erase userdata and cache (and format
                                            if supported by partition type)
  -u                                        do not first erase partition before
                                            formatting
  -s <specific device>                      specify device serial number
                                            or path to device port
  -l                                        with "devices", lists device paths
  -p <product>                              specify product name
  -c <cmdline>                              override kernel commandline
  -i <vendor id>                            specify a custom USB vendor id
  -b <base_addr>                            specify a custom kernel base address.
                                            default: 0x10000000
  -n <page size>                            specify the nand page size.
                                            default: 2048
  -S <size>[K|M|G]                          automatically sparse files greater
                                            than size.  0 to disable
esteban@dronix:~/WORKING_DIRECTORY$
```

Choosing our hardware

In the previous chapters, we learned how to obtain the source code, how the build system works, and how to build our first custom Android system for the emulator. The only things we know about real hardware are that Android is primarily used on smartphones and tablets and that we can certify our hardware according to the Android **Compatibility Definition Document (CDD),** with all its constraints and rules. The truth is that Android CDD aims to provide guidelines to bring to the market devices that are compliant with Google Mobile Services requirements. This is crucial information because it gives us the freedom to choose different hardware if our goal is not to develop a smartphone or a tablet for the main consumer market.

In the last two years, the amount of devices not being a smartphone or a tablet, but being able to run Android has increased enormously. There is a whole new ecosystem of te so-called development boards that can run Android or Ubuntu Linux, for instance. Most of these boards are not CDD compliant—they don't have apps such as Google Play Store, YouTube, Google Maps, and so on, but they still run Android and they can still be tested against Android CTS. This is a great opportunity for manufactures or advanced users who want to experiment.

This scenario is now possible because the actual hardware requirements to boot Android are getting very minimal nowadays. Keep in mind that Android is based on the Linux Kernel and the system itself has a few similarities if we strip away the Google apps ecosystem. Nowadays, most of the boards that are equipped with enough hardware to run Linux have a good chance of running Android as well.

Hardware architectures

The most popular hardware architecture we find in the Android market is definitely the ARM family, with its ARMv7 and ARMv8-A. Over time, the x86 and MIPS platforms received official support and they have gained market shares in recent months. As a further note, Android 5 Lollipop introduced support for 64-bit architectures.

Minimum requirements

In a fashion that reminds us of minimal requirements just for playing games, even Android as its own. For instance, Android 5.1 requires at least 512 MB RAM if it is going to be installed on a device with a standard display density device. Otherwise, you will need at least 1.8GB RAM if you are planning to port it to a device with a high density display.

The previous versions are less demanding when it comes to RAM. Android 4.4 KitKat, for instance, requires only 512 MB RAM. Unfortunately, KitKat comes with other constraints—there is no support for 64-bit architectures and a OpenGL ES 2.0 GPU is necessary.

Lots of other hardware components, such as cameras, GPS sensors, accelerometers, gyroscopes, touchscreens, and so on, are very common, but they are absolutely optional—if your device does not need a camera, you can just save money. You can tailor your system, starting from a very minimal system, up to what is specifically needed for your use cases.

System on Chip – SoC

The coming of advanced embedded systems, such as smartphones and tablets, created a huge demand for new embedded chips—more and more small and powerful. When you think about a computer, you think about CPUs, motherboards, video cards, and lots of external devices. In the embedded world, you think about SoC.

SoC stands for SYSTEM on Chip and it goes beyond the simple concept of a CPU. Most of the current SoC solutions embed a multicore CPU, RAM controller, ROMs, EEPROMs or Flash memories, USB support, Ethernet support, USART, SPI, and even a power management system. Everything is contained in one single chip, as shown in the next screenshot of an example SoC architecture:

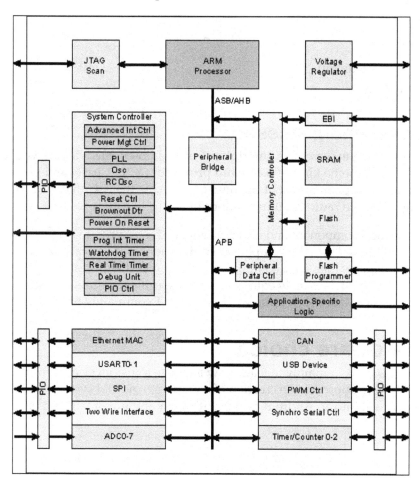

As you can imagine, the immediate advantage of this approach is the small size of the system. We can now have powerful, more and more feature complete and complex systems, with smaller and smaller power consumption in a smaller and smaller package, to satisfy every need that the market has.

The biggest players here are as follows:

- Samsung
- Qualcomm
- Huawei
- Mediatek
- Nvidia
- Intel
- Freescale
- Texas Instrument
- Broadcom

The baseband processor

If you are planning to develop a smartphone or a radio-enabled device, you are going to deal with some kind of **baseband processor (BP)**. A baseband processor is a separated component; most of the time it is outside the SoC that is in charge of everything related to radio communications.

The BP is a critical component and it's kept separate for security reasons. Governments have strict policies about radio component certifications and basically, every Government requires that these components are equipped with read-only firmwares. Due to its nature, a BP is usually equipped with a specific real-time operating system and communicates with the external world via an AT commands-based serial bus.

Our hardware choice

The goal of this book in mainly to teach how to create a custom system for an existing device and how to approach the creation of a working Android system for a device that can be turned into an Android device with a fair amount of will and effort.

We are going to use two popular devices in this journey:

- Google Nexus 6 by Motorola
- UDOO by Aidilab and SECO

Motorola Nexus 6

In the second chapter, we learned about Google devices — smartphones, tablets, and so on. In this chapter, we will work with their latest smartphone currently available — the Nexus 6.

Nexus 6, codename Shamu, is currently the top device available by Google. Its technical specifics are impressive:

- Qualcomm® Snapdragon™ 805 with quad-core 2.7 GHz CPU
- Display QHD AMOLED, 5.96" 2,560 x 1,440 (493 ppi), 16:9
- Back camera: 13 MP, LED flash, f/2.0
- Front camera: 2 MP
- GPU: Adreno 420
- Wireless: 802.11ac 2x2 (MIMO)
- Bluetooth: 4.1
- NFC
- RAM: 3 GB
- Storage: 32 GB or 64 GB
- Sensors: GPS, gyroscope, accelerometer, light sensor, barometer

- Networking:
  - GSM: 850/900/1,800/1,900 MHz
  - Band WCDMA: 1/2/4/5/6/8/9/19
  - Band LTE: 1/3/5/7/8/9/19/20/28/41
  - CA DL: B3-B5, B3-B8
- Battery: 3,220 mAh, wireless charging systems

The following screenshot shows the internal structure—SoCs, battery, display panel:

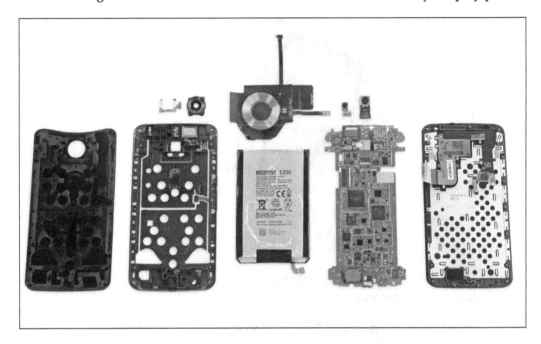

Nexus 6 is obviously a fully CDD and CTS-compliant platform. It's shipped with the full Google Apps package and will be our reference as a certified device.

UDOO Quad

Completely different compare to the Nexus 6, UDOO is not a smartphone or a Google certified device—there are no Google Apps here. It's a so-called Single Board Computer—a development and experimentation board that can be equipped with Android or Ubuntu Linux. UDOO will be our reference board to prove that we can create a working Android system out of hardware that's pretty different from a smartphone.

Let's have a look at its technical specifics:

- Freescale ARM i.MX6 Cortex A9 Quad core 1GHz CPU
- GPU Vivante GC 2000 + Vivante GC 355 + Vivante GC 320
- Atmel SAM3X8E ARM Cortex-M3 CPU (same as Arduino Due)
- 76 fully available GPIO: 62 digital + 14 digital/analog
- RAM: DDR3 1GB
- Ethernet up to 1,000Mbit/s
- On board micro SD card as primary storage
- HDMI port
- LVDS port
- Wi-Fi module
- SATA interface
- RTC module
- CSI camera connection
- 2 USB ports
- 2 x 3.5" ports for mic and speakers

As you can see, there are no sensors—there is no fancy light sensor or gyroscope, no accelerometer, and no GPS. There is no Baseband Processor either—we can't make phone calls, but we have more than enough to run Android on it!

 You have surely spotted the Atmel microprocessor. Basically, UDOO comes with an embedded Arduino microprocessor that can be used to push your experimentations even further—go for it!

Compiling Android for a real-world device

By now, you know everything you need to know about the build system and how to retrieve the source code. Retrieving the proper source code for Google official devices is no big deal, but life isn't always so easy. Working with many different devices, you will certainly come across a manufacturer who is not willing to give the source code away. They are not legally forced to release it. This is an unfortunate scenario that, hopefully, will be considered bad marketing and will disappear in the future.

For our example, instead, we are going to play with two devices that offer great support and that will magnificently serve the purpose.

Nexus 6

The first device we are going to explore is the official Google Nexus 6 by Motorola. We have already had an overview of the device. If you want to push it even further, you can refer to the official Motorola Nexus 6 web page:

```
http://www.motorola.in/consumers/View-all-Mobile-Phones/Nexus-6-by-
Motorola/nexus-6-in.html
```

In the second chapter, we learned how to retrieve the source code for Google official devices. The only thing we need to know now is the specific tag to refer:

```
android-5.1.1_r14
```

The moment we have the source code, we can set up the environment with the setup script and run the `lunch` command to specifically target our Nexus 6. The next screenshot shows how we are choosing device number 16, Nexus 6— codename Shamu:

```
aosp_shamu_userdebug
```

Here is the output:

```
 ✕  ─  ☐    esteban@dronix: ~/WORKING_DIRECTORY
                        esteban@dronix: ~/WORKING_DIRECTORY 80x32
    16.  aosp_shamu-userdebug
    17.  full_fugu-userdebug
    18.  aosp_fugu-userdebug
    19.  aosp_deb-userdebug
    20.  aosp_tilapia-userdebug
    21.  aosp_flo-userdebug
    22.  aosp_grouper-userdebug

Which would you like? [aosp_arm-eng] 16

============================================
PLATFORM_VERSION_CODENAME=REL
PLATFORM_VERSION=5.1.1
TARGET_PRODUCT=aosp_shamu
TARGET_BUILD_VARIANT=userdebug
TARGET_BUILD_TYPE=release
TARGET_BUILD_APPS=
TARGET_ARCH=arm
TARGET_ARCH_VARIANT=armv7-a-neon
TARGET_CPU_VARIANT=krait
TARGET_2ND_ARCH=
TARGET_2ND_ARCH_VARIANT=
TARGET_2ND_CPU_VARIANT=
HOST_ARCH=x86_64
HOST_OS=linux
HOST_OS_EXTRA=Linux-3.19.0-28-generic-x86_64-with-Ubuntu-15.04-vivid
HOST_BUILD_TYPE=release
BUILD_ID=LMY48I
OUT_DIR=out
============================================

esteban@dronix:~/WORKING_DIRECTORY$ ▊
```

For security and copyright reasons, the source base we acquired does not contain everything we need to build the system. Real-world devices, unlike the emulator, come with proprietary software components that must be downloaded separately. For instance, our Nexus 6 has proprietary software by three of its component manufacturers:

- **Broadcom**: NFC, Bluetooth, and Wi-Fi
- **Motorola**: Media, audio, thermal, touchscreen, and sensors
- **Qualcomm**: GPS, audio, camera, gesture, Graphics, DRM, video, and sensors

The software components are distributed as binary files and can be downloaded at https://developers.google.com/android/nexus/drivers, by looking for Nexus 6, build codename LMY48M. Download the three files and extract them into your WORKING_DIRECTORY. The next screenshot shows the content of your download folder, with the three downloaded files:

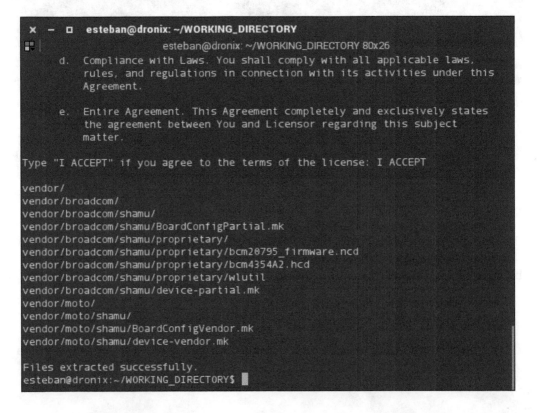

```
✕ — ▢    esteban@dronix: ~/WORKING_DIRECTORY
             esteban@dronix: ~/WORKING_DIRECTORY 80x3
-rwxr-x--x 1 esteban esteban    277666 Aug  4 21:45 extract-broadcom-shamu.sh
-rwxr-x--x 1 esteban esteban 126717305 Aug  4 21:46 extract-moto-shamu.sh
-rwxr-x--x 1 esteban esteban  25835995 Aug  4 21:46 extract-qcom-shamu.sh
```

Every one of the downloaded packages contains a script, once you extract the content. The moment you run this script, it will show you a license you need to accept in order to continue. The next screenshot shows you the process for the extract-broadcom-shamu.sh file:

```
$ chmod +x extract-broadcom-shamu.sh
$ ./extract-broadcom-shamu.sh
```

```
✕ — ▢    esteban@dronix: ~/WORKING_DIRECTORY
             esteban@dronix: ~/WORKING_DIRECTORY 80x26
      d.   Compliance with Laws. You shall comply with all applicable laws,
           rules, and regulations in connection with its activities under this
           Agreement.

      e.   Entire Agreement. This Agreement completely and exclusively states
           the agreement between You and Licensor regarding this subject
           matter.

Type "I ACCEPT" if you agree to the terms of the license: I ACCEPT

vendor/
vendor/broadcom/
vendor/broadcom/shamu/
vendor/broadcom/shamu/BoardConfigPartial.mk
vendor/broadcom/shamu/proprietary/
vendor/broadcom/shamu/proprietary/bcm20795_firmware.ncd
vendor/broadcom/shamu/proprietary/bcm4354A2.hcd
vendor/broadcom/shamu/proprietary/wlutil
vendor/broadcom/shamu/device-partial.mk
vendor/moto/
vendor/moto/shamu/
vendor/moto/shamu/BoardConfigVendor.mk
vendor/moto/shamu/device-vendor.mk

Files extracted successfully.
esteban@dronix:~/WORKING_DIRECTORY$ ▮
```

These three scripts are the final configuration step before launching the actual build process. After we have accepted all the three licenses, we can run our trusted `make` command and, patiently, wait for the build process to complete.

When the build process is over, the `out/target/product/shamu/` folder will contain your first Android build for the Google Nexus 6.

UDOO Quad

UDOO is one of the most popular development boards on the market. The hardware is top notch, the user community is great, it's well documented and it's the perfect workbench for an infinite number of experiments.

UDOO is not a Google device, so there is no chance we could use the source code we already have to create out custom Android system. We must stick to the source code that UDOO manufacturers provide the advanced users with. You can download the source code from the following link:

```
http://download.udoo.org/files/Sources/UDOO_Android_4.4.2_Source_
v1.0.tar.gz
```

Once you have downloaded the file, you can extract it using your terminal and the following command:

```
$ tar zxf  UDOO_Android_4.4.2_Source_v1.0.tar.gz
```

 As you have already figured out, the last available version of the UDOO Android source base is KitKat. When our adventure is over, you could try to port Lollipop to this platform as a new challenging Android project.

The extracted files and folders look exactly like the official Android folder structure we saw for the Nexus 6. The only real difference is that UDOO provides us with the source code for almost every component—you will find the bootloader source code and even the Linux kernel source code. Both bootloader and kernel will be compiled during the building process, unlike the Nexus 6 scenario, where we got them as precompiled files. The Android system, bootloader, and kernel will be combined to create the final image set we will need to deploy to our UDOO.

Setup

Before launching the `envsetup` script, we need to configure the environment to be able to build the bootloader. We will learn a lot about the bootloader in the next sections. For now, you just need to open up your Terminal and run these commands:

```
$ export ARCH=arm
```

```
"$ export CROSS_COMPILE=$PWD/prebuilts/gcc/linux-x86/arm/arm-eabi-
4.6/bin/arm-eabi-
```

```
$ export PATH=$PWD/bootable/bootloader/u-boot-imx/tools:$PATH
```

```
$ source build/envsetup.sh
```

As the last configuration step, we need to set up the build system to properly generate the system image for our UDOO:

```
~$: lunch udoo-eng
```

Bootloader

Everything is in place. We can now compile the bootloader. Open a Terminal and navigate to the `bootloader` folder:

```
$ cd bootbable/bootloader/uboot-imx
```

This folder contains the executable to perform the bootloader compilation. Run it like this:

```
$ ./compile -c
```

The previous command will show a configuration dialog, like the one in the next screenshot. You will select the hardware configuration you are targeting—CPU, RAM, and so on. When everything is properly configured, the compilation process will be performed and it will generate the bootloader binary images:

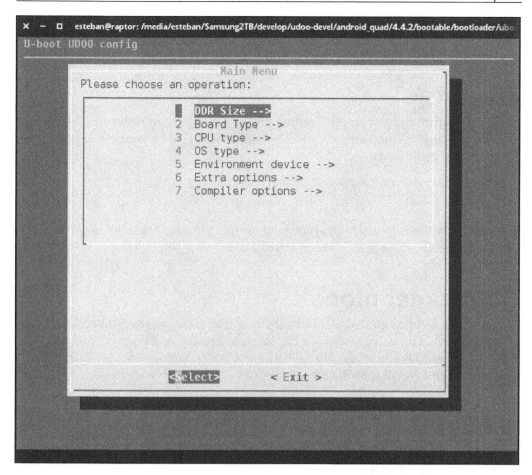

System

Once we have the bootloader images, we can go back to the source code root folder and launch the main system image build process, using the following command:

```
$ make
```

This could take a while, so be patient. As usual, when the compilation is over, you will find all the binary images you will need in the out/ folder, ready to be installed to our hardware and bring it to live.

Kernel

The Linux kernel will be compiled automatically during the Android system building process. If you want, you can also build the kernel by yourself, using the following commands:

```
$ make -C kernel_imx imx6_udoo_android_defconfig
$ make bootimage
```

The process will generate a brand new boot.img in the out/ folder. You can find the specific kernel file in kernel_imx/arch/arm/boot.

Bootloader mode

The previous sections guided you to your first system images, ready to be flashed to your hardware. These images will be deployed to the device memory. The Nexus 6 has an internal Nand memory. The UDOO has a pretty standard SD card. The first step of the deployment is switching the device into the bootloader mode.

Bootloader mode is a particular state of the device that allows us to transfer and deploy a system image to the device itself, using the fastboot utility. Every device running Android has this mode, but not every device will let us access it. Some devices come with a locked bootloader, for security reasons or simply because of a short-sighted manufacturer.

Obviously, we will be able to access the bootloader on our devices: Google is a generous manufacturer and every Nexus device comes with an unlocked or unlockable bootloader; UDOO, as a development board, is designed to be developer friendly, as well.

Nexus devices

Every Nexus device will let us to access bootloader mode, but every device will do it in its own way. According to the model, we will need a specific sequence of steps to boot the device in bootloader mode. The following table shows how to do it for every Nexus device. Be sure to turn off your device and unplug the USB cable, pick the model from the table, and press the right buttons:

Device	Keys
shamu	Press and hold *Volume Down*, then press and hold *Power*
fugu	Press and hold *Power*
volantis	Press and hold *Volume Down*, then press and hold *Power*
hammerhead	Press and hold both *Volume Up* and *Volume Down*, then press and hold *Power*
flo	Press and hold *Volume Down*, then press and hold *Power*
deb	Press and hold *Volume Down*, then press and hold *Power*
manta	Press and hold both *Volume Up* and *Volume Down*, then press and hold *Power*
mako	Press and hold *Volume Down*, then press and hold *Power*
grouper	Press and hold *Volume Down*, then press and hold *Power*
tilapia	Press and hold *Volume Down*, then press and hold *Power*
phantasm	Power the device, cover it with one hand after the LEDs light up and until they turn red
maguro	Press and hold both *Volume Up* and *Volume Down*, then press and hold *Power*
toro	Press and hold both *Volume Up* and *Volume Down*, then press and hold *Power*
toroplus	Press and hold both *Volume Up* and *Volume Down*, then press and hold *Power*
panda	Press and hold *Input*, then press *Power*
wingray	Press and hold *Volume Down*, then press and hold *Power*
crespo	Press and hold *Volume Up*, then press and hold *Power*
crespo4g	Press and hold *Volume Up*, then press and hold *Power*

For our Nexus 6, we need to press *Volume Down* then also press *Power* and keep both pressed. The smartphone will boot and you will land on a screen like the one in the following screenshot:

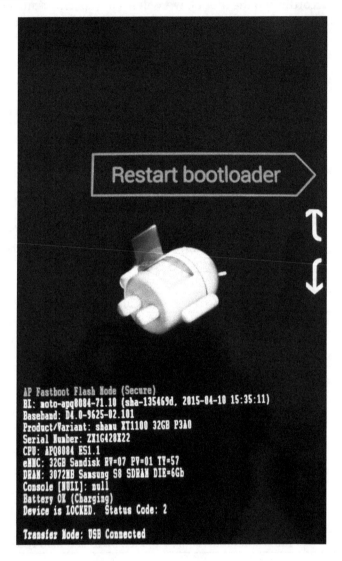

Here we are in Bootloader Mode!

The first thing you will notice is the quite explicit:

Device is LOCKED

As we said, Nexus devices come with an unlockable bootloader. We just need to connect the device to our computer with a standard USB cable, open a terminal and run the following command:

```
$ fastboot oem unlock
```

You will see a notice message that will warn you that unlocking the bootloader will erase everything on your device. Yes, it will. That's unfortunate, but, from a security and system point of view, it's necessary.

 This is the right moment to think about a data backup. You can still abort the process, restart your smartphone, save your data and try again. We will wait for you!

If you are brave enough and you just don't need all those pictures of little kitties on your phone anymore, just select YES and the bootloader will unlock smoothly. If for any reason you'd like the bootloader to lock again, you can use the following command:

```
$ fastboot oem lock
```

The moment we unlocked the bootloader, we gained full control of the Nand memory — we can erase partitions or flash the system images we have created. Unfortunately, Google does not release the source code of the bootloader, so we wouldn't know how they implement the whole fastboot protocol. Luckily for us, we are going to figure it out thanks to UDOO. The UDOO manufacturer provides us with the full source base, even the one for the bootloader.

UDOO family boards

UDOO comes as an open book. We can access every partition on its memory, with basically zero effort. There is no such thing as a "button ninja combination" to switch to bootloader mode. We can use a serial connection to analyze the whole boot process, stop it, and interact with it using the control console:

1. Connect the serial interface
2. Stop the boot sequence
3. Access the uboot console
4. Run fastboot

We now have the fastboot server ready to go. With the server in place, we will be able to connect to fastboot from our computer, using the fastboot client we already know.

This process could seem a bit harder than the one from Nexus. That's true. The fact is that UDOO does not ship with a default secret bootloader like the Nexus or any other mainstream smartphone on the market does. UDOO is mainly a development board and, as with lots of such devices, gives you the freedom and power to choose the bootloader you prefer. However, in an effort to be more developer friendly, UDOO can perfectly work with the most popular open source bootloader solution — uboot.

The uboot solution is fully compliant with the standard requirements for a bootloader to properly launch an operating system — hardware initialization, memory test, and so on. It also implements the fastboot protocol and the extraction of the kernel contained in the boot.img, generated by the build system. These last two features make it fully compatible with Android.

Flashing Android images

Here we are. Every piece of the puzzle is in place — you can finally move forward to installing your brand new custom Android version onto your device.

 As a reminder, we built the so-called stock version of the Android system: you won't find any of the Google apps in here — no YouTube, no Google Play Store.

Nexus 6

After the build process is complete, you will find all the system images you need in the **out/target/product/shamu** folder:

- system.img: This is, well, the system image. It contains the whole operating system — Android Framework, system native libraries, and the system utility app, such as Calc or Clock.

- recovery.img: This image contains what we are going to place in the *Recovery* partition. It contains a kernel and the recovery software itself.

- boot.img: This image contains the Linux Kernel and a small RamDisk. This image will be placed in the boot partition and will contain all the files needed to initialize the system: init.rc, for instance, and every other component needed to start the system.

Every partition can be flashed using a specific partition image and an appropriate command. Switch your Nexus into bootloader mode, plug the USB cable, and let's flash a few partitions. Launch your Terminal, navigate to `out/target/product/shamu`, and execute these commands:

```
:$ fastboot flash system system.img
:$ fastboot flash boot boot.img
:$ fastboot flash recovery recovery.img
:$ fastboot reboot
```

The last command will reboot your device and your brand new custom Android version will come to life! This first version of the system will definitely look bare without Google Play Store. With no possibility of installing applications, there is very little we can do with a device, indeed. No sad faces, please! In the next chapters, we will learn how to acquire and install the Google apps we need and how to customize our system.

As a final note, in this first run, we used the Linux Kernel provided by Google — we didn't compile it from sources. In the next chapters, we will learn how to do it and take full control.

UDOO

As usual, UDOO is slightly different. We have a few possible paths to achieve our goal, but first things first — partitions. The first step is to prepare the SD card with the proper partitions set. Unlike the Nexus and its pre-partitioned Nand memory, ready to be flashed, with UDOO we have full control of the system, even of the memory partitioning.

Freedom and power come with responsibility — we need to create the proper partitions before being able to install the system. Being developer friendly, the UDOO development team provides a handy script to speed up the job. The root folder of your UDOO working directory contains a `make_sd.sh` file. Insert the UDOO SD card in your computer and detect the disk number:

- On Linux, using `df -f`, you should look for something like `/dev/mmcblkX`
- On OS X, using `diskutil list` you should look for something like `/dev/rdisksX`

A super easy trick is to insert the SD card and note down all the disk numbers. Extract the SD card and figure out the one that is now missing! Once you have detected the disk number, you can run the script like this by specifying the proper disk name:

```
$ ./make_sd.sh /dev/mmcblkX
```

The script will automatically erase the SD card, create the partition structure, and copy all the files the build system generated and deployed in out/. This could take a while, depending on the speed of your SD card.

As we saw, developing for a Google device is pretty straightforward: we download the source code and start configuring the system to achieve our built images. We end up with a stock version of the system we can later decide to customize as we like. Developing or porting Android to a new hardware is a totally different matter: it is quite different and requires a bit of effort and commitment.

When you decide to set out for a journey like this, the first crucial step is choosing the proper hardware platform. The market offers a large collection of vendors and every vendor offers his own particular solutions—different SoC, different on-board sensors, cheap low-end boards, or hyper-fast expensive boards. There is no place in this book for discussion about choosing an expensive board or not. We focus on the developer and their world and, as a professional, 99% of the time they will find themselves working with a so-called reference board.

A **reference board** is a particular kind of development board that every vendor offers to its potential clients. Usually, a reference board ships with everything possible on-board—tons of sensors, tons of external devices, tons of connectors, and possible purposes. The final goal is to provide developers with a board that can truly show off the full potential of the SoC and the whole hardware solution. Everything is tailored to make developers' life easy: the Linux Kernel source code is provided, the hardware components specifications are provided, and the documentation is provided.

The UDOO board we played with in the chapter can be considered close to a reference board. It does not have every possible sensor, but it's easily expandable with external sensors and we know how to communicate with those sensors because the platform is open and easy to debug. An easy way to debug our software and hardware is crucial to make our developing time effective.

UDOO comes with a handy micro-USB connection that is also a Serial-to-USB converter. Using this connection, we can interact with the board at one of the lowest level monitors and manipulate the boot sequence. To properly connect to the board console, we need to install a specific software on our computer: a modem control and terminal emulator named minicom.

You can install it on Ubuntu using apt-get:

```
$ sudo apt-get install minicom
```

You can install it on OS X using brew:

```
$ brew install minicom
```

When we have `minicom`, we can connect the turned-off UDOO to the USB port and run the following command on our Terminal:

```
$ minicom -b 115200 -D /dev/ttyUSB0
```

`ttyUSB0` is the system device that the operating system associated to the UDOO connection. It could be different on your system, that is `ttyUSB1`, `ttyUSB2`, according to the hardware configuration, other connected USB devices, and so on. A bit of trial and error could be necessary.

We can now plug the power cable in and turn on the board. If the connection is properly configured, you will see the boot sequence as shown in the following screenshot:

```
✕  —  ☐   esteban@dronix: /media/esteban/Samsung2TB/lavoro/mygw
                    esteban@dronix:/media/esteban/Samsung2TB/mygw 80x35
U-Boot 2009.08-svn75 (Jan 27 2015 - 07:05:07)

CPU: Freescale i.MX6 family TO1.2 at 792 MHz
Thermal sensor with ratio = 177
Temperature:   28 C, calibration data 0x5624d369
mx6q pll1: 792MHz
mx6q pll2: 528MHz
mx6q pll3: 480MHz
mx6q pll8: 50MHz
ipg clock      : 66000000Hz
ipg per clock  : 66000000Hz
uart clock     : 80000000Hz
cspi clock     : 60000000Hz
ahb clock      : 132000000Hz
axi clock    : 264000000Hz
emi_slow clock: 132000000Hz
ddr clock      : 528000000Hz
usdhc1 clock   : 198000000Hz
usdhc2 clock   : 198000000Hz
usdhc3 clock   : 198000000Hz
usdhc4 clock   : 198000000Hz
nfc clock      : 24000000Hz
Board: i.MX6Q-UDOO: unknown-board Board: 0x63012 [POR]
Boot Device: NOR
I2C:    ready
DRAM:   1 GB
MMC:    FSL_USDHC: 0,FSL_USDHC: 1,FSL_USDHC: 2,FSL_USDHC: 3
In:     serial
Out:    serial
Err:    serial
Net:    got MAC address from IIM: 00:c0:08:88:af:5b
FEC0 [PRIME]
Hit any key to stop autoboot:  0
MX6Q UDOO U-Boot >
CTRL-A Z for help | 115200 8N1 | NOR | Minicom 2.7 | VT102 | Offline | ttyUSB0
```

We can monitor the boot sequence and interact with the system in a few interesting ways. The one we are interested in now is stopping the boot sequence and switching to bootloader mode.

During the boot sequence, you will see a message suggesting how to stop the boot sequence itself and access `uboot`. Once you are in, run `fastboot` as shown in the following screenshot:

```
 ×  —  ☐   esteban@dronix:/media/esteban/Samsung2TB/lavoro/mygw
                    esteban@dronix:/media/esteban/Samsung2TB/lavoro/mygw 80x10
MX6Q UDOO U-Boot >
MX6Q UDOO U-Boot >
MX6Q UDOO U-Boot >
MX6Q UDOO U-Boot > fastboot
fastboot is in init.......flash target is MMC:2
USB Mini b cable Connected!
fastboot initialized
USB_SUSPEND
CTRL-A Z for help | 115200 8N1 | NOR | Minicom 2.7 | VT102 | Offline | ttyUSB0
```

We can now flash the system images we have:

```
$ fastboot flash system system.img
$ fastboot flash boot boot.img
$ fastboot flash recovery recovery.img
$ fastboot reboot
```

Having the serial connection still on, when the system reboots, we can enjoy all the system messages that the boot sequence provides: system initialization and Linux kernel loading, until we reach Android loading and finish to Android system console prompt. This is the beauty and the power of having deep access to and knowledge about your system and your hardware. The following screenshot shows a part of the boot sequence in the precise moment of kernel deployment:

```
✕  —  ☐   esteban@dronix: /media/esteban/Samsung2TB/lavoro/mygw
                esteban@dronix: /media/esteban/Samsung2TB/lavoro/mygw 80x34
Net:    got MAC address from IIM: 00:c0:08:88:af:5b
FEC0 [PRIME]
Hit any key to stop autoboot:  0
kernel  @ 10808000 (4339648)
ramdisk @ 11800000 (499845)
kernel cmdline:
        use uboot command line:
        console=ttymxc1,115200 init=/init video=mxcfb0:dev=ldb,LDB-WVGA,if=RGB66
6,bpp=32 video=mxcfb1:off video=mxcfb2:off fbmem=28M vmalloc=400M androidboot.co
nsole=ttymxc1 androidboot.hardware=freescale mem=1024M

Starting kernel ...

Initializing cgroup subsys cpuset
Initializing cgroup subsys cpu
Linux version 3.0.35-svn73 (udoo@ubuntu) (gcc version 4.6.x-google 20120106 (pre
release) (GCC) ) #2 SMP PREEMPT Thu Jan 22 02:43:19 PST 2015
CPU: ARMv7 Processor [412fc09a] revision 10 (ARMv7), cr=10c53c7d
CPU: VIPT nonaliasing data cache, VIPT aliasing instruction cache
Machine: i.Mx6 UDOO Board
Ignoring unrecognised tag 0x41000901
Memory policy: ECC disabled, Data cache writealloc
CPU identified as i.MX6Q, silicon rev 1.2
PERCPU: Embedded 7 pages/cpu @c14d5000 s5536 r8192 d14944 u32768
Built 1 zonelists in Zone order, mobility grouping on.  Total pages: 223232
Kernel command line: console=ttymxc1,115200 init=/init video=mxcfb0:dev=ldb,LDB-
WVGA,if=RGB666,bpp=32 video=mxcfb1:off video=mxcfb2:off fbmem=28M vmalloc=400M a
ndroidboot.console=ttymxc1 androidboot.hardware=freescale mem=1024M
PID hash table entries: 2048 (order: 1, 8192 bytes)
Dentry cache hash table entries: 65536 (order: 6, 262144 bytes)
Inode-cache hash table entries: 32768 (order: 5, 131072 bytes)
Memory: 640MB 240MB = 880MB total
Memory: 878772k/878772k available, 169804k reserved, 491520K highmem
Virtual kernel memory layout:
```

Summary

In this chapter, you have built and installed your first Android system for a real-world device. You now know a lot more about Google Nexus 6 and UDOO board. You have learned how to use ADB and Fastboot. You have learned how to interact with a development board using a serial connection and tools such as minicom, monitoring, and manipulating the boot sequence.

In the next chapter, we will dig into the Linux kernel building and customization.

5
Customizing Kernel and Boot Sequence

In the previous chapter, we created and deployed our first custom version of Android. We created a version for a commercial smartphone, the Google Nexus 6, and a more hard-core version for a development board, the Udoo Quad. We learned about more development tools, such as ADB and Fastboot. We focused on the debugging tools, mastering the serial connection, and the boot sequence.

In this chapter, we will dive into the system—from the kernel customization to the boot sequence. You will learn how to retrieve the proper source code for Google devices, how to set up the build environment, how to build your first custom version of the Linux kernel, and deploy it to your device. You will learn about:

- Toolchain overview
- How to configure the host system to compile your own Linux kernel
- How to configure the Linux kernel
- Linux kernel overview
- Android boot sequence
- The Init process

An overview of the Linux kernel

In *Chapter 1*, *Understanding the Architecture*, we learned how Android has been designed and built around the Linux kernel. One of the reasons to choose the Linux kernel was its unquestioned flexibility and the infinite possibilities to adjust it to any specific scenario and requirement. These are the features that have made Linux the most popular kernel in the embedded industry.

Linux kernel comes with a GPL license. This particular license allowed Google to contribute to the project since the early stages of Android. Google provided bug fixing and new features, helping Linux to overcome a few obstacles and limitations of the 2.6 version. In the beginning, Linux 2.6.32 was the most popular version for the most part of the Android device market. Nowadays, we see more and more devices shipping with the new 3.x versions.

The following screenshot shows the current build for the official Google Motorola Nexus 6, with kernel 3.10.40:

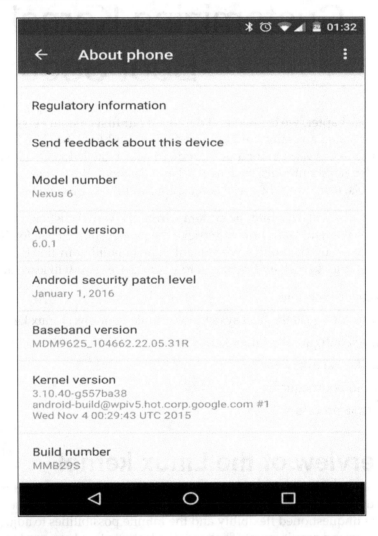

The Android version we created in the previous chapters was equipped with a binary version of the Linux kernel. Using an already compiled version of the kernel is the standard practice: as we have seen, AOSP provides exactly this kind of experience.

As advanced users, we can take it a step further and build a custom kernel for our custom Android system. The Nexus family offers an easy entry into this world as we can easily obtain the kernel source code we need to build a custom version. We can also equip our custom Android system with our custom Linux kernel and we will have a full-customized ROM, tailored for our specific needs.

In this book, we are using Nexus devices on purpose — Google is one of the few companies that formally make available the kernel source code. Even if every company producing and selling Android devices is forced by law to release the kernel source code, very few of them actually do it, despite all the GPL license rules.

Obtaining the kernel

Google provides the kernel source code and binary version for every single version of Android for every single device of the Nexus family.

The following table shows where the binary version and the source code are located, ordered by device code name:

Device	Binary location	Source location	Build configuration
shamu	device/moto/shamu-kernel	kernel/msm	shamu_defconfig
fugu	device/asus/fugu-kernel	kernel/x86_64	fugu_defconfig
volantis	device/htc/flounder-kernel	kernel/tegra	flounder_defconfig
hammerhead	device/lge/ hammerhead-kernel	kernel/msm	hammerhead_defconfig
flo	device/asus/flo-kernel/kernel	kernel/msm	flo_defconfig
deb	device/asus/flo-kernel/kernel	kernel/msm	flo_defconfig
manta	device/samsung/manta/kernel	kernel/exynos	manta_defconfig
mako	device/lge/mako-kernel/kernel	kernel/msm	mako_defconfig
grouper	device/asus/grouper/kernel	kernel/tegra	tegra3_android_defconfig
tilapia	device/asus/grouper/kernel	kernel/tegra	tegra3_android_defconfig
maguro	device/samsung/tuna/kernel	kernel/omap	tuna_defconfig
toro	device/samsung/tuna/kernel	kernel/omap	tuna_defconfig
panda	device/ti/panda/kernel	kernel/omap	panda_defconfig
stingray	device/moto/wingray/kernel	kernel/tegra	stingray_defconfig

Device	Binary location	Source location	Build configuration
wingray	device/moto/wingray/kernel	kernel/tegra	stingray_defconfig
crespo	device/samsung/crespo/kernel	kernel/samsung	herring_defconfig
crespo4g	device/samsung/crespo/kernel	kernel/samsung	herring_defconfig

As in *Chapter 4*, *Moving to real-world hardware*, we are going to work with the Motorola Nexus 6, code name `Shamu`.

Both the kernel binary version and the kernel source code are stored in a git repository. All we need to do is compose the proper URL and clone the corresponding repository.

Retrieving the kernel's binary version

In this section, we are going to obtain the kernel as a binary, prebuilt file. All we need is the previous table that shows every device model, with its codename and its binary location that we can use to compose the download of the URL. We are targeting Google Nexus 6, codename `shamu` with binary location:

```
device/moto/shamu-kernel
```

So, to retrieve the binary version of the Motorola Nexus 6 kernel, we need the following command:

```
$ git clone https://android.googlesource.com/device/moto/shamu-kernel
```

The previous command will clone the repo and place it in the `shamu-kernel` folder. This folder contains a file named `zImage-dtb` — this file is the actual kernel image that can be integrated in our ROM and flashed into our device.

Having the kernel image, we can obtain the kernel version with the following command:

```
$ $ dd if=kernel bs=1 skip=$(LC_ALL=C grep -a -b -o $'\x1f\x8b\x08\x00\
x00\x00\x00\x00' kernel | cut -d ':' -f 1) | zgrep -a 'Linux version'
```

Output:

```
 ×  −  □    esteban@dronix: ~/code/embedded_android/shamu-kernel
            esteban@dronix: ~/code/embedded_android/shamu-kernel 81x11
esteban@dronix:~/code/embedded_android/shamu-kernel$ dd if=zImage-dtb bs=1 skip=
$(LC_ALL=C grep -a -b -o $'\x1f\x8b\x08\x00\x00\x00\x00\x00' zImage-dtb | cut -d
':' -f 1) | zgrep -a 'Linux version'


Linux version 3.10.40-g33175b0 (android-build@vpak2.mtv.corp.google.com) (gcc ve
rsion 4.8 (GCC) ) #1 SMP PREEMPT Thu Oct 22 22:49:19 UTC 2015
7238548+0 records in
7238548+0 records out
7238548 bytes (7,2 MB) copied, 9,95393 s, 727 kB/s
esteban@dronix:~/code/embedded_android/shamu-kernel$
```

The previous screenshot shows the command output: our kernel image version is 3.10.40 and it has been compiled with GCC version 4.8 on October the the twenty-second at 22:49.

Obtaining the kernel source code

As for the binary version, the previous table is critical also to download the kernel source code. Targeting the Google Nexus 6, we create the download URL using the source location string for the device codename `shamu`:

kernel/msm.git

Once we have the exact URL, we can clone the GIT repository with the following command:

```
$ git clone https://android.googlesource.com/kernel/msm.git
```

Git will create an `msm` folder. The folder will be strangely empty—that's because the folder is tracking the `master` branch by default. To obtain the kernel for our Nexus 6, we need to switch to the proper branch.

There are a lot of available branches and we can check out the list with the following command:

```
$ git branch -a
```

The list will show every single branch, targeting a specific Android version for a specific Nexus device. The following screenshot shows a subset of these repositories:

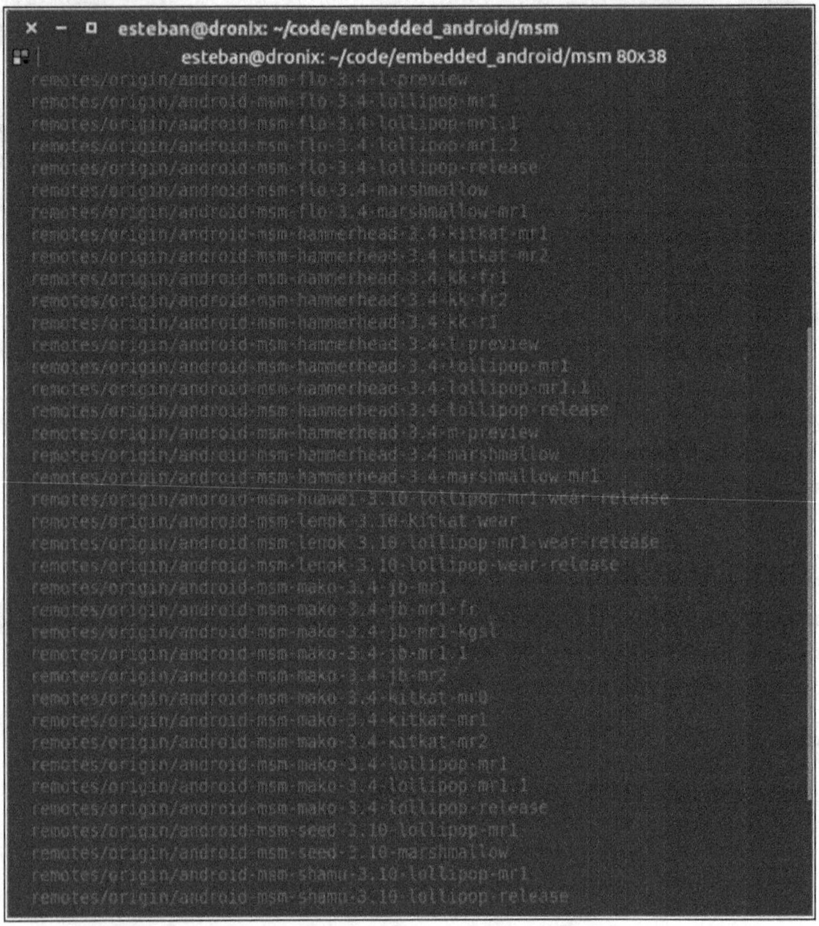

Now that you have the branch name, for your device and your Android version, you just need to checkout the proper branch:

```
$ git checkout android-msm-shamu-3.10-lollipop-release
```

The following screenshot shows the expected command output:

```
x  -  □    esteban@dronix: ~/code/embedded_android/msm
              esteban@dronix: ~/code/embedded_android/msm 80x7

esteban@dronix:~/code/embedded_android/msm$ git checkout android-msm-shamu-3.10-
lollipop-release
Branch android-msm-shamu-3.10-lollipop-release set up to track remote branch and
roid-msm-shamu-3.10-lollipop-release from origin.
Switched to a new branch 'android-msm-shamu-3.10-lollipop-release'
esteban@dronix:~/code/embedded_android/msm$
```

Setting up the toolchain

The toolchain is the set of all the tools needed to effectively compile a specific software to a binary version, enabling the user to run it. In our specific domain, the toolchain allows us to create a system image ready to be flashed to our Android device. The interesting part is that the toolchain allows us to create a system image for an architecture that is different from our current one: odds are that we are using an x86 system and we want to create a system image targeting an ARM (Advanced RISC Machine) device. Compiling software targeting an architecture different from the one on our host system is called **cross-compilation**.

The Internet offers a couple of handy solutions for this task—we can use the standard toolchain, available with the AOSP (Android Open Source Project) or we can use an alternative, very popular toolchain, the Linaro toolchain. Both toolchains will do the job—compile every single C/C++ file for the ARM architecture.

As usual, even the toolchain is available as precompiled binary or as source code, ready to be compiled. For our journey, we are going to use the official toolchain, provided by Google, but when you need to explore this world even more, you could try out the binary version of Linaro toolchain, downloadable from www. linaro.org/download. Linaro toolchain is known to be the most optimized and performing toolchain in the market, but our goal is not to compare toolchains or stubbornly use the best or most popular one. Our goal is to create the smoothest possible experience, removing unnecessary variables from the whole building a custom Android system equation.

Getting the toolchain

We are going to use the official toolchain, provided by Google. We can obtain it with Android source code or downloading it separately. Having your trusted Android source code folder at hand, you can find the toolchain in the following folder:

```
AOSP/prebuilts/gcc/linux-x86/arm/arm-eabi-4.8/
```

This folder contains everything we need to build a custom kernel — the compiler, the linker, and few more tools such as a debugger.

If, for some unfortunate reason, you are missing the Android source code folder, you can download the toolchain using the following git command:

```
$ git clone https://android.googlesource.com/platform/prebuilts/gcc/
linux-x86/arm/arm-eabi-4.8
```

Preparing the host system

To successfully compile our custom kernel, we need a properly configured host system. The requirements are similar to those we satisfied to build the whole Android system in the previous chapter:

- Ubuntu
- Linux kernel source code
- Toolchain
- Fastboot

Ubuntu needs a bit of love to accomplish this task: we need to install the ncurses-dev package:

```
$ sudo apt-get install ncurses-dev
```

Once we have all the required tools installed, we can start configuring the environment variables we need. These variables are used during the cross-compilation and can be set via the console. Fire up your trusted Terminal and launch the following commands:

```
$ export PATH=<toolchain-path>/arm-eabi-4.8/bin:$PATH
$ export ARCH=arm
$ export SUBARCH=arm
$ export CROSS_COMPILE=arm-eabi-
```

Configuring the kernel

Before being able to compile the kernel, we need to properly configure it. Every device in the Android repository has a specific branch with a specific kernel with a specific configuration to be applied.

The table on page 2 has a column with the exact information we need — Build configuration. This information represents the parameter we need to properly configure the kernel build system. Let's configure everything for our Google Nexus 6. In your terminal, launch the following command:

```
$ make shamu_defconfig
```

This command will create a kernel configuration specific for your device. The following screenshot shows the command running and the final success message:

```
 x  -  □    esteban@dronix: ~/code/embedded_android/msm
              esteban@dronix: ~/code/embedded_android/msm 80x20

esteban@dronix:~/code/embedded_android/msm$ make shamu_defconfig
  HOSTCC   scripts/basic/fixdep
  HOSTCC   scripts/kconfig/conf.o
  HOSTCC   scripts/kconfig/zconf.tab.o
In file included from scripts/kconfig/zconf.tab.c:2503:0:
scripts/kconfig/menu.c: In function 'get_symbol_str':
scripts/kconfig/menu.c:567:18: warning: 'jump' may be used uninitialized in this
 function [-Wmaybe-uninitialized]
     jump->offset = r->len - 1;
                  ^

scripts/kconfig/menu.c:528:19: note: 'jump' was declared here
   struct jump_key *jump;
                    ^

  HOSTLD   scripts/kconfig/conf
drivers/usb/gadget/Kconfig:897:warning: defaults for choice values not supported
#
# configuration written to .config
#
esteban@dronix:~/code/embedded_android/msm$ █
```

Once the .config file is in place, you could already build the kernel, using the default configuration. As advanced users, we want more and that's why we will take full control of the system, digging into the kernel configuration. Editing the configuration could enable missing features or disable unneeded hardware support, to create the perfect custom kernel, and fit your needs.

Luckily, to alter the kernel configuration, we don't need to manually edit the `.config` file. The Linux kernel provides a graphical tool that will allow you to navigate the whole configuration file structure, get documentation about the single configurable item, and prepare a custom configuration file with zero effort.

To access the configuration menu, open your terminal, navigate to the `kernel` folder and launch the following command:

```
$ make menuconfig
```

The following screenshot shows the official Linux kernel configuration tool — no frills, but very effective:

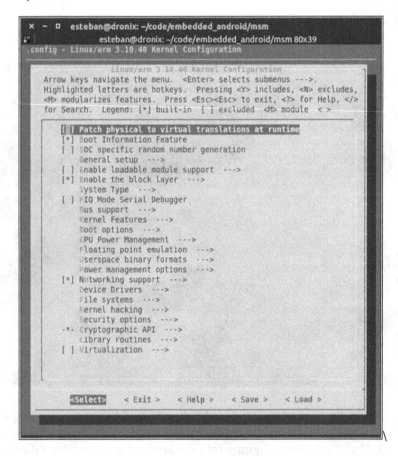

In the upper half of the screenshot, you can see the version of the kernel we are going to customize and a quick doc about how you can navigate all those menu items: you navigate using the *arrow* keys, you enter a subsection with the *Enter* key, you select or deselect an item using *Y*/*N* or *Spacebar* to toggle.

With great power comes great responsibility, so be careful enabling and disabling features — check the documentation in `menuconfig`, check the Internet, and, most of all, be confident. A wrong configuration could cause a freeze during the boot sequence and this would force you to learn, to create a different configuration and try again.

As a real-world example, we are going to enable the FTDI support. Future Technology Devices International or FTDI is a worldwide known semiconductor company, popular for its RS-232/TTL to USB devices. These devices come in very handy to communicate to embedded devices using a standard USB connection. To enable the FTDI support, you need to navigate to the right menu by following these steps:

`Device Drivers|USB support|USB Serial Converter support`

Once you reach this section, you need to enable the following item:

`USB FTDI Single Port Serial Driver`

The following screenshot shows the correctly selected item and gives you an idea of how many devices we could possibly support (this screen only shows the USB Serial Converter support):

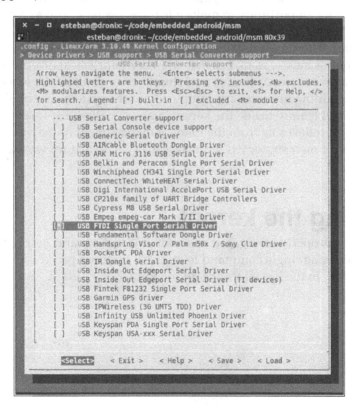

Once you have everything in place, just select **Exit** and save the configuration, as shown in the following screenshot:

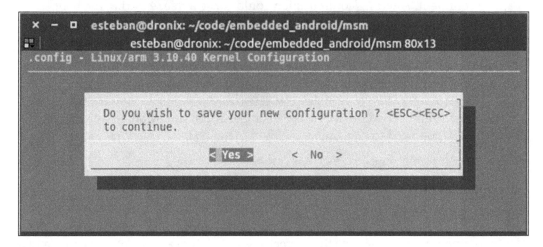

With the exact same approach, you can add every new feature you want. One important note, we added the FTDI package merging it into the kernel image. Linux kernel gives you the opportunity to make a feature available also as a module. A module is an external file, with .ko extension, that can be injected and loaded in the kernel at runtime. The kernel modules are a great and handy feature when you are working on a pure Linux system, but they are very impractical on Android. With the hope of having a modular kernel, you should code yourself the whole module loading system, adding unnecessary complexity to the system. The choice we made of having the FTDI feature inside the kernel image penalizes the image from a size point of view, but relieves us from the manual management of the module itself. That's why the common strategy is to include every new feature we want right into the kernel core.

Compiling the kernel

Once you have a properly configured environment and a brand new configuration file, you just need one single command to start the building process. On your terminal emulator, in the kernel source folder, launch:

```
$ make
```

The `make` command will wrap up the necessary configuration and will launch the compiling and assembling process. The duration of the process heavily depends on the performance of your system: it could be one minute or one hour. As a reference, an i5 2.40 GHz CPU with 8 GB of RAM takes 5-10 minutes to complete a clean build. This is incredibly quicker than compiling the whole AOSP image, as you can see, due to the different complexity and size of the code base.

Working with non-Google devices

So far, we have worked with Google devices, enjoying the Google open-source mindset. As advanced users, we frequently deal with devices that are not from Google or that are not even a smartphone. As a real-world example, we are going to use again a UDOO board: a single-board computer that supports Ubuntu or Android. For the time being, the most popular version of UDOO is the UDOO Quad and that's the version we are targeting.

As for every other device, the standard approach is to trust the manufacturer's website to obtain kernel source code and any useful documentation for the process: most of all, how to properly flash the new kernel to the system. When working with a custom kernel, the procedure is quite consolidated. You need the source code, the toolchain, a few configuration steps, and, maybe, some specific software package to be installed on to your host system. When it comes to flashing the kernel, every device can have a different procedure. This depends on how the system has been designed and which tools the manufacturing team provides. Google provides `fastboot` to flash our images to our devices. Other manufactures usually provide tools that are similar or that can do similar things with little effort.

The UDOO development team worked hard to make the UDOO board fully compatible with `fastboot` — instead of forcing you to adjust to their tools, they adjusted their device to work with the tools you already know. They tuned up the board's bootloader and you can now flash the `boot.img` using `fastboot`, like you were flashing a standard Google Android device.

To obtain the kernel, we just need to clone a git repository. With your trusted terminal, launch the following command:

```
$ git clone http://github.com/UDOOBoard/Kernel_Unico kernel
```

Once we have the kernel, we need to install a couple of software packages in our Ubuntu system to be able to work with it. With the following command, everything will be installed and put in place:

```
$ sudo apt-get install build-essential ncurses-dev u-boot-tools
```

Time to pick a toolchain! UDOO gives you a few possibilities—you can use the same toolchain you used for the Nexus 6 or you can use the one provided by the UDOO team itself. If you decide to use the UDOO official toolchain, you can download it with a couple of terminal commands. Be sure you have already installed `curl`. If not, just install it with the following command:

```
$ sudo apt-get install curl
```

Once you have `curl`, you can use the following command to download the toolchain:

```
$ curl http://download.udoo.org/files/crosscompiler/arm-fsl-linux-
gnueabi.tar.gz | tar -xzf
```

Now, you have everything in place to launch the build process:

```
$ cd kernel
```

```
$ make ARCH=arm UDOO_defconfig
```

The following is the output:

```
 ×  —  □    esteban@dronix: /media/esteban/Samsung2TB/develop/udoo-devel/kernel
         esteban@dronix: /media/esteban/Samsung2TB/develop/udoo-devel/kernel 80x11
  HOSTCC   scripts/basic/fixdep
  HOSTCC   scripts/kconfig/conf.o
  SHIPPED  scripts/kconfig/zconf.tab.c
  SHIPPED  scripts/kconfig/lex.zconf.c
  SHIPPED  scripts/kconfig/zconf.hash.c
  HOSTCC   scripts/kconfig/zconf.tab.o
  HOSTLD   scripts/kconfig/conf
#
# configuration written to .config
#
esteban@dronix:/media/esteban/Samsung2TB/develop/udoo-devel/kernel$ 
```

The previous screenshot shows the output of the configuration process. When the default `.config` file is ready, you can launch the build process with the following command:

```
$ make -j4 CROSS_COMPILE ../arm-fsl-linux-gnueabi/bin/arm-fsl-linux-
gnueabi- ARCH=arm uImage modules
```

When the build process is over, you can find the kernel image in the `arch` folder:

```
$ arch/arm/boot/uImage
```

As for the Nexus 6, we can customize the UDOO kernel using `menuconfig`. From the kernel source folder, launch the following command:

```
$ make ARCH=arm menuconfig
```

The following screenshot shows the UDOO kernel configuration menu. It's very similar to the Nexus 6 configuration menu. We have the same combination of keys to navigate, select and deselect features, and so on:

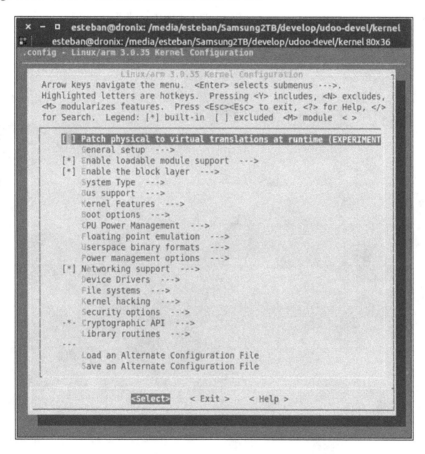

Working with UDOO, the same warnings we had with the Nexus 6 apply here too — be careful while removing components from the kernel. Some of them are just meant to be there to support specific hardware, some of them, instead, are *vital* for the system to boot. As always, feel free to experiment, but be careful about gambling!

This kind of development device makes debugging the kernel a bit easier compared to a smartphone. UDOO, as with a lot of other embedded development boards, provides a serial connection that enables you to monitor the whole boot sequence. This comes in handy if you are going to develop a driver for some hardware and you want to integrate it into your kernel or even if you are simply playing around with some custom kernel configuration. Every kernel and boot-related message will be printed to the serial console, ready to be captured and analyzed.

The next screenshot shows the boot sequence for our UDOO Quad board:

As you can see, there is plenty of debugging information, from the board power-on to the Android system prompt.

Driver management

Since version 2.6.x, Linux gives the developer the opportunity to compile parts of the kernel as separated modules that can be injected into the core, to add more features at runtime. This approach gives flexibility and freedom: there is no need to reboot the system to enjoy new features and there is no need to rebuild the whole kernel if you only need to update a specific module. This approach is widely use in the PC world, by embedded devices such as routers, smart TVs, and even by our familiar UDOO board.

To code a new kernel module is no easy task and it's far from the purpose of this book: there are plenty of books on the topic and most of the skill set comes from experience. In these pages, you are going to learn about the big picture, the key points, and the possibilities.

Unfortunately, Android doesn't use this modular approach: every required feature is built in a single binary kernel file, for practical and simplicity reasons. In the last few years there has been a trend to integrate into the kernel even the logic needed for Wi-Fi functionality, that was before it was loaded from a separated module during the boot sequence.

As we saw with the FTDI example in the previous pages, the most practical way to add a new driver to our Android kernel is using `menuconfig` and building the feature as a core part of the kernel.

In the next chapter, we will dig deeper in this topic and add new features to our kernel that are not present in the default configuration.

Altering the CPU frequency

Overclocking a CPU is one of the most loved topics among advanced users. The idea of getting the maximum amount of power from your device is exciting. Forums and blogs are filled with discussions about overclocking and in this section we are going to have an overview and clarify a few tricky aspects that you could deal with on your journey.

Every CPU is designed to work with a specific clock frequency or within a specific frequency range. Any modern CPU has the possibility to scale its clock frequency to maximize performance when needed and power consumption when performance is not needed, saving precious battery in case of our beloved mobile devices. Overclocking, then, denotes the possibility to alter this working clock frequency via software, increasing it to achieve performance higher than the one the CPU was designed for.

Contrary to what we often read on unscrupulous forum threads or blogs, overclocking a CPU can be a very dangerous operation: we are forcing the CPU to work with a clock frequency that formally hasn't been tested. This could backfire on us with a device rebooting autonomously, for its own protection, or we could even damage the CPU, in the worst-case scenario.

Another interesting aspect of managing the CPU clock frequency is the so-called underclock. Leveraging the CPU clock frequency scaling feature, we can design and implement scaling policies to maximize the efficiency, according to CPU load and other aspects. We could, for instance, reduce the frequency when the device is idle or in sleep mode and push the clock to the maximum when the device is under heavy load, to enjoy the maximum effectiveness in every scenario. Pushing the CPU management even further, lots of smartphone CPUs come with a multicore architecture: you can completely deactivate a core if the current scenario doesn't need it.

The key concept of underclocking a CPU is adding a new frequency below the lowest frequency provided by the manufacturer. Via software, we would be able to force the device to this frequency and save battery. This process is not riskless. We could create scenarios in which the device has a CPU frequency so low that it will result in an unresponsive device or even a frozen device. As for overclocking, these are unexplored territories and only caution, experience and luck will get you to a satisfying result.

An overview of the governors

Linux kernel manages CPU scaling using specific policies called **governors**. There are a few pre-build governors in the Linux kernel, already available via `menuconfig`, but you can also add custom-made governors, for your specific needs.

The following screenshot shows the `menuconfig` section of Google Nexus 6 for CPU scaling configuration:

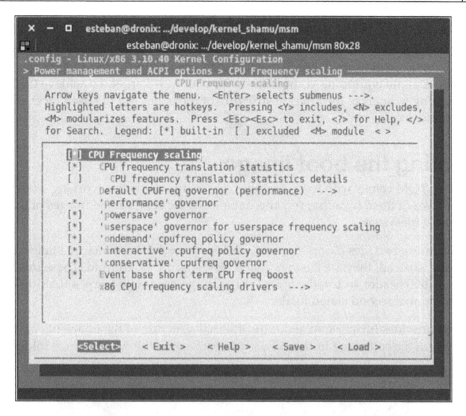

As you can see, there are six prebuild governors. Naming conventions are quite useful and make names self-explanatory: for instance, the performance governor aims to keep the CPU always at maximum frequency, to achieve the highest performance at every time, sacrificing battery life.

The most popular governors on Android are definitely the ondemand and interactive governors: these are quite common in many Android-based device kernels. Our reference device, Google Nexus 6, uses interactive as the default governor.

As you would expect, Google disallows direct CPU frequency management, for security reasons. There is no quick way to select a specific frequency or a specific governor on Android. However, advanced users can satisfy their curiosity or their needs with a little effort. In the next chapter, you will learn more about CPU management, but, for now, let's customize your boot image.

Customizing the boot image

So far, you learned how to obtain the kernel source code, how to set up the system, how to configure the kernel, and how to create your first custom kernel image. The next step is about equipping your device with your new kernel. To achieve this, we are going to analyze the internal structure of the boot.img file used by every Android device.

Creating the boot image

A custom ROM comes with four .img files, necessary to create a working Android system. Two of them (system.img and data.img) are compressed images of a Linux compatible filesystem.

The remaining two files (boot.img and recovery.img) don't contain a standard filesystem. Instead, they are custom image files, specific to Android. These images contain a 2KB header sector, the kernel core, compressed with gzip, a RAMdisk, and an optional second stated loader.

Android provides further info about the internal structure of the image file in the boot.img.h file contained in the mkbootimg package in the AOSP source folder.

The following screenshot shows a snippet of the content of this file:

```
esteban@dronix: ~/code/embedded_android/core/mkbootimg
          esteban@dronix: ~/code/embedded_android/core/mkbootimg 80x31
} __attribute__((packed));

/*
**  +-----------------+
**  | boot header     | 1 page
**  +-----------------+
**  | kernel          | n pages
**  +-----------------+
**  | ramdisk         | m pages
**  +-----------------+
**  | second stage    | o pages
**  +-----------------+
**
** n = (kernel_size + page_size - 1) / page_size
** m = (ramdisk_size + page_size - 1) / page_size
** o = (second_size + page_size - 1) / page_size
**
** 0. all entities are page_size aligned in flash
** 1. kernel and ramdisk are required (size != 0)
** 2. second is optional (second_size == 0 -> no second)
** 3. load each element (kernel, ramdisk, second) at
**    the specified physical address (kernel_addr, etc)
** 4. prepare tags at tag_addr.  kernel_args[] is
**    appended to the kernel commandline in the tags.
** 5. r0 = 0, r1 = MACHINE_TYPE, r2 = tags_addr
** 6. if second_size != 0: jump to second_addr
**    else: jump to kernel_addr
*/

#if 0
                                                       57,5         75%
```

As you can see, the image contains a graphical representation of the `boot.img` structure. This ASCII art comes with a deeper explanation of sizes and pages.

To create a valid `boot.img` file, you need the kernel image you have just built and a ramdisk. A ramdisk is a tiny filesystem that is mounted into the system RAM during the boot time. A ramdisk provides a set of critically important files, needed for a successful boot sequence. For instance, it contains the `init` file that is in charge of launching all the services needed during the boot sequence.

There are two main ways to generate a boot image:

- We could use the `mkbootimg` tool
- We could use the Android build system

Using `mkbootimg` gives you a lot of freedom, but comes with a lot of complexity. You would need a serious amount of command-line arguments to properly configure the generating system and create a working image. On the other hand, the Android build system comes with the whole set of configuration parameters already set and ready to go, with zero effort for us to create a working image. Just to give you a rough idea of the complexity of `mkbootimg`, the following screenshot shows an overview of the required parameters:

Playing with something so powerful is tempting, but, as you can see, the amount of possible wrong parameters passed to mkbootimg is large. As pragmatic developers, dealing with mkbootimg is not worth the risk at the moment. We want the job done, so we are going to use the Android build system to generate a valid boot image with no effort.

In the previous chapters, you created a custom version of the whole system using Android source code and a properly configured build system. We are going to take advantage of all the work that we have already done to complete this new step. All that you need to do is export a new environment variable, pointing to the kernel image you have created just a few pages ago. With your trusted terminal emulator, launch:

```
$ export TARGET_PREBUILT_KERNEL=<kernel_src>/arch/arm/boot/zImage-dtb
```

Once you have set and exported the TARGET_PREBUILT_KERNEL environment variable, you can launch:

```
$ make bootimage
```

A brand new, fully customized, boot image will be created by the Android build system and will be placed in the following folder:

```
$ target/product/<device-name>/boot.img
```

With just a couple of commands, we have a brand new boot.img file, ready to be flashed. Using the Android build system to generate the boot image is the preferred way for all the Nexus devices and for all those devices, such as the UDOO, that are designed to be as close as possible to an official Google device.

For all those devices on the market that are compliant to this philosophy, things start to get tricky, but not impossible. Some manufactures take advantage of the Apache v2 license and don't provide the whole Android source code. You could find yourself in a scenario where you only have the kernel source code and you won't be able to leverage the Android build system to create your boot image or even understand how boot.img is actually structured.

In these scenarios, one possible approach could be to pull the boot.img from a working device, extract the content, replace the default kernel with your custom version, and recreate boot.img using mkbootimg: easier said than done.

Right now, we want to focus on the main scenario, dealing with a system that is not fighting us. In the upcoming chapters, you will learn how to fight back and take full control of the system.

Upgrading the new boot image

Once you have your brand new, customized boot image, containing your customized kernel image, you only need to flash it to your device. We are working with Google devices or, at least, Google-compatible devices, so you will be able to use `fastboot` to flash your `boot.img` file to your device.

To be able to flash the image to the device, you need to put the device in `fastboot mode`, also known as `bootloader mode`. Every device has its own way to reach this mode, so, according to the device you are using, you can examine the table in *Chapter 4, Moving to Real-World Hardware* with all the steps to reach the fastboot mode.

Once your device is in fastboot mode, you can connect it via USB to your host computer. Fire up a terminal emulator and launch the command to upgrade the boot partition:

```
$ sudo fastboot flash boot boot.img
```

In a few seconds, `fastboot` will replace the content of the device boot partition with the content of your `boot.img` file. When the flashing process is successfully over, you can reboot your device with:

```
$ sudo fastboot reboot
```

The device will reboot using your new kernel and, thanks to the new USB TTL support that you added a few pages ago, you will be able to monitor the whole boot sequence with your terminal emulator.

Android boot sequence

To fully understand all Android internals, we are going to learn how the whole boot sequence works: from the power-on to the actual Android system boot. The Android boot sequence is similar to any other embedded system based on Linux: in a very abstract way, after the power-on, the system initializes the hardware, loads the kernel, and finally the Android framework. Any Linux-based system undergoes a similar process during its boot sequence: your Ubuntu computer or even your home DSL router.

In the next sections, we are going to dive deeper in to these steps to fully comprehend the operating system we love so much.

Internal ROM – bios

When you press the power button on your device, the system loads a tiny amount of code, stored inside a ROM memory. You can think about this as an equivalent of the BIOS software you have in your PC. This software is in charge of setting up all the parameters for CPU clock and running the RAM memory check. After this, the system loads the bootloader into memory and launches it.

An overview of bootloader

So far, the bootloader has been loaded into the RAM memory and started. The bootloader is in charge of loading the system kernel into the RAM memory and launching it, to continue the boot sequence.

The most popular bootloader software for Android devices is U-Boot, the Universal Bootloader. U-Boot is widely used in all kinds of embedded systems: DSL routers, smart TVs, infotainment systems, for example. U-boot is open source software and its flexibility to be customized for any device is definitely one of the reasons for its popularity.

U-boot's main task is to read the kernel image from the boot partition, load it into the RAM memory, and run it. From this moment on, the kernel is in charge of finishing the boot sequence.

You could think about U-boot on Android like GRUB on your Ubuntu system: it reads the kernel image, decompresses it, loads it into the RAM memory, and executes it. The following diagram gives you a graphical representation of the whole boot sequence as on an embedded Linux system, an Android system, and a Linux PC:

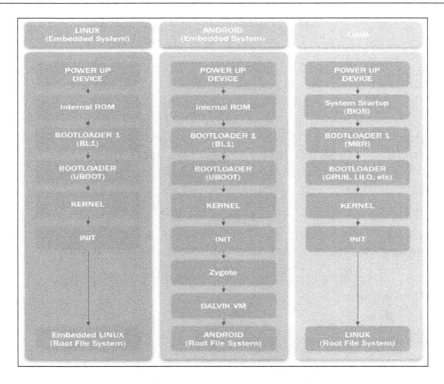

The kernel

After the bootloader loads the kernel, the kernel's first task is to initialize the hardware. With all the necessary hardware properly set up, the kernel mounts the ramdisk from `boot.img` and launches `init`.

The Init process

In a standard Linux system, the `init` process takes care of starting all the core services needed to boot the system. The final goal is to complete the boot sequence and start the graphical interface or the command line to make the system available to the user. This whole process is based on a specific sequence of system scripts, executed in a rigorous order to assure system integrity and proper configuration.

Android follows the same philosophy, but it acts in a different way. In a standard Android system, the `ramdisk`, contained in the `boot.img`, provides the `init` script and all the scripts necessary for the boot.

The Android init process consists of two main files:

- init.rc
- init.${ro.hardware}.rc

The `init.rc` file is the first initialization script of the system. It takes care of initializing those aspects that are common to all Android systems. The second file is very hardware specific. As you can guess, `${ro.hardware}` is a placeholder for the reference of a particular hardware where the boot sequence is happening. For instance, `${ro.hardware}` is replaced with `goldfinsh` in the emulator boot configuration.

In a standard Linux system, the init sequence executes a set of bash scripts. These bash scripts start a set of system services. Bash scripting is a common solution for a lot of Linux systems, because it is very standardized and quite popular.

Android systems use a different language to deal with the initialization sequence: Android Init Language.

The Android init language

The Android team chose to not use Bash for Android init scripts, but to create its own language to perform configurations and services launches.

The Android Init Language is based on five classes of statements:

- Actions
- Commands
- Services
- Options
- Imports

Every statement is line-oriented and is based on specific tokens, separated by white spaces. Comment lines start with a # symbol.

Actions

An Action is a sequence of commands bound to a specific trigger that's used to execute the particular action at a specific moment. When the desired event happens, the Action is placed in an execution queue, ready to be performed.

This snippet shows an example of an Action statement:

```
on <trigger> [&& <trigger>]*
  <command>
  <command>
  <command>
```

Actions have unique names. If a second Action is created with the same name in the same file, its set of commands is added to the first Action commands, set and executed as a single action.

Services

Services are programs that the init sequence will execute during the boot. These services can also be monitored and restarted if it's mandatory they stay up. The following snippet shows an example of a service statement:

```
service <name> <pathname> [ <argument> ]*
  <option>
  <option>
  . . .
```

Services have unique names. If in the same file, a service with a nonunique name exists, only the first one is evaluated as valid; the second one is ignored and the developer is notified with an error message.

Options

Options statements are coupled with services. They are meant to influence how and when init manages a specific service.

Android provides quite an amount of possible options statements:

- `critical`: This specifies a device-critical service. The service will be constantly monitored and if it dies more than four times in four minutes, the device will be rebooted in Recovery Mode.
- `disabled`: This service will be in a default stopped state. init won't launch it. A disabled service can only be launched manually, specifying it by name.
- `setenv <name> <value>`: This sets an environment variable using `name` and `value`.

- `socket <name> <type> <perm> [ <user> [ <group> [ <seclabel> ] ] ]`: This command creates a Unix socket, with a specified `name`, (`/dev/socket/<name>`) and provides its file descriptor the specified service. `<type>` specifies the type of socket: `dgram`, `stream`, or `seqpacket`. Default `<user>` and `<group>` are 0. `<seclabel>` specifies the SELinx security context for the created socket.

- `user <username>`: This changes the username before the service is executed. The default username is `root`.

- `group <groupname> [ <groupname> ]*`: This changes the group name before the service is executed.

- `seclabel <seclabel>`: This changes the SELinux level before launching the service.

- `oneshot`: This disables the service monitoring and the service won't be restarted when it terminates.

- `class <name>`: This specifies a service class. Classes of services can be launched or stopped at the same time. A service with an unspecified `class` value will be associated to the default class.

- `onrestart`: This executes a command when the service is restarted.

- `writepid <file...>`: When a services forks, this option will write the process ID (PID) in a specified file.

Triggers

Triggers specify a condition that has to be satisfied to execute a particular action. They can be event triggers or property triggers. Event triggers can be fired by the trigger command or by the `QueueEventTrigger()` function. The example event triggers are `boot` and `late-init`. Property triggers can be fired when an observed property changes value. Every Action can have multiple Property triggers, but only one Event trigger; refer to the following code for instance:

```
on boot && property:a=b
```

This Action will be executed when the `boot` event is triggered and the property a is equal to b.

Commands

The Command statement specifies a command that can be executed during the boot sequence, placing it in the `init.rc` file. Most of these commands are common Linux system commands. The list is quite extensive. Let's look at them in detail:

- `bootchart_init`: This starts bootchart if it is properly configured. Bootchart is a performance monitor and can provide insights about the boot performance of a device.

- `chmod <octal-mode-permissions> <filename>`: This changes file permissions.

- `chown <owner> <group> <filename>`: This changes the owner and the group for the specified file.

- `class_start <serviceclass>`: This starts a service specified by its class name.

- `class_stop <serviceclass>`: This stops and disables a service specified by its class name.

- `class_reset <serviceclass>`: This stops a service specified by its class name. It doesn't disable the service.

- `copy <src> <dst>`: This copies a source file to a new destination file.

- `domainname <name>`: This sets the domain name.

- `enable <servicename>`: This starts a service by its name. If the service is already queued to be started, then it starts the service immediately.

- `exec [<seclabel>[<user>[<group> ]* ]] -- <command> [ <argument> ]*`: This forks and executes the specified command. The execution is blocking: no other command can be executed in the meantime.

- `export <name> <value>`: This sets and exports an environment variable.

- `hostname <name>`: This sets the hostname.

- `ifup <interface>`: This enables the specified network interface.

- `insmod <path>`: This loads the specified kernel module.

- `load_all_props`: This loads all the system properties.

- `load_persist_props`: This loads the persistent properties, after the successful decryption of the `/data` partition.

- `loglevel <level>`: This sets the kernel log level.

- `mkdir <path> [mode] [owner] [group]`: This creates a folder with the specified name, permissions, owner, and group. The defaults are 755 as permissions, and root as owner and group.

- `mount_all <fstab>`: This mounts all the partitions in the `fstab` file.

- `mount <type> <device> <dir> [ <flag> ]* [<options>]`: This mounts a specific device in a specific folder. A few mount flags are available: `rw`, `ro`, `remount`, `noatime`, and all the common Linux mount flags.

- `powerctl`: This is used to react to changes of the `sys.powerctl` system parameter, critically important for the implementation of the reboot routing.

- `restart <service>`: This restarts the specified service.

- `rm <filename>`: This deletes the specified file.

- `rmdir <foldername>`: This deletes the specified folder.

- `setpropr <name> <value>`: This sets the system property with the specified name with the specified value.

- `start <service>`: This starts a service.

- `stop <service>`: This stops a service.

- `swapon_all <fstab>`: This enables the swap partitions specified in the fstab file.

- `symlink <target> <path>`: This creates a symbolic link from the target file to the destination path.

- `sysclktz <mins_west_of_gtm>`: This sets the system clock.

- `trigger <event>`: This programmatically triggers the specified event.

- `wait <filename > [ <timeout> ]`: This monitors a path for a file to appear. A timeout can be specified. If not, the default timeout value is 5 seconds.

- `write <filename> <content>`: This writes the specified content to the specified file. If the file doesn't exist, it creates the file. If the file already exists, it won't append the content, but it will override the whole file.

Imports

Imports specify all the external files that are needed in the current file and imports them:

```
import <path>
```

The previous snippet is an example of how the current init script can be extended, importing an external init script. `path` can be a single file or even a folder. In case *path* is a folder, all the files that exists in the first level of the specified folder will be imported. The command doesn't act recursively on folders: nested folders must be imported programmatically one by one.

Summary

In this chapter, you learned how to obtain the Linux kernel for your device, how to set up your host PC to properly build your custom kernel, how to add new features to the kernel, build it, package it, and flash it to your device.

You learned how the Android boot sequence works and how to manipulate the init scripts to customize the boot sequence.

In the next chapter, you will learn how to *cook* your first custom ROM, how to root your device, and replace the recovery partition.

6
"Cooking" Your First ROM

In *Chapter 5*, *Customizing Kernel and Boot Sequence*, we took an amazing journey into the Linux kernel — now you know how to obtain the right version for your device and how to build it. We got great satisfaction customizing and building your own kernel version, specific for your device — we added new drivers for your hardware and removed those that were unnecessary. You finally learned about the boot sequence.

In this chapter, we will enter the *modding* world and we will move forward with your first customized ROM. You will learn how to set up the system and how to create a custom ROM. We will see an overview of the most popular ROMs, and all the tools you need and how to use them.

The following topics will be covered in the chapter:

- History of Android modding (Cyanogenmod)
- Custom recovery
- Root access
- Kitchen and other tools

History of custom ROMs

First things first — What does "Custom ROM" mean?

Most Android devices come with so-called *NAND memories*. A NAND memory is a particular type of flash memory. A flash memory is based on transistors, instead of rotating disks, like in old hard drives. This type of memory is completely electrically managed — it can be written and erased and can store data indefinitely (not volatile). Knowing this, we may think that everything is writable on Android. Well, not exactly!

The acronym ROM stands for Read-Only Memory. This type of memory is often used in embedded systems to safely store all those files that are part of the core system. In an effort to guarantee the highest system integrity possible, developers must be sure that the core system stays intact over device reboots and possible failures. That's why the core system is stored in a type of memory that can only be written once—Read-Only Memory, to be precise. With time, the Android hacking community took the acronym and transformed it. Nowadays, in saying Custom ROM, you are simply saying "My own custom Android system for this specific device," and this is the meaning we will use in the following pages.

As for the Linux kernel, Android is one of the most popular open source projects currently developed. Free to use and customizable, used by millions of people, Android is the base element for hundreds of customized operating systems—most of them were experiments, some were custom versions fixing particular bugs for specific scenarios, and others were optimized versions of the original system.

In the beginning, the modding community was very scattered—lots of lone wolves, hacking in their dark rooms. Over time, most of them converged into more social environments, combining their efforts in forums and communities, creating modding teams to provide users with better and more reliable ROMs.

In *Chapter 5*, *Customizing Kernel and Boot Sequence*, we saw how to create a custom version of Android working with the source code. We were able to radically alter the original system to create our version, perfectly fitting our needs, so what's all this hype about modding? Why couldn't we just grab the source code and customize our system? The truth is that, unfortunately, Google is a needle in a haystack. Most of the other manufacturers play the whole open source game a bit differently and it is not always possible to rebuild a system from scratch, due to the lack of provided source code.

Luckily for us, Android customization can be achieved by following a *different path*—going straight to the system memory partition, decompiling the components, and making customizations, or so-called **surface modifications**.

A totally different game is played in the Linux kernel field. As you can remember, Android and the Linux kernel have different licenses—Android is distributed under the Apache License v2, while the Linux kernel is distributed under the GPL license. The GPL license is stricter about modification and redistribution and the manufacturers have a hard time keeping the kernel *secret*. That's why the Linux kernel is always available and modders can add, remove, and improve whatever aspect they want—new drivers, improved power management, improved CPU management, and so on.

When you look at the whole custom ROM idea, you end up thinking that you see custom ROMs everywhere and every day—manufacturer's ROM. If we think that the *really pure* Android system is the one shipped with Nexus devices, we realize that manufacturers are the *first modders*, turning the original system into something often completely different. Just think about Samsung or HTC custom UI. Those are huge modifications to the UI. Think about those devices that have an AM/FM radio—again, serious customization. Some manufacturers have gone so far with customizations over the years that they eventually made their device incompatible even with Google Play Store.

In the following pages, we will see an overview of the most popular custom ROMs to try to understand why they are so loved by advanced users.

Cyanogenmod

One of the undisputedly most popular Android custom ROMs is Cyanogenmod. It's one of the oldest ones and it brings features and performance that cannot be found in the official Android system:

Since the beginning, just after the first public releases of Android open source code, the Cyanogen team started back-porting the latest Android version to old devices. They basically overcame manufacturers' *business decisions* to leave old devices with old Android versions and made an effort to give new glory to so-called *legacy devices*.

During the years, the Cyanogenmod team added and tuned tons of features, and this approach attracted thousands of users. The improvements have been so good that often the official Google Android team merged them into the official Android source base, in the real open source community spirit.

As said earlier, the Cyanogenmod team didn't start the project from scratch. They used the Android Open Source Project and enhanced it. Using a different approach to lots of other customizers, they decided that the whole project had to be available as open source code, allowing everybody to enjoy all the features, learn from the source code, and contribute to the project itself. Over the years, the community has grown significantly, and lots and lots of blog posts, tutorials, and practical guides have invaded the web-sphere, making Cyanogenmod one of the most popular custom ROMs currently available.

This is a list of the most-loved features that Cyanogenmod currently provides:

- **Theming support**: The whole system UI can be customized with user-made themes that can be applied to the system at runtime
- **FLAC support**: Free Lossless Audio Codec is one of the many audio codecs available on the system
- **Bigger APN (Access Point Network) list**: Lots of different APNs have been added over time, making it easy to quickly set up an Internet connection on a multitude of devices
- **OpenVPN client**: The popular VPN software is available and ready to be used
- **Enriched Power Off menu**: The Power Off menu contains new actions such as Reboot, Recovery Mode Reboot, and so on

Some other features include:

- Support for Wi-Fi, Bluetooth, and USB tethering
- CPU Overclock management and system-wide performance enhancements
- Advanced management of Soft Buttons
- New Toggle Buttons in the system notification menu such as GPS, Bluetooth, and Wi-Fi
- Advanced Application permissions management, for a meticulously secured system
- System-wide graphics enhancements
- Increased performance and reliability, as stated by the team, compared to any other Android system derived from the official Google vanilla one

In April 2013, Cyanogenmod went from community project to an actual company. Despite this, the open source nature is still one of the main core values of the company. So far, it counts 17 employees working full-time on the project. In the last three years, they received a few donations from third-party partners, such as Benchmark Capital and Redpoint Ventures, pushing the development of an easier Cyanogenmod installation process.

In 2014, Cyanogenmod announced a partnership with OnePlus, a smartphone manufacturer, to distribute their devices with a pre-installed Cyanogenmod. According to their analytics, Cyanogenmod is currently used by 50 million devices.

Building Cyanogenmod

Inspired by Google AOSP, Cyanogenmod provides an official website where you can download the project source code and access the support forum: `www.cyanogenmod.org`.

The website also provides a complete list of every supported device. Unlike Google AOSP, which formally supports only Nexus devices, Cyanogenmod is available for dozens of different devices.

The Cyanogenmod build system is the exact same one you already mastered in the previous chapters. Knowing that, we leave it as an exercise to download and build your own Cyanogenmod version to fully understand how far Android AOSP can be customized and improved.

Installing a pre-build version

Being an open source project, you could build Cyanogen from source. If you want a quicker solution, Cyanogenmod provides pre-built installable versions of the system for a plethora of devices. Just check the website and look for one of your devices — chances are that it's on the list of supported devices.

Once you find that your device is supported, you can pick one of the many versions available. The release cycle is very different from Google's. One of the most *adventurous* features of the whole Cyanogenmod world is the **nightly build** — every night, an automatic system starts a new build with the latest contribution to the source code repository. These are tricky versions, which must be considered unstable, but will contain all the new things that the development team adds to the system daily — *only for the brave!*

In addition to the different release cycle, Cyanogenmod also uses a different version naming convention. The team uses tags to specify the different versions of the ROM:

- **Nightly**: As Already explained.

- **Experimental**: This is the version currently under testing.

- **M Snapshot, or Milestone Snapshot**: This is more stable than a nightly, but still to be considered unstable.

- **Release Candidate**: This is the final step before reaching the *stable* state. This is the first release that it would be *wise* to use on a daily basis on your device.

- **Stable**: This is the final state, targeting all users.

The Android Open Kang Project

Android Open Kang Project, also known as AOKP, is an open source project born in 2011 with the goal of providing an alternative to official Google Android for smartphones and tablets:

As you can imagine, the Kang team didn't create the system from scratch. They used the Android Open Source Project by Google as a starting point, as Cyanogenmod did. This particular Android version targets high-end smartphones and tablets and improves a few aspects to make the system more efficient and customizable. These are some of its main pros, which are the reason why more and more users decide to switch to AOKP.

One of the aspects that users love is that the AOKP team focused on making the system as light as possible. They stripped away every unnecessary app and basically left just the official Google apps, to create the smallest possible system.

Most of the smartphones and tablets nowadays contain lots and lots of *esthetical* features that could slow down the system and are heavy on the eye. These types of apps are called **bloatware** and are usually pre-installed system apps that are impossible to remove from the system. AOKP made getting rid of these useless apps one of its main goals.

The Kang team works very hard to guarantee the maximum level of customization for the user's system. AOKP provides a **ROM Control** menu to customize lots of aspects of the system, from UI customization to behavior customizations. A large amount of energy has been spent in the gesture management domain, and one of the coolest features is the possibility to launch any desired app with a finger gesture instead of tapping on an icon.

As with Cyanogenmod, AOKP also provides plenty of documentation and downloads on their website at `http://aokp.co`. Again, you can check out the source code and build it yourself, or try out an already built version.

Here is a quick list of the goodies you can find in AOKP:

- **Vibration Pattern**: Every contact can be associated to a particular vibration pattern
- **Navigation Ring**: The Android lock screen can be customized with user-chosen apps to quickly access them even with a locked device
- **LED Control**: The system LED behavior can be customized in terms of color, blinking, and duration to create custom notifications for your custom scenarios
- **Custom Toggles**: The notification area can be customized with different toggle buttons to create the perfect setup that fits your needs

The following image shows two screenshots from the actual system:

- The first one shows how to customize the **Navigation Ring**
- The second one shows how to customize the **Vibration** pattern

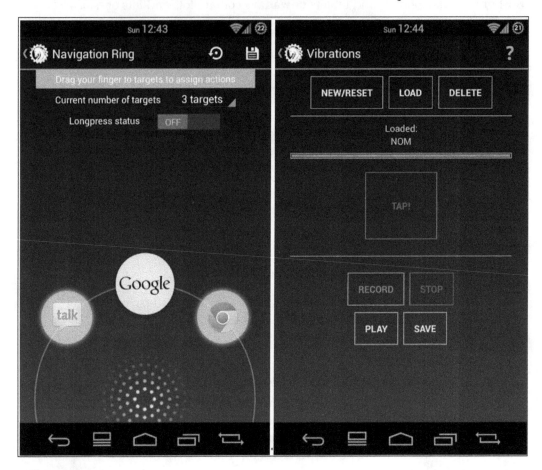

Installing AOKP

AOKP versioning is different from Google's and Cyanogenmod's. AOKP provides only too versions:

- Nightlies
- Milestones

Nightlies are the equivalent of Cyanogenmod's nightly build. Indeed, this is just a build automatically generated every night by the AOKP build system. This is to be considered highly unstable and only to be installed for testing purposes.

By contrast, Milestones are stable builds, meant to be installed for stable daily usage.

To keep the community engaged, the Kang team created **AOKP PUSH**, an app that keeps the phone updated with new builds and also includes the ability to install a system update, when available. As a final note, like Cyanogenmod, AOKP is completely free and open to your contributions.

Minor ROMs

In the previous sections, we saw an overview of the two most popular custom ROMs available nowadays for Android smartphones and tablets. As you can imagine, this is just the tip of the iceberg — over the years, dozens of different custom ROMs have been developed and released. Lots of them target specific scenarios to solve specific issues or satisfy specific needs of their users, improving the Android system in their own way. Most of them are not built from scratch, but are based on already available systems that have been customized and redistributed.

Most of the available custom ROMs target a specific device, to solve device-specific issues and improve usability and performance. **DroniX** (`https://goo.gl/R3c9pJ`), for instance, a project created by the authors of this very book, targeted a specific device, the Huawei Ideos U8150, a low-end device that became very popular at the time. The development team focused on performance and squeezed every available Megahertz from the Ideos CPU. With the Kernel source code available, we were able to improve CPU frequencies and governors. Better power management meant better battery management, with better performance and increased battery life.

As always, be careful when you try out custom ROMs. Some of them could be very *extreme* and could be dangerous for your devices. This is unfortunate, but it's a real scenario. There is no magic for *cooking* a custom ROM, and there are a lot of things that can go wrong. Things like extreme overclocking, for instance, are dangerous, and a wise user should distrust ROMs that try to sell these kinds of features. Experimenting with Android can be fun, satisfying, and challenging, but it must be done with knowledge and wisdom.

We can't list here every custom ROM available in the wild. What we can do is to point you in the right direction: `http://www.xda-developers.com/`. This is probably the most famous forum to get the latest news and the latest crazy things.

Overview of OEM customizations

Even if they are not commonly considered custom ROMs, all the Android variants distributed by manufacturers can be considered to have heavy customizations. We witness these every day—every time you look at a Samsung device, you know that it's not pure Android.

From the system launcher to the Settings menu, every single component of these systems is heavily customized by the OEM and very far from the official Google version. In some cases, the system is so different that the average user doesn't know that he is using the same Android 5 system, for instance.

This is a list of the most popular OEM customizations to demonstrate how a system can be modified and how different the same Android version can look on devices by different manufactures.

Samsung – TouchWiz

TouchWiz is a graphical interface, optimized for touch interfaces. It has been developed by Samsung and its technical partners. Often, it's incorrectly defined as a "custom operating system", but technically speaking, it's just a heavy customization of the Android UI.

The first version of TouchWiz was released in 2010, for Android 2.1 and BADA, an operating system created by Samsung for its smartphones and tablets. The current version is TouchWiz 5 and we can find lots of improvements, added over the years. In the beginning, TouchWiz was just a *different UI*. Today, it's a collection of custom system applications, customized UI widgets, and lots of new settings and features, such as sound profiles, power management, toggles, and so on. The following screenshot shows the home screen and the applications drawer:

Huawei EMUI

Under the influence of Samsung's work, Huawei also provides its own version of Android UI for its devices. As with Samsung, they started with a customized UI and added lots of features, such as theme customization — icons, colors, fonts, and lock screen. The notification area has been customized and improved, too.

One of the most useful new features is definitely the advanced power management. It provides three possible setups: Ultra, Smart, and Normal. Ultra is the *extreme* setup — one click, and you can turn off every sensor but the bare minimum ones, aiming to achieve the longest possible battery life. Smart tries to automatically manage the power usage as much as possible. Normal is all about performance — the battery won't last long, but the device will work at full speed.

The following image shows the Hawei EMUI home screen:

HTC Sense

In 2009, HTC release the first version of its customized UI for smartphones. It targeted Android and Windows Mobile with a shared graphical user experience to not confuse users.

The most popular feature in HTC is the big collection of home widgets, but there are other features that are just as interesting, such as a tracking system for use if the device is stolen. This system allows the user to make remote operations on the device to locate it or wipe the memory, or simply lock it. It's even possible to show a custom message on the lock screen, with an address or a reward to reobtain the device.

The following screenshot shows the home screen of HTC Sense 7:

LG Optimus UI

LG, like others, provides a customized UI—user-picked images for the system icons, colors, and a few custom settings. An interesting feature is the **vocal command** to take a picture and the ability to pick the best picture from a burst of photo photos.

The following image shows the home screen and the customized notification area:

Xiaomi MIUI

This is definitely the heaviest customized system and it has one specific feature that none of the previous ones have—it's open source! Xiaomi began to work on MIUI with Android 2.3.7 and Cyanogenmod 7—those two were the core of the system. Over the years, they created a custom ROM that is way more than just a customized UI, adding more and more features.

In 2011, Xiaomi jumped into the market, switching from system customizer to device manufacturer, with high-end, low-cost devices, equipped with its MIUI system.

The following image shows the MIUI home screen and app store:

Unfortunately, this is a popular trend—an easy method for branding and to assure customer loyalty, but it's not always the recommended way to go.

There are other manufacturers that prefer to ship their devices with a vanilla Android—Motorola, for instance. Motorola's branding approach is to add just a couple of *by Motorola* apps. These are usually utility apps, aiming to enrich the user experience while keeping the system clean.

Motorola's strategy also has one big pro—a system very close to Google's original one means faster updates. Every time Google releases a new Android version, Motorola devices receive system updates as well in a few days. This is very unusual for most of the other manufacturers, somehow doomed to stay on old Android versions due to the huge amount of work necessary to update such a heavily customized system.

An overview of Android recovery

One of the most important parts of the whole Android architecture is the `Recovery` partition. A recovery partition is very common in embedded systems, and we saw an overview of it in previous chapters. As we know, the so-called `Recovery` is a minimal runtime system, completely decoupled from the main Android system and totally self-sufficient. Its main goal is to guarantee system integrity and provide the necessary tools to fix common minor issues and restore a properly working system.

With an Android vanilla `Recovery`, we can:

- Update the Android system
- Wipe the data partition and the cache partition

Wiping the data and cache partition is a common practice if we want to restore our device to the factory defaults, for instance, in order to have a clean system to start experimenting on something specific, or if we just want to sell it.

Diving into Android recovery

The Android `Recovery` system is completely standalone. This means that whatever might happen to the main Android system, `recovery` will be always able to restore a working system.

To achieve this level of resilience, `recovery` contains its own Linux kernel and its own `rootfs`. The following screenshot shows how `recovery` actually lives near the Android system, but is completely separate:

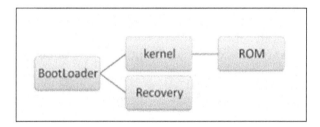

The previous screenshot shows how access to the `recovery` is bound to the `BootLoader`. The `BootLoader` is unable to decide if the current boot sequence is going to end with a running `recovery` or a running Android system.

Recovery mode can be accessed with a button combination when the device is turned off. For our reference device, Google Nexus 6, you can take the following steps:

1. Press and hold *Volume Down, Volume Up* and *Power buttons* simultaneously.

2. Release all buttons when the `Fastboot Mode` menu appears.

3. Use the *Volume* buttons until the upper part of the screen displays the `Recovery Mode` text.

4. Press *Power* to select `Recovery Mode` — after that you will see an Android icon laid on its back.

5. Press and hold the *Power* button, then press the *Volume Up* button once.

Once you have landed on the recovery main screen, you can navigate using the *Volume* buttons and confirm your choice using the *Power* button.

The options you will find in the recovery menu could vary, but an Android vanilla `recovery` will definitely provide these options:

- **Reboot system now**: This option will restart the system.

- **Apply update from ADB**: Android Debug Bridge can be used from a host computer to upload an official Google system update. Only certified updates can be uploaded and applied this way due to security measures enforced by the recovery to guarantee system integrity.

- **Wipe cache partition**: This option will erase the *cache* partition. This partition usually contains the system's temporary data and app cache data. Deleting this file will free quite an amount of disk space, without losing user data or apps.

- **Wipe data/factory reset**: This option will erase the volatile memory and restore the original factory system. Everything that is not strictly system-related will be deleted: videos, music, documents, user apps, and so on. The cache partition will be erased as well.

The following screenshot show a stock Android recovery:

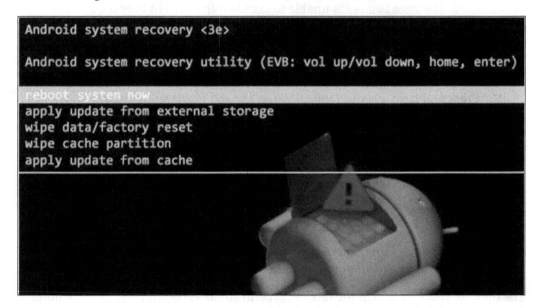

```
Android system recovery <3e>

Android system recovery utility (EVB: vol up/vol down, home, enter)

reboot system now
apply update from external storage
wipe data/factory reset
wipe cache partition
apply update from cache
```

Installing an alternative recovery

As with the whole Android system, even the recovery source code is available for study and modifications and, over the years, the Android community has developed alternatives that can be used in place of the Android stock recovery.

All these alternatives aim to improve and add more features to the stock recovery. The most common features are:

- **Ability to save and restore system backups**: NANDroid is extremely useful for experimenting with custom systems and adventurous configurations
- **Ability to install custom ROMs**: Probably the most important among the added features, from a custom ROM developer's point of view
- **Enhanced UI and UXD**: Some of these custom recoveries provide support for the touchscreen, instead of the default *Volume/Power* button navigation

The most popular recovery alternatives are:

- Clockworkmod
- 4EXT
- Amon Ra Recovery
- Team Win Recovery Project (TWRP)

Every one of them is different in some way—look and feel, advanced features, and so on, but all of them provide a clear way to allow the advanced user to install custom ROMs.

Clockworkmod

This is definitely one of the most popular custom recoveries in the game. It's often called CWM, and has been developed by Koushik "*Koush*" Dutta. He started with the ancient Android 2.1 recovery source code and, since then, he has kept on adding features.

One of the main features is the NANDroid backup, which allows the user to safely save and restore the whole system structure. Another interesting feature is the ability to connect to the recovery shell from a computer, via ADB. A critically important feature is the ability to update the system using unofficial update packages. Unlike the stock recovery, Clockworkmod ignores all signature certificates, knowing that only an advanced user would try to flash a custom-made update package.

Clockworkmod recovery can be easily installed using the specific app distributed via Google Play Store, or manually, as we will see.

To install it manually on your trusted Nexus device, you can use `fastboot`. Follow these steps to install Clockworkmod recovery:

1. First thing to do—download it. The Clockworkmod website has a complete list of supported devices and specific download files: `https://www.clockworkmod.com/rommanager`.

2. Once you have the file, decompress it and you will have a `.img` file.

3. Now, put your device in `fastboot` mode, as we saw in previous chapters, fire up a terminal, and use the following command to flash the `.img` file to the recovery partition:

   ```
   $~: sudo fastboot flash recovery recovery.img
   ```

4. Once the brand new recovery has been installed, you can reboot the device straight to recovery mode with the following command:

   ```
   $~: sudo fastboot reboot recovery
   ```

From this moment on, we can install custom ROMs or perform a total system backup.

It's also possible to recompile the Clockworkmod source code from scratch, since the project is open source. You can also find a custom recovery source code in the custom Cyanogenmod ROM that we have discussed in previous paragraphs. Building Cyanogenmod from the source code follows the same steps you already followed to build official Android: the build system and the build setup are the same. Applying the same know-how as for vanilla Android, you can easily create a Cyanogenmod system image and a Clockworkmod custom recovery.

Here's a screenshot of the Clockworkmod UI:

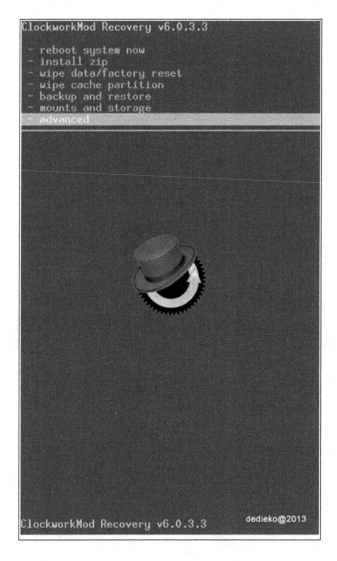

TWRP – Team Win Recovery Project

One alternative to the famous Clockworkmod recovery is TWRP, which stands for Team Win Recovery Project. One of the most important features of this recovery mod is support for touchscreens.

In this way, you can interact with the recovery mod directly using the screen, like you normally do using Android, which is very convenient, especially if we compare it to the volume keys used in all the other recovery mods. The graphical interface is pretty usable, with big buttons that show all the various options (they are very similar to the ones in the Clockwork mod). Using TWRP, you can install unofficial ROMs and also perform a complete system backup.

The project was born on 30th July 2011 and is an open source project— also, here you can either download a binary for your device or recompile from source code.

You can find more information on the official website at `http://teamw.in/`.

Here are some screenshots of TWRP:

Connecting to the recovery shell using ADB

Custom recovery can be operated using their standard UI, as we saw, and using an ADB connection. This feature is not available in the stock recovery and will be very useful during our experiments.

Once the custom recovery is installed, fire up a terminal and run the following command:

```
~$: adb devices
```

ADB will list all the available devices, as shown in the following screenshot:

Knowing that there is just a single device, we can simply use the following command to connect to the recovery shell:

```
~$: adb shell
```

You will be prompted with a # symbol, which lets you know that you have administrator powers as a *root* user. Being a *root* user gives you the opportunity to do advanced tasks, such as mount the `system/` in *read/write mode* and add or remove any file you want, without starting the whole Android system.

Device permissions

As we have seen in previous chapters, Android is based on Linux, so it also inherits the part that concerns user permissions. As with a standard Linux system, Android also manages everything through groups and users. In the default configuration, it's not possible to obtain administrator (root) access, in order to prevent tampering with the system. Also, with access to the whole operating system, it's easy to corrupt the system itself, accidentally or deliberately (for example, to steal user data using a virus).

Every Android app, when installed on the system, generates a new user and group, and inter-app communications are performed according to Android SDK constraints and protocols. Sometimes, though, it's useful to have complete control over the device, like, for example, when installing apps that manage CPU frequency and the CPU governor.

Now let's see how to obtain root access and what the implications of rooting the device are.

Root access

Root access enables the users of smartphones, tablets, and other devices with Android OS installed to obtain privileged access, also called root access, to the whole Android operating system. As we have already mentioned, Android uses a Linux kernel, so obtaining root access is very similar to obtaining administrator (superuser) access to a regular Linux or Unix-like OS, such as FreeBSD or Mac OS X.

Often, the reason for obtaining root access is to overcome the limits imposed on the device by the hardware producers. As a root user, you have the ability to modify or replace system apps and change the settings. Also, you can use the apps that require root permissions themselves, enabling you to execute operations that would otherwise be inaccessible to normal Android users. Rooting the device, that is, obtaining root access, can also help if you want to totally remove the device OS and replace it with another, maybe more recent, one.

In the following paragraphs, we will see how to obtain root access, which is the key precondition for installing the custom ROM.

SuperSu

To use root permissions in Android apps, an independent developer known as Chainfir Jorrit Jongma has developed a library that enables you to use them from your app and therefore execute root-level operations. Everything is open source and you can explore the documentation regarding the API at the official website of the developer: `https://su.chainfire.eu`.

If you would like to check out the library source code, you can find it (and contribute) here: `https://github.com/Chainfire/libsuperuser`.

Obtaining root access

Now it's time to see how to obtain root permissions on our device in practice. Unfortunately, it's not that simple, and there are various ways to obtain root permissions on a device. Every device has its quirks, and hence a different procedure to execute in order to obtain root permissions. Generally, we can say that if there's a possibility of installing a recovery mod, then there's also a possibility of installing everything necessary to become root. We just need to copy the right files to the system partition that is mounted as read-only by default, so we can access it either by making an ad hoc system partition using the source files, or — in cases when we don't have the Android source code — by mounting the partition in read/write mode through one of the custom recovery mods we described previously.

Up till now, we haven't talked about the legal issues regarding modifying the software present on the device. In general, it is not illegal to install custom ROMs onto our devices, except that there's the possibility of invalidating the device warranty. As far as the Nexus devices are concerned, there's no problem whatsoever; they are being sold for the purposes of software development, so the product warranty isn't tied to the software but to the hardware instead.

Chef toolkit

One of the main goals of this book is to help you realize your own version of a ROM customization. In the dictionary of modders, the act of modifying a version of Android in order to produce one's own ROM customization is often referred to with the verb *to cook* and the word *kitchen*.

"Cooking one's own ROM" means to modify the stock version of Android installed on one's device, with the aim of creating a new one.

For this reason, all the tools that might help to make the development of a ROM customization easier are called **Chef toolkit**.

As discussed in the previous chapters, it is indeed possible to create one's own ROM version starting from the source code, but this is not always possible, as some device manufacturers do not release their source code. In all those cases, we need to act on the system partitions, often directly on the binaries that build the internal core, both on the application framework and on the filesystem utilities.

In the next paragraphs, we will learn how to cook a ROM starting from binary images, beginning from the environment and analyzing the development tools that will help us carry out our first ROM customization.

Preparing the environment

Before we can start developing the ROM, we most certainly need to prepare an adequate environment on our computer. Android can be used with basically all the most recent operating systems, from Windows, to Linux, to OS X.

We always refer to Ubuntu, as we did in the previous chapters when we dealt with compiling Android from the source code. Therefore, all you need to start is a computer with a recent version of Ubuntu installed on it. Besides that, we suggest to also install a good text editor for developers—it could either be VIM from the command line, or graphic editors such as ATOM, SublimeText, and so on. We will mostly work from the console, using different scripts and tools in order to finalize our first custom ROM.

Android kitchen

One of the *chef's* most important tools is undoubtedly the `Kitchen`. Although we are stealing our analogies from the world of cooking, we are actually focusing on the preparation of our first Android customization—the first step is obtaining the system binary images.

We refer to as the `Android Kitchen` the set of tools that are usually used, such as the scripts to be used in a shell, and which help the developer perform automated tasks, such as decompressing and editing the system images that build a ROM, decompiling APK packets, sometimes adding the root privileges to the ROM, and so on.

Of course, many different kitchens exist online, each one with its own peculiarities. We will study some of them and we will try to perform simple actions in order to get our first custom ROM ready to be flashed onto our device.

One of the most popular `Android Kitchens` is **dsixda**. The project is formally "retired," but it has been forked by lots of users and the development is still ongoing. It's open source and you can download it or fork it and contribute to the project starting from `https://github.com/dsixda/Android-Kitchen`.

The dsixda `kitchen` is based on a suite of `Bash` scripts and tools to provide an easy method to perform the most common *cooking* operations:

- Add Busybox
- Add root permissions
- Customize the boot screen

These are just few of the possible operations available in its console menu. This kitchen is compatible with Windows, Linux, and OS X. We are going to use it with our trusted Ubuntu. Once you have downloaded the kitchen (`https://github.com/dsixda/Android-Kitchen/archive/0.224.zip`), uncompress it into a folder, enter the folder, and run the following:

```
$: ./menu
```

This command will fire up the main menu, as shown in the following screenshot:

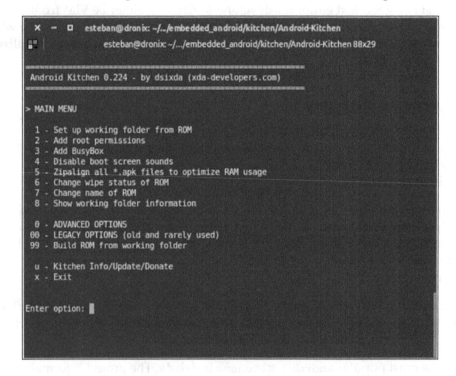

The dsixda kitchen manipulates two specific partitions—system and boot-respectively compressed in `system.img` and `boot.img` files. In the following sections, we will dig into extracting these partitions and customizing them.

Other developers' tools

Many other different tools could come in handy for the developer, of course strictly depending on one's specific needs. A **hexadecimal editor** would certainly be very useful for the analysis of binary images, while simple graphics editing software would help when it comes to modifying icons or other graphical aspects of the ROM, as well as for preparing the whole environment for compiling the Linux kernel, and possibly Android applications to add to the ROM.

We usually prepare the environment as if we had to compile Android from the source together with the Linux kernel, so that we definitely have all the necessary tools to build our custom ROM.

Manipulating DEX files with APKTool

Working with an Android system, it's quite common to need to manipulate DEX files. DEX stands for **Dalvik Executable** and these files are used by Android Virtual Machine. To easily manipulate these files, you can use APKTool by Ryszard Wiśniewski and Connor Tumbleson. The tools are open source and you can download them at `http://ibotpeaches.github.io/Apktool/`.

APKTool is written in Java, so you need a JVM to use it. Once you have the APKTool `jar` file in place, fire up a terminal and run the following:

```
$: java -jar apktool_2.0.3.jar
```

Replace the version with yours, if necessary. The following screenshot shows the initial help menu of the tool:

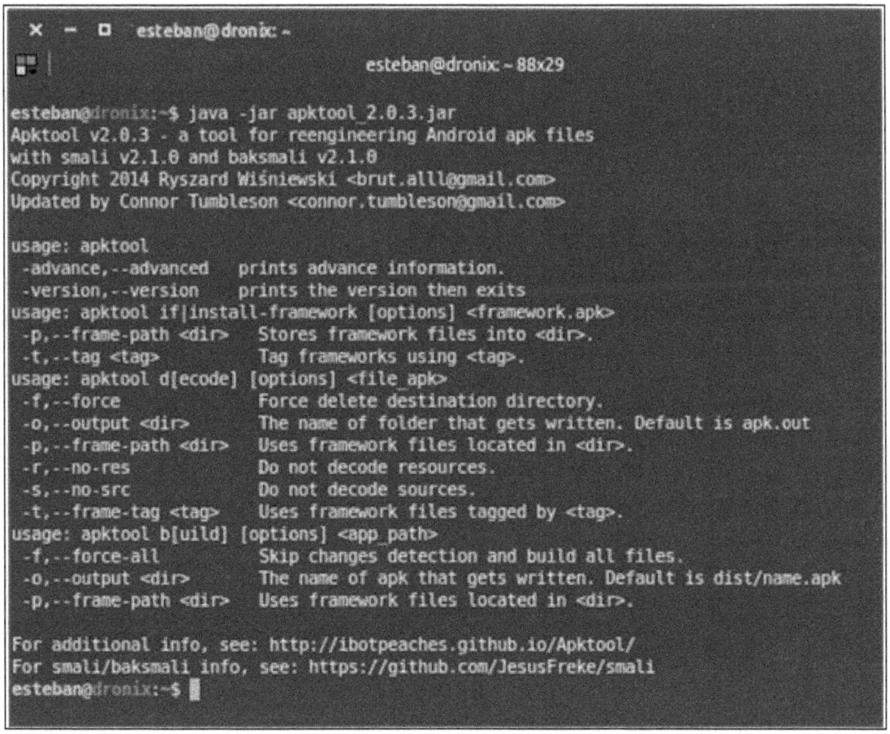

APKTool is based on two other tools — smali and baksmali, to assemble and disassemble the files. It requires an initial setup to work properly: framework-res.apk position. You must specify where APKTool must look to obtain this file. framework-res.apk is part of the Android system and can be extracted from a running Android device, using our trusted ADB:

```
~$ adb pull /system/framework/framework-res.apk .
```

The previous command will copy the APK from the Android device into the current folder. Once we have the file in place, we can tell APKTool where to find it:

```
~$ apktool if {path to framework-res.apk}
```

Now that everything is configured, we can try to decompile and customize an APK, using the following command:

```
~$ apktool d myapk.apk path_destination_decompilation
```

The APK content will be placed in the destination folder we specified and we can edit any file we want. After all our modifications, we can *recompress* the folder into an APK file with the following command:

```
~$ apktool b path_decompiled_files new_apk_mod.apk
```

Once the new APK is ready, we can copy it to the device with a file transfer app or using ADB push, as we saw in the previous chapters.

Cooking our first ROM

So far, we have seen an overview of the suite of tools we need to create a custom ROM from a binary system image. The most important of all is the kitchen, and it needs system.img and boot.img partition files to properly do its job.

If you are targeting Google devices, this is an easy game. Google provides system source code for its devices, so we can always build our .img files from the source, as we learned in previous chapters. We can also grab the .img files from the official system installation packages that Google also provides for its devices at every new release of the Android system.

If you are targeting a device that's not a Nexus, things become more adventurous. Most of the time you don't have the system source code; often you don't even have the downloadable system images. As you will see in the next sections, there is always a way to obtain every last piece of the puzzle to create our custom ROM.

Gathering the ingredients

The list is quite short. All you need is:

- Kernel source code, if you want to customize the system at core level
- `system.img`
- `boot.img`

The two `.img` files may be provided by the manufacturer, like Google does, or can be manually dumped from a running device system memory. The first scenario is the *lucky* one; the second one is more advanced and requires a bit of creativity. This is the scenario we are going to explore in greater depth, because, if you are lucky enough to have the manufactured system restore file, you simply need to decompress it into a folder and you will get the `.img` files you are looking for.

Dumping system partitions

To create a dump of the system memory, you will need to access the system with root privileges. As we already know, there are a few ways to gain root privileges—device-specific rooting, installing a custom recovery, and so on. Pick the technique you prefer.

Once you have root privileges, fire up a terminal and connect to your device shell with the following command:

```
~$: adb shell
```

The system will welcome us with a # symbol. We can now proceed with dumping the partitions. To get an overview of the partitions structure, you can use the following command:

```
~ # cat /proc/partitions
```

The following screenshot shows the output for a standard Google Nexus 6 device:

```
 ×  –  □    esteban@dronix: ~

                                          esteban@dronix: ~ 97x51
root@shamu:/ # cat /proc/partitions
major minor  #blocks  name

    7      0      32768 loop0
  179      0   30535680 mmcblk0
  179      1     114688 mmcblk0p1
  179      2      16384 mmcblk0p2
  179      3        384 mmcblk0p3
  179      4         56 mmcblk0p4
  179      5         16 mmcblk0p5
  179      6         32 mmcblk0p6
  179      7       1024 mmcblk0p7
  179      8        256 mmcblk0p8
  179      9        512 mmcblk0p9
  179     10        500 mmcblk0p10
  179     11       4156 mmcblk0p11
  179     12        384 mmcblk0p12
  179     13       1024 mmcblk0p13
  179     14        256 mmcblk0p14
  179     15        512 mmcblk0p15
  179     16        500 mmcblk0p16
  179     17          4 mmcblk0p17
  179     18        512 mmcblk0p18
  179     19       1024 mmcblk0p19
  179     20       1024 mmcblk0p20
  179     21       1024 mmcblk0p21
  179     22       1024 mmcblk0p22
  179     23      16384 mmcblk0p23
  179     24      16384 mmcblk0p24
  179     25       2048 mmcblk0p25
  179     26      32768 mmcblk0p26
  179     27        256 mmcblk0p27
  179     28         32 mmcblk0p28
  179     29        128 mmcblk0p29
  179     30       8192 mmcblk0p30
  179     31       1024 mmcblk0p31
  259      0       2528 mmcblk0p32
  259      1          1 mmcblk0p33
  259      2          8 mmcblk0p34
  259      3      16400 mmcblk0p35
  259      4       9088 mmcblk0p36
  259      5      16384 mmcblk0p37
  259      6     262144 mmcblk0p38
  259      7      65536 mmcblk0p39
  259      8       1024 mmcblk0p40
  259      9    2097152 mmcblk0p41
  259     10   27807616 mmcblk0p42
  179     32       4096 mmcblk0rpmb
  254      0   27807616 dm-0
root@shamu:/ #
root@shamu:/ #
```

The number of partitions is almost overwhelming, but we need to focus just on the system partition and the boot partition. We know that the partitions we are interested in are there, among all those listed partitions. Now, we have to figure out which of those partitions is actually system/ and which is boot/.

The relationship between a physical partition and its role in the Android architecture is shown with the following command:

```
~ # ls /dev/block/platform/msm_sdcc.1/by-name
```

The previous command will show something like this:

```
~ # . . .
~ # ... recovery -> /dev/block/mmcblk0p35
~ # ... system   -> /dev/block/mmcblk0p41
~ # ... boot     -> /dev/block/mmcblk0p37
~ # ... userdata -> /dev/block/mmcblk0p42
~ # . . .
```

As you can see, it shows every relevant partition and its role. We can easily figure out that the physical mccblk0p41 will become our system.img and mmcblk0p37 will become our boot.img file.

We will take advantage of the /sdcard partition to store the dumps, and we will create the dumps using the utility dd:

```
~ # dd if=/dev/block/mmcblk0p41 of=/sdcard/system.img
```

With the previous command, you are copying the whole system partition into a single file on the SD card. This process can take a while—be patient. Once you have the system.img file, you can move on to creating the boot.img file, with the following command:

```
~ # dd if=/dev/block/mmcblk0p37 of=/sdcard/boot.img
```

You now have the two most important files to create a custom ROM. Let's start customizing them.

Modifying an Android system binary image

Follow these steps to modify an Android system binary image:

1. Let's start with system.img. First of all, you need to bring it on to your host computer:

   ```
   ~$ adb pull /sdcard/system.img .
   ```

2. Then, you need to create a mount point to mount the image into it:

   ```
   ~$ mkdir system_mount_point
   ```

3. Now you can mount it as a common image file:

   ```
   ~$ mount -o loop system.img system_mount_point
   ```

On old devices, the filesystem used for `system.img` was `yaffs`. Over the years, the Android system migrated to an `ext4` filesystem, also very common on lots of Linux systems. Chances are that you are working with an `ext4` filesystem right now.

Entering the mount point with `cd` and listing the files with `ls`, you will see a folder structure similar to the one in the next image:

```
 ×  –  □   esteban@dronix: ~/develop/system_mount_point

                         esteban@dronix: ~/develop/system_mount_point 98x19
esteban@dronix:~/develop/system_mount_point$ ll
total 180
drwxr-xr-x. 14 root     root       4096 gen 31 18:35 ./
drwxrwxr-x   3 esteban  esteban    4096 feb  4 02:12 ../
drwxr-xr-x. 68 root     root       4096 gen 31 18:35 app/
drwxr-xr-x.  3 root        2000    8192 gen 31 18:35 bin/
-rw-r--r--.  1 root     root       4770 gen  1  2009 build.prop
drwxr-xr-x. 15 root     root       4096 gen 31 18:35 etc/
drwxr-xr-x.  2 root     root       8192 gen  1  2009 fonts/
drwxr-xr-x.  4 root     root       4096 gen  1  2009 framework/
drwxr-xr-x.  6 root     root       8192 gen 31 18:35 lib/
drwx------.  2 root     root       4096 gen  1  1970 lost+found/
drwxr-xr-x.  3 root     root       4096 gen  1  2009 media/
drwxr-xr-x. 61 root     root       4096 gen  1  2009 priv-app/
-rw-r--r--.  1 root     root     105126 gen  1  2009 recovery-from-boot.bak
drwxr-xr-x.  9 root     root       4096 gen  1  2009 usr/
drwxr-xr-x.  8 root        2000    4096 gen  1  2009 vendor/
drwxr-xr-x.  2 root        2000    4096 gen 31 18:35 xbin/
esteban@dronix:~/develop/system_mount_point$ 
```

You can now navigate the folders tree and study the structure, removing or adding the file you want. One interesting file to study is `build.prop`. This file contains juicy information about the system and its configuration. It's a very hardware-specific file, due to the infinite possibilities for customizing an Android system, but most of the variants share common details, such as memory heap size, display density, device code name, manufacturer name, Android framework SDK version, Android system version, and so on. There is even information about the system build time and the default ringtone for notifications and calls. There are plenty of little customizations with which you can play and experiment. For heavier modifications, keep reading and get ready for what's coming in the next chapter.

Modifying an Android binary boot image

As you already learned from the previous chapters, the boot image is a bit different from a system image. First of all, it doesn't contain a filesystem we can mount on our host system: the boot image has to be *decompressed*.

To decompress the boot image, you are going to use the specific menu item in the `Android Kitchen` from the previous pages. The boot image is a key component of a custom ROM: that's where the kernel is and where the `init` scripts are. It's the perfect spot to place a system customization that must be applied before the Android system starts, such as the CPU governor setup.

To start working with the boot image, just copy the file into the `Kitchen` folder, fire up the menu, and start picking the options you want from the menu:

- Changing the ROM name can be the perfect first step
- Add root permissions
- `zipalign` the APK files for faster reading and loading
- `deodexk` the APK file for easy file manipulation, paying the price of slower loading

Once you are satisfied with the modifications, use the `kitchen` to generate an update file. This is a `.zip` file that can be flashed to the device using the custom recovery and represents your first custom ROM—congratulations!

Flashing our custom ROM

You have your `.zip` file and your customized system partition, and you are thrilled to have flashed them to your device.

To flash the system partition, we can use `fastboot`. First, you must unmount the partition itself using the following command:

```
~$ umount system_mount_point
```

Before we start experimenting with the system partition, it's always wise to do a system backup:

> *"Be prepared. You never know."*

Now, you can put the device in Fastboot mode, according to the specific sequence of your device. For our reference device, Google Nexus 6, the sequence is:

1. Power off
2. Press *Volume Up, Volume Down*, and *Power* at the same time
3. Release when the `Fastboot` menu appears

The device is now ready to receive the new system partition. Flash it with the following command:

```
~ $ fastboot flash system system.img
```

Your brand new system partition is in place! If your modifications were very extreme and adventurous, you could end up in a *bootloop* — the system keeps on rebooting and never ends the boot sequence. Stock system images distributed by manufacturers, or your own backups, come in very handy in this unfortunate scenario.

 If you are working with a Samsung device and you have a Windows system, you can check out Samsung Odin, a GUI tool to flash your ROMs and root your devices.

The final step is to flash the .zip file you generated with the kitchen. The file is generated according to a specific file structure and it's ready to be passed to your custom recovery. The recovery will treat it as a "system update" even if it's a completely brand new, customized system.

First of all, reboot your system in recovery mode. You can do it with a button sequence or using ADB, with the following command:

```
$: adb reboot recovery
```

Once the device is in recovery mode, navigate with the volume buttons and select **Apply update from ADB**. This will put the device in waiting mode. Go back to your terminal and navigate to the .zip file generated with the kitchen. Finally, load the file to the device:

```
$: adb sideload filename.zip
```

Congratulations! Your first custom ROM is *live* on your device. Now, go back to customize it even more!

Summary

This chapter taught us what a custom ROM is. We started from a description of the currently existing, most relevant projects, and we have proceeded deep into the details. We have also had a look at some very important components, such as *Android Recovery*, both the stock ones and those that have been modified. Finally, as we did in the previous chapters, we have adopted a practical approach, learning how to prepare a suitable environment for Android customization. We have also studied the different tools that are generally used to perform this task, and, in the end, we have applied the concepts we just learned through a simple example of creating a custom ROM. In the next chapter, we will be diving deeper into every single aspect of a ROM, using practical examples to show how to customize and increase the performance of your ROM.

7
Tailoring Your Personal Android System

In the previous chapter, you learned about the most popular custom Android ROMs. We started to dive deep and analyze those parts of the system involved in the modding process, to effectively understand where to customize and how to do it, mastering the Android modding toolset.

In this chapter, we will go even further, diving deeper into every single aspect of a ROM, using practical examples to show how to customize and increase the performance of your ROM.

The main topics of this chapter are:

- Hacking the Android framework
- Adding new Android applications to the build system
- Adding new Linux-native apps, using the Android source code, or editing an existing binary ROM image
- Optimizing the system to better support custom hardware, with focus on the application layer and on the kernel layer.

Receiving over the air updates – OTA

Every Android device is, by design, able to receive updates over time. These can be system updates—when a new Android version has been released, or security updates—when some critical vulnerability has been fixed and Google is distributing the patch. Once the update has been received, every device is able to decompress and apply this update, following the required procedure.

These types of updates are called OTA, or over the air updates, because they can be downloaded and applied by the Android device itself, without the support of a host PC. These updates are typically going to patch operating system features, working in the so-called *read-only* part of the system. No user app will ever be affected by these updates— apps installed via the Google Play Store are completely safe.

Android will asynchronously notify you when a new OTA is available. Most of the time you will receive a notification if connected to a Wi-Fi network and if your battery is above 50% to ensure a possible fast download and a safe updating process. When an update is available, a new system notification will appear in the Status Bar notification area. Once the notification is clicked, Android will show you details about the update, as shown in the following image:

OTA updates can be grouped into these three categories:

- Full system updates
- Incremental system updates
- Single update packages

Updating the whole system

As you can guess, this family of updates will bring up the whole system to a new version. They contain a whole system image, with system, boot, and recovery partitions.

To install these updates, the system needs to be able to properly boot the Recovery system and simply read and apply the update file.

Even if it is a full system update, the user partition is not affected and no app or user data is erased.

Updating the system incrementally

These updates are somewhat smaller than the full system ones and their goal is to apply patches to specific system components. Being tailored for a specific version of the operating system and a specific version of the file to be patched, these updates cannot be randomly applied to available devices.

To enforce this constraint, before installing such update files, the system checks for the correct file versions and any other possible requirement needed by the update. If some requirement is not satisfied, Android notifies the user with an error icon and the update procedure is aborted.

Applying a single component update

An OTA update package is a standard .zip file containing a META-INF/com/Google/Android/update-binary file. Once Android has verified the ZIP file signature, it decompresses the file in /tmp and executes it. A few arguments are passed to the command line. These are:

- Update-binary API version number
- The command line file descriptor, to communicate with the command line, to send progress updates to the UI
- The filename

In the same folder as `update-binary`, there is another interesting file—`updater-binary`. This file contains the sequence of actions to perform to install the update. All these actions are expressed in `Edify`, a custom **Domain Specific Language (DSL)** that Google created for this task. As is usual in the open source world, Google documented everything about this language and you can find the documentation in `/bootable/recovery/edify`.

The truth is that Recovery can execute every statically-linked binary named `update-library`. Leveraging this opportunity, lots of developers prefer to use different languages, which they are more familiar with, to perform all the operations needed to apply the update.

In the next pages we will see examples of both possible scenarios, using Google's Edify or a custom solution.

Creating over the air updates

Google provided plenty of developer tools to generate the different types of OTA. If you want to generate a *Full Update OTA*, the following two steps are required:

1. Generate a ZIP file containing the full update files
2. Generate the OTA package with all the necessary toolsets for the update

To generate the `zip` file containing the chosen target files, navigate to the `root` folder of the AOSP sources and run the following commands:

```
. build/envsetup.sh && lunch aosp-shamu
mkdir dist_output
make dist DIST_DIR=dist_output
```

If the process has been successful, we should have the `zip` file containing the target files in the directory `dist_output`. As an example, let's try listing the folder content with the following command:

```
ls -l dist_output/*target_files*
```

Now we should see a `.zip` file that will also have in its name the name of the target we are compiling for.

At this point, you only need to generate the OTA package containing all the necessary files for the update. Among the available tools, there's a utility that will help us do so, through the following command:

```
./build/tools/releasetools/ota_from_target_files \
    dist_output/aosp_shamu-target_files-eng.esteban.zip
ota_update.zip
```

As shown here, you'll find the screen with the generated OTA package and the command output:

```
x  -  □   esteban@axm0: ~/code/personal/WORKING_DIRECTORY
                            esteban@axm0: ~/code/personal/WORKING_DIRECTORY 110x12
unzipping target target-files...
(using device-specific extensions from target_files)
loaded device-specific extensions from /tmp/targetfiles-1c8BvE/META/releasetools.py
using prebuilt recovery.img from IMAGES...
using prebuilt boot.img from IMAGES...
putting script in bin/install-recovery.sh
no bootloader.img in target_files; skipping install
no radio.img in target_files; skipping install
done.
esteban@axm0:~/code/personal/WORKING_DIRECTORY$ ls -l ota_update.zip
-rw-rw-r-- 1 esteban esteban 206846478 Apr 17 19:09 ota_update.zip
esteban@axm0:~/code/personal/WORKING_DIRECTORY$ ▮
```

Now we have our OTA package ready to be installed on *development devices*, because the default OTA is signed with *test keys*. If you want to provide your users with an installable OTA package, you need to sign the OTA with your *own private keys*, using the specific option provided by the OTA-generation tool.

In order to generate an **incremental OTA**, the procedure is nearly the same, except that you also need to indicate the ZIP file containing the previous OTA version. The command will be something like the following:

```
./build/tools/releasetools/ota_from_target_files \
    -i PREVIOUS-aosp-shamu-target_files.zip \
    dist_output/aosp-shamu-target_files.zip
incremental_ota_update.zip
```

As for our previous example, you'll get a ZIP file containing the incremental backup.

Finally, there are no predefined tools for the composition of the Update OTA package, as it's up to us to decide what to install/update through the update script, which we will examine in detail later.

OTA internals

As anticipated in the previous section, an OTA package contains a binary file in its folder tree:

```
META-INF/com/google/android/update-binary
```

This binary file is generated by Android's build system, in the `bootable/recovery/updater` folder, and it is used to properly perform the update.

The binary contains internal routines and an interpreter for the scripting language called `Edify`. This language supports a set of ad hoc commands in order to allow the correct execution of a system update without affecting the integrity of the system itself. You can find an example of an Edify script in one of the OTA ZIP files you have just generated, at:

```
META-INF/com/google/android/updater-script
```

Shown here is an example screenshot for an Edify script:

Usually, we don't need to manually write any Edify code, because in a standard scenario there are automated tools that generate the correct OTA packages containing all the necessary files, but it could be useful to manually modify them when debugging, or in case we are building our custom ROM from binaries and we need to customize the installation on the flash memory of the relative files.

Let's have a look at the Edify syntax in the next section.

Edify syntax

The first thing to know is that Edify evaluates every expression as all string type values. An empty string is considered as `false` in a Boolean context, while any other value is considered as `true`. To recapitulate, Edify supports all the following expression types:

```
(expr )
expr + expr  # string concatenation, not integer addition
expr == expr
expr != expr
expr && expr
expr || expr
! expr
if expr then expr endif
if expr then expr else expr endif
function_name(expr, expr,...)
expr; expr
```

Every string that contains the following type of character, which of course are not reserved words, are considered as string literal:

```
a-z, A-Z, 0-9, _, :, /, .
```

With reserved words, we refer to words such as `if` `else`, and `endif`.

Constant strings can also be written using *double-quotes*, in order to create strings with spaces or other characters not listed in the previous example, such as the following:

```
\n, \t,
```

It can also be respectively written as follows for the new line and tab:

```
\", \\
```

As an escape character, we use " and \ in a string written with *double-quotes*.

The operators are simply short-circuiting, that is, the right side isn't even considered if the logic result is determined by the left side of the expression. The syntax can be very concise, as shown in the following snippet; the two lines are equivalent:

```
a1 && a2
if a1 then a2 endif
```

The `;` character is a sequence point, meaning that what's at its left is considered before, and what's at its right is considered after.

Let's see a richer example:

```
show_progress(0.750000, 0);
ui_print("Android Shamu");
mount("ext4", "EMMC", "/dev/block/…/system", "system");
unmount("/system");
```

The interpreter contains all the functions that are necessary to complete a correct update. Unless differently specified, the functions usually render `true` in case of success and `false` in case of error.

The language provides utility methods to control the flow and manage edge situations. If, for example, we want to trigger an error to block the installation, we can use the following functions:

```
abort();
assert();
```

As you can expect, in case you want to add a new feature, you can do that by modifying the sources, but before that, let's have a look at some of the most useful functions already available:

- `abort([msg])`: This method gives you the opportunity to abort the currently running script. It also takes a string argument, `msg`, that can be shown to the user as further information about the abort.

- `assert(expr[, expr, ...])`: This method takes a list of expressions as argument and evaluates them one by one. If any of these expressions fail, or returns `false`, the whole script execution stops. The system also shows an "Assert failed" message and the assert text that just failed.

- `apply_patch(src_file, tgt_file, tgt_sha1, tgt_size, patch1_sha1, patch1_blob, [...])`: This method takes a `patch1_blob` file and applies it as a binary patch to the source file `src_file` to produce the target `tgt_file`.

- `delete_recursive([dirname, ...])`: This function takes a list of folder names as argument and deletes them, also deleting every single file they contain.

- `file_getprop(filename, key)`: This method can be considered as a properties file inspector. It takes a couple of arguments, a filename and a key, and scans the file as if it were a property file, looking for the provided key. If the key is found, its value is returned.

- `format(fs_type, partition_type, location, fs_size, mount_point)`: This method provides a powerful way to format partitions.

- `ifelse(cond, e1[, e2])`: This method represents the common `it-then-else` computer science statement.

- `is_mounted(mount_point)`: This method helps to detect mounted partitions.

- `mount(fs_type, partition_type, name, mount_point)`: This method mounts a filesystem of `fs_type` at `mount_point`.

- `rename(src_filename, tgt_filename)`: This method takes two arguments, to perform a renaming from `src_filename` to `tgt_filename`.

- `run_program(path[, arg, ...])`: This method executes the binary at path, passing `args`, and it returns the program's exit status.

- `sleep(secs)`: This method takes an integer, `secs`, as an argument and pauses the execution for `secs` seconds.

- `symlink(target[, source, ...])`: This method takes a `target` file and a list of `sources` and creates all sources as *symlinks* to target.

- `unmount(mount_point)`: This is the counterpart of `mount`. This method unmounts the filesystem mounted at `mount_point`.

- This is just a subset of all the available commands. If you are curious about the whole list, you can check the official Google documentation at `http://source.android.com/devices/tech/ota/inside_packages.html`.

We are now able to modify — or create from scratch — an *Edify* script for an Update installation. This knowledge will turn out to be very useful with the custom ROM, especially when the sources are not available, in case you want to modify the system through a custom recovery, installing specific files in the read-only system partitions.

OTA for custom ROM

As already anticipated, out of the OTA concept we get a convenient system for the custom ROM installation. The reason for this is that most custom ROMs are distributed as *Update* ZIP packages, to be fed to the custom Recovery, which will then take care of the package installation in the system. Analyzing the OTA structure — as we did in the previous section — we can intuitively understand how to organize a specific package to install a modified version of Android. In fact, through an ad hoc Edify script, it is possible to format and reinstall all the files that are contained in any system partition, in order to distribute your own modified Android version.

This task is left as an exercise to the reader as it can be achieved with the knowledge acquired so far.

Advanced ROM customization

In the previous chapters, you have made your first steps within the custom ROMs world; we have discovered what's already available online and analyzed the most characteristic aspects in detail. In this chapter we will go in deep and learn how to modify the most internal parts of Android's framework.

Custom ROMs are often associated with those "*hackers*" who add the most unexpected features and then share everything online, but it doesn't always happen like that.

As explained in the previous chapters, many device manufacturers propose their own modified Android version, which is nothing but an Android custom ROM.

This is a very important aspect, as this book is addressed both to the previously mentioned *hackers* and to those who use all this knowledge in their daily work—a *hacker* will often work with binary ROM, and rarely with sources, while the professional will certainly have the sources at their disposal, as well as all the relevant tools to make the development of additional features possible.

In the following section, we will try to explain the two different approaches to customization in a simple way. These are: from the sources and from binary.

ROM customization from binary

To modify a ROM starting from binary, we regrettably have few available choices. As we don't have the sources to generate the different images, we can only modify the filesystem, adding utilities and new apps, or making aesthetic changes to colors and icons, starting from the framework binary.

We can use the tools we saw in the previous chapter and apply all the required changes, then, when we are done, we can generate a package `update.zip` with the correct Edify script, that allows the installation of new features.

Furthermore, we can also add new applications both in *Java* and *C*, or enhance the system image adding a `BASH` environment, or copy in the `/system` partition updated application like *Gmail* or *Maps*, that might eat space in the `/data` partition.

Even if the possibilities are limited in this kind of scenario, starting from a binary image, we can try some optimization and tweak, as we will see in the upcoming sections.

Customizing ROM from source

If you have the source code, you can do almost anything, but as you know,

"With great power comes great responsibility" – Uncle Ben, Spider-Man.

The first step is to identify the part we want to modify, and consequently, its repository. Let's take, for example Android's Settings menu, which we will keep as a master example to modify our ROM. The source code of Settings.apk is in the following path:

```
packages/apps/Settings
```

Once the source code path, and so, the repository, have been identified, the best way to start your customization is to mirror the repository on your server, where you will then operate the changes to the code.

In order to make sure your repository is part of the Android system, you need to update the manifest.xml, so that when you sync again with *"repo"*, you will clone your own Settings version, and not Android's.

After that, you need to create another personal repository, where you'll keep your manifest, modifying the following line:

```
<project path="packages/apps/Settings"
name="platform/packages/apps/Settings" groups="pdk-fs" />
```

Here you see where the code will be locally downloaded:

```
project path="packages/apps/Settings"
```

And here, its remote location:

```
name="platform/packages/apps/Settings"
```

You'll notice that there isn't a link in the remote position, because we'll use the default one, defined at the top as follows:

```
<remote name="aosp" fetch=".." />
<default revision="refs/tags/android-6.0.0_r6" remote="aosp"
sync-j="4" />
```

As you can see, fetch refers to the parent folder ".." instead of an absolute path. The best thing to do to simplify our work is to add a remote as follows:

```
<remote  name="my_repo-github"
fetch="git://github.com/my_personal_repo/" />
```

In this way, we have defined our remote, and we only have to fix the `Settings` line like this:

```
<project path="packages/apps/Settings" name="my_repo_Settings"
remote="my_repo-github" />
```

We now have all the necessary configuration in place to proceed with the development: we have our separate repository, where we can develop the code, but most importantly, thanks to the modification in the manifest, we don't have to touch the remaining managed parts of the system managed by Google, so that the update of other components of Google is made simple and smooth.

Adding new packages to Android's build system

The first step is to add a package to Android's build system, so that, when we perform our build, it will be automatically compiled and added to the ROM, just as it happens with other applications. We can work on two levels: adding a system app as a compiled binary app, written in *C*, or adding a system app as an *Application Layer* that runs on Android Dalvik Machine and ships as an APK.

In order to create an Android application, the first thing to do is to prepare the environment for writing the code and generate the APK file that will be executed by Android's internal virtual machine. We are going to develop a standard Android app using Java, Android Studio, and Android SDK.

Adding a package by binary

While developing a custom ROM, you might need to add binary executables or applications you don't have the source code for. For example, you might want to add a particular application as the default application for a specific task, so that when the user boots the ROM, the application is already installed into the system. We can refer to the `Facebook` application as an example of this.

To successfully add a new application to your system image, you just need to get the `APK` file and copy it in the right ROM directory. You can do that with an `update.zip file`, adding the right Edify script, which will install the new APK — as we'll see later in more detail — or, as already anticipated in the previous chapters, you can perform the entire operation through Android's build system.

The first step is to write the correct `Android.mk`; let's imagine we have our APK file at the following path:

`<aosp-root>/package/app/myapkfolder/`

Once your APK is in place, you need to create an `Android.mk` file and add the following snippet:

```
LOCAL_PATH := $(call my-dir)
include $(CLEAR_VARS)
LOCAL_MODULE_TAGS := optional
LOCAL_MODULE := < your app folder name >
LOCAL_SRC_FILES := < app apk filename >
LOCAL_MODULE_CLASS := APPS
LOCAL_MODULE_SUFFIX := $(COMMON_ANDROID_PACKAGE_SUFFIX)
include $(BUILD_PREBUILT)
```

Analyzing the snippet, you will notice a couple of placeholders you will need to replace with your actual values. After that you'll need to create a new entry in the `commons.mk` file, situated in:

```
build/target/product
```

Add the new APK installation-related line, as follows:

```
PRODUCT_PACKAGES += < what you have defined in LOCAL_MODULE >
```

At this point, you only have to recompile the AOSP to find the new APK in the system, preinstalled among the other system apps.

Another very common and handy way to add a precompiled app to our ROM is doing it with the help of the Android update system. Provided that you have already installed a custom recovery image—which will make all your operations easier—to add a new binary to Android's `/system/xbin` directory, you only need to create an `update.zip` with an Edify script inside to perform the right operations.

Here you'll see an Edify script that performs a precompiled app installation in the target folder `/system/xbin`. The script is contained in:

```
META-INF/com/google/android/
```

The script contains the following code:

```
ui_print("Edify Script for binary installation");
ui_print("Flashing a binary");
show_progress(0.700000, 0);
ui_print("mounting /system");
mount("ext4", "EMMC", "/dev/block/system", "/system");
ui_print("");
ui_print("Installing binary");
package_extract_dir("system", "/system");
ui_print("unmounting system");
```

```
unmount("/system");
ui_print("unmounted system");
ui_print("Operations completed!");
```

The internal structure of the `update.zip` file will look like this:

```
update.zip
---> META-INF/com/google/android/update-script
---> META-INF/com/google/android/updater-script
---> system/xbin/mybinary
```

Once the update package has been created, you only need to apply it through the recovery custom that is installed on your device. As you have surely noted, the same approach, *"edify script + update.zip + recovery"*, is used over and over, and this shows how Android's update system is solid and flexible and comes in handy for a huge number of tasks and scenarios; but we can go even further.

There's yet another procedure, that we might define as *"dirty"*, which allows even more complex installations. You would still use the procedure of the update package, but instead of using the Edify syntax, which might often be inconvenient and not so powerful for advanced scenarios, you will redefine the content of the `update-script` binary.

As you know, this binary, that by default contains the interpreter to execute the Edify script, is launched by the system. This *"dirty"* technique consists of replacing this binary with a shell script that performs the operations you need. With this alternative approach, you have the very powerful shell scripting language at your disposal, and let's consider that some recovery custom includes the Bash—as shell—which will hence work as the interpreter.

The following is an example of the `busybox` installation in the Android system, using an ad hoc `update.zip`, with a shell script that operates the installation:

```
#!/sbin/sh

FD=$2

ui_print() {
  echo -n -e "ui_print $1\n" > /proc/self/fd/$FD
  echo -n -e "ui_print\n" > /proc/self/fd/$FD
}

set_perm() {
  chown $1:$2 $4
```

```
   chmod $3 $4
}

ui_print "- Mounting /system"
mount /system

ui_print "- Installing BusyBox"
unzip -o "$3" busybox -d /system/xbin

ui_print "- Setting right permissions -"
set_perm 0 2000 0755 /system/xbin/busybox

ui_print "- Symlinking BB applets"
for i in $(/system/xbin/busybox --list); do
  busybox ln -sf busybox "/system/xbin/$i"
done

ui_print "- Unmounting /system"
umount /system

ui_print "- BusyBox Installation complete -"
```

This script will replace our `update-script` and will operate the binary installation. As a result, the update package will have the following structure:

```
update.zip
---> META-INF/com/google/android/update-script
---> busybox
```

Thus, we can perform the most complex installations, and it turns out to be one of the most used methods by the Android ROM "modders".

Adding packages by source code

In *Chapter 3, Setup and Build – the Emulator Way*, we broadly explained how to add new packages to the build system from source. In this section, we will make a real example by creating a `Hello World` application, with the help of Android Studio, which we will import and compile together with the entire Android system.

First, we need to create a base application with Android Studio.

For the installation instructions, please read the following link: `http://developer.android.com/sdk/index.html`.

When your system is ready, launch the IDE and create a new project:

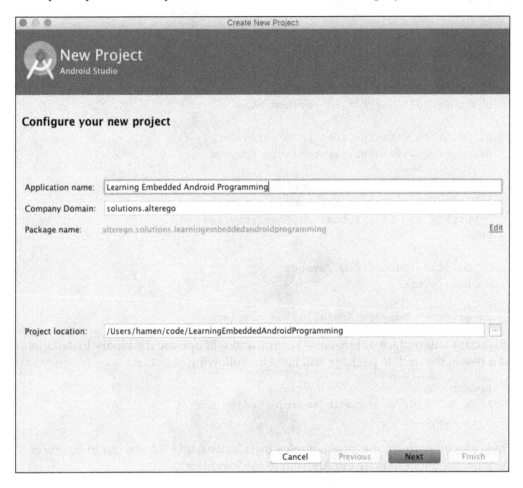

The previous image shows how to specify an app name, a domain, and a path folder for our Android project. Once you have entered all the data, you can click **Next** and move to the API level selection, as shown here:

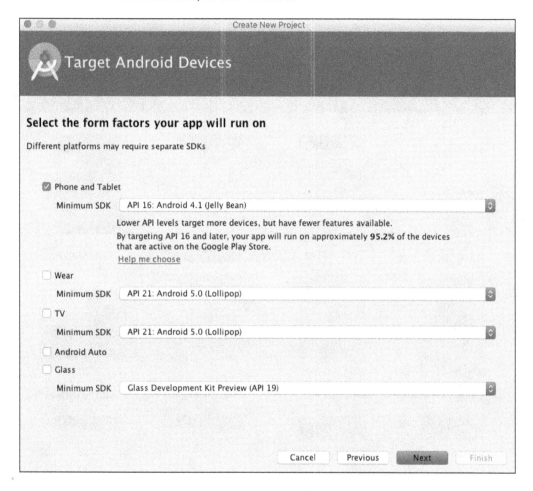

As shown in the previous image, by default Android Studio will target API 16 to cover more than 95% of the market. This value doesn't really matter in our scenario, because this app will be installed only in our custom ROM, that is probably Android 6. Let's move to the next screen—Activity Picker:

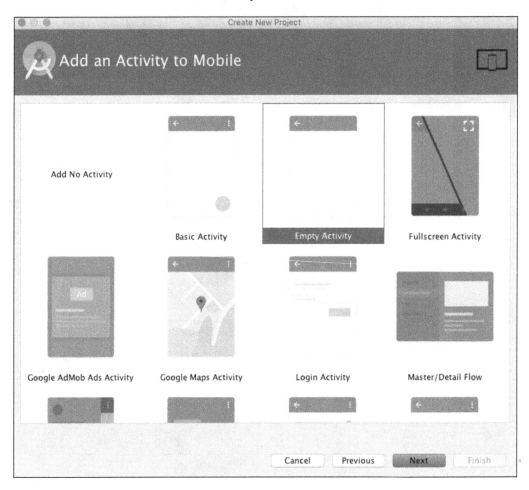

The previous image shows the plethora of possible activities we can easily add to our apps. For this example, we will use just an **Empty Activity**, to keep things simple:

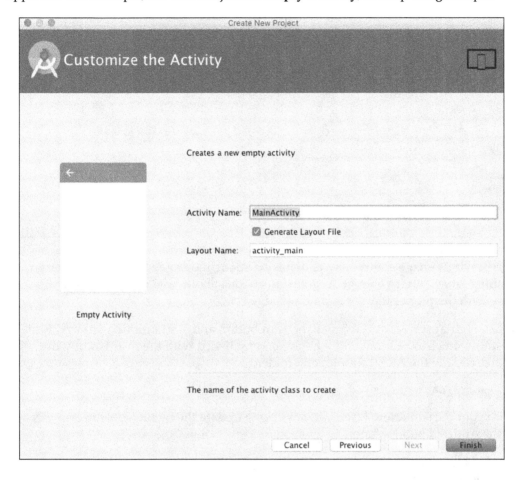

The previous image shows how to rename our brand new activity—`MainActivity` will do the job flawlessly. Just click **Finish** and Android Studio will bring you to the editor screen to add some code to your `Hello, World` app:

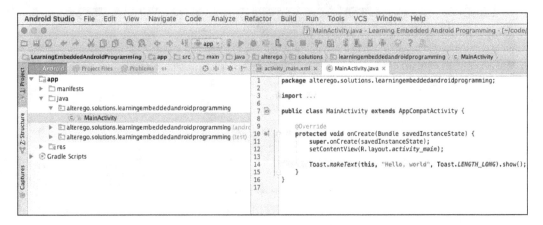

The previous image shows how to display a `Toast` message when our app starts; nothing fancy, but it's enough to give you an idea about how things can be made easy with the proper tool set and knowledge.

When your app is ready, just click the **Run** button and start building your APK file. Test it as much as you can and when you are satisfied with the results, copy the source code to the AOSP source code folder:

```
<aosp>/package/apps/Myapp
```

With your current know-how, you are able to update the manifest file to add this app to the Android build system.

The final touch is the `Android.mk` file. For this `Hello,World` example, just create a new file as follows:

```
<aosp>/package/apps/Myapp/Android.mk
```

Add the following snippet:

```
LOCAL_PATH := $(call my-dir)
include $(CLEAR_VARS)

# Build all java files in the java subdirectory
LOCAL_SRC_FILES := $(call all-subdir-java-files)
```

```
# Name of the APK to build
LOCAL_PACKAGE_NAME := LocalPackage

# Tell it to build an APK
include $(BUILD_PACKAGE)
```

Using Android's build system, you are now able to build and package your own Android apps for your custom ROM.

Hacking the Android framework

In *Chapter 6, "Cooking" Your First ROM*, we had a look at a few heavily-customized versions of Android, and lots of these customizations were related to the User Interface. UI customization is a tricky topic due to the *personal taste* factor involved: many users love a *"pure Android"* UI, many other users love the idea of a *"different Android"* UI, far from the mainstream UI experience.

In this section, we are giving you free will and the chance to choose between a vanilla Android and a customized one. You will learn how to make small customizations, to the status bar or to the colors, for example, or big customizations, like adding a new item to the **Settings** menu to properly set up the custom features of your custom ROM.

Customizing the boot sequence UI

The graphical appearance of the ¾|+ boot sequence is definitely one of the most popular customizations you'd like to do and often the one that your users will ask for and will love.

During the boot sequence, a standard Android device will show:

- The Splash image
- The Boot animation

The Splash image is a static image that the system shows in the first seconds after Power On. On a Google Nexus device, the Splash image looks like the following image:

The image shows the Google brand and a lock. As we already learned, the lock represents the status of the *bootloader*—locked or unlocked. The Splash image is associated to the initial phases of the boot—typically, the system shows the Splash image from the Power On to the completion of the bootloader and Linux kernel setup sequence.

Customizing the ¾¦+ Splash image is no easy thing, because even if theoretically it's just an image, or a sequence of images, stored on the NAND memory, every manufacturer uses a custom approach to accomplish this goal and they are very unwilling to document how we could revert their work. What is extremely easy for them, having plenty of tools and knowledge about their system, becomes hours and hours of reverse engineering for us, with unpredictable results and effects on the stability of the whole system.

Turning our attention to the boot animation, we can see that the boot animation is that sequence of images, most of the time animated, that any Android device shows during the startup sequence, right after the Splash image and until the Android system completes boot. Many manufacturers customize this animation to enforce their brand, and you will do the same with your *own brand*. From a technical point of view, the moment you see the boot animation, the kernel has been loaded, the partitions have been mounted, and Android is starting to boot.

This sequence of images is way easier to customize compared to the Splash image. This is due to the fact that, even if the majority of the device has a custom boot animation, every single one of them respect very strict known requirements – that means that we have documentation for this!

As with lots of Android components, the boot animation comes as a standard `.zip` file and is placed in the `/system/media/` folder or in the `/data/local/`. All we need to customize the boot animation is to grab it, edit it as we like, and place it back – piece of cake!

To retrieve the file, we can use our trusted `adb`. Fire up your terminal and run the following command:

```
adb pull /system/media/bootanimation.zip .
```

Of course, if the file is not there, try the second possible location, as we said previously. Once you have the file on your host computer, you can decompress it and you will see the same folder structure as shown in the following image:

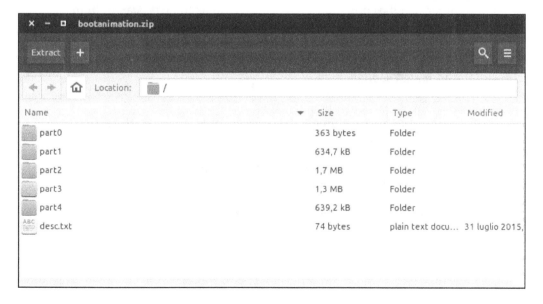

All those part* folders contain the images that create the animation, and the desc. txt file contains the instructions to properly perform the animation.

Open the desc.txt file with your preferred text editor and you will see something like the following image:

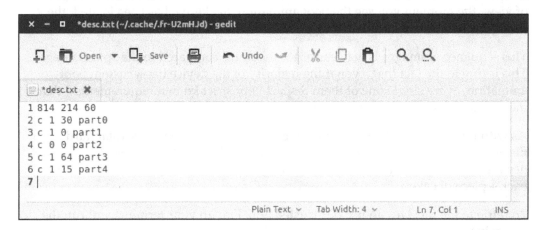

The first row specifies the resolution and the frame rate at which the animation will be displayed. Lines 2 to 6 specify how to show the different parts of the animation.

The first letter, "c", stands for "continue", and instructs the system to keep playing the sequence even if the boot sequence is completed.

The first number specifies how many times the part has to be repeated. In the example, just once, or infinite time (using 0 as the value to indicate an infinite loop). The second number specifies how many seconds will be waited before starting the next part. The last token of the row specifies the folder containing the images to show to create the animated sequence.

Now that you know about the inner structure of the bootanimation.zip file and how to set up the sequence, it's time to be creative and replace all those boring images to create your own awesome animation!

Once you are satisfied, it's time to create a new bootanimation.zip file. Fire up your terminal and run the following command:

```
zip -r -0 bootanimation.zip part0 part1 partX desc.txt
```

Carefully, replace `partx` with the correct sequence of folders you have in your animated sequence. To try out your brand new boot animation, just upload the `zip` file to `/data/local/` folder using `adb`. You could even create a custom `update.zip` and flash it to your device using Recovery. It's up to you.

> FFMPEG is a handy tool to extract images from a video to create your animated sequence. Fire up a terminal and run the following:
>
> ```
> ffmpeg -i "path_file" -r 1 -s 1024x768 -f image2
> "path_images-=.jpg"
> ```
>
> The previous command specifies a few interesting parameters: `-r 1` to capture a frame every second, `-s` to specify a resolution for the final images, and `-f image2` to actually capture a frame and save it as an image. As always, you can refer to `-h` for further documentation.

Customizing the Android Settings menu

One great feature of Android is modularity: most of the system features are actually Android apps, developed and maintained separately. The Android `Settings` menu, for instance, is just an Android app itself, called `Settings.apk`, and, being part of the AOSP, can be freely customized, according to our needs. In the next pages, you will learn how to work on `Settings.apk` to add your custom menu item.

Open your terminal emulator, and from your `WORKING_DIRECTORY` containing Android source code, navigate to:

```
WORKING_DIRECTORY/packages/apps/Settings
```

This folder contains the source code of the vanilla `Settings` menu; this is your starting point for the customization.

This is a crucial example, because, when you are working on a custom ROM, you are improving the system, adding new features, or enhancing existing ones. Your new features will probably need some level of setup and placing all the possible configuration options where the user expects them, that is, the `Settings` menu, which is a fundamental point for a great user experience.

The following image shows the vanilla Android `Settings` menu, the object of our customization:

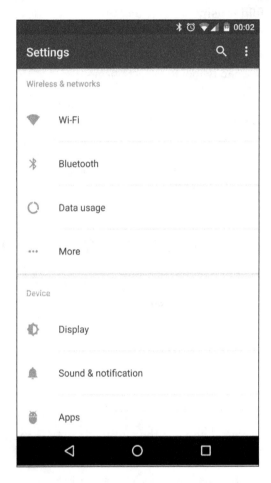

Once you are in the `Settings` menu app folder, `packages/apps/Settings`, you can start editing files to add your new menu item. Let's start with adding a few strings. With your preferred editor — Android Studio, Atom, SublimeText, and so on — edit `res/values/strings.xml` and add the following lines:

```
<!-- Settings main menu category heading. Embedded Android Settings. [CHAR LIMIT=40] -->
<string name="header_category_custom">Embedded Android Settings </string>
<string name="custom_settings_title">Embedded Android</string>
<string name="custom_settings">My Settings</string>
<string name="custom_settings_display">subTitle</string>
```

The `strings.xml` file contains the list of every text string used in the `Settings` app; it's the perfect starting point for your customization and gives you an idea about naming conventions and structure.

Once you are satisfied with the string file, create a new `.java` file named `CustomSettings.java` and place it in the `src/com/android/settings` folder. This will contain all the logic we need. The following image shows a snippet of a custom `PreferenceFragment` you can create:

```java
package com.embedded.android;

import android.os.Bundle;
import android.preference.Preference;
import android.preference.PreferenceFragment;
import android.widget.Toast;

import com.android.settings.R;

public class CustomSettings extends PreferenceFragment {
    private String mDisplayTypeKey;

    @Override
    public void onCreate(Bundle savedInstanceState) {
        super.onCreate(savedInstanceState);

        Toast.makeText(getActivity(), "My settings", Toast.LENGTH_LONG).show();
    }
}
```

This `Fragment` will load a specific layout file that you need to create. Let's call it `custom_settings.xml` and populate it as shown in the next image:

```xml
<PreferenceScreen xmlns:android="http://schemas.android.com/apk/res/android"
    android:key="custom_settings_general"
    android:title="@string/custom_settings_title">

</PreferenceScreen>
```

Now you need to add a few lines to the `AndroidManifest.xml`. Navigate to the `root` folder and edit the `AndroidManifest.xml` file as follows:

```xml
<activity android:name="Settings$CustomSettingsActivity"
    android:configChanges="orientation|keyboardHidden|screenSize"
    android:label="@string/custom_settings"
    android:taskAffinity="">
    <intent-filter>
        <action android:name="android.intent.action.MAIN" />
        <category android:name="android.intent.category.DEFAULT" />
        <category android:name="com.android.settings.SHORTCUT" />
    </intent-filter>
    <meta-data android:name="com.android.settings.FRAGMENT_CLASS"
        android:value="com.embedded.android.CustomSettings" />
    <meta-data android:name="com.android.settings.TOP_LEVEL_HEADER_ID" />
</activity>
```

Navigate to the main `src/` folder and open `Settings.java`. This file contains every `Activity` available in the `Settings` menu. Here you can add your own `Activity`, as shown in the next image:

```java
package com.android.settings;

import com.android.settings.applications.AppOpsSummary;

/**
 * Top-level Settings activity
 */
public class Settings extends SettingsActivity {

    /*
     * Settings subclasses for launching independently.
     */
    public static class CustomSettingsActivity extends SettingsActivity { /* empty */ }
    public static class BluetoothSettingsActivity extends SettingsActivity { /* empty */ }
    public static class WirelessSettingsActivity extends SettingsActivity { /* empty */ }
    public static class SimSettingsActivity extends SettingsActivity { /* empty */ }
    public static class TetherSettingsActivity extends SettingsActivity { /* empty */ }
    public static class VpnSettingsActivity extends SettingsActivity { /* empty */ }
    public static class DateTimeSettingsActivity extends SettingsActivity { /* empty */ }
    public static class StorageSettingsActivity extends SettingsActivity { /* empty */ }
    public static class WifiSettingsActivity extends SettingsActivity { /* empty */ }
    public static class WifiP2pSettingsActivity extends SettingsActivity { /* empty */ }
    public static class InputMethodAndLanguageSettingsActivity extends SettingsActivity { /* empty */ }
    public static class KeyboardLayoutPickerActivity extends SettingsActivity { /* empty */ }
    public static class InputMethodAndSubtypeEnablerActivity extends SettingsActivity { /* empty */ }
    public static class VoiceInputSettingsActivity extends SettingsActivity { /* empty */ }
    public static class SpellCheckersSettingsActivity extends SettingsActivity { /* empty */ }
    public static class LocalePickerActivity extends SettingsActivity { /* empty */ }
    public static class UserDictionarySettingsActivity extends SettingsActivity { /* empty */ }
    public static class HomeSettingsActivity extends SettingsActivity { /* empty */ }
    public static class DisplaySettingsActivity extends SettingsActivity { /* empty */ }
    public static class DeviceInfoSettingsActivity extends SettingsActivity { /* empty */ }
    public static class ApplicationSettingsActivity extends SettingsActivity { /* empty */ }
    public static class ManageApplicationsActivity extends SettingsActivity { /* empty */ }
    public static class AppOpsSummaryActivity extends SettingsActivity {
        @Override
        public boolean isValidFragment(String className) {
            if (AppOpsSummary.class.getName().equals(className)) {
                return true;
            }
            return super.isValidFragment(className);
        }
    }
}
```

The `src/` contains a `SettingsActivity.java` file. At the beginning of this you will find a field, `String` array, named `ENTRY_FRAGMENTS`. These are all the `Fragments` that can be loaded by the `Activity` files in the `Settings` menu. The list is quite impressive, and on Android Marshmallow, it contains about 70 `Fragments`; in your Android version, it will contain one more entry: yours. Add your `CustomSettings` class to the array, as shown in the following screenshot:

```
private static final String[] ENTRY_FRAGMENTS = {
        WirelessSettings.class.getName(),
        WifiSettings.class.getName(),

        .
        .
        .
        ApnSettings.class.getName(),
        CustomSettings.class.getName()
};
```

We are almost there. The next thing we need to do is compile the new package with the following command:

```
:$ mm
```

Once we have created the new package, we can create a new update file and flash it using Recovery. On the next boot, we will see our brand new menu item in the **Settings** screen, as shown in the next screenshot:

Enhancing the system performance

Lots of the custom ROMs that you can find on the Net bring performance enhancements, extended battery life, and lots of small tweaks. Most of these enhancements can be achieved with a surgical tuning of the `build.prop` file.

Customizing the system property file

The Android `build.prop` file contains details about a variety of system settings that are applied to the system during the boot sequence. Before diving into its customization, we need an overview about its internal structure.

Open a terminal and connect to your device using the following command:

```
:$ adb shell
```

Navigate to the `/system` folder and open the `build.prop` file. The content will look like the following snippet:

```
ro.product.model=Nexus 6
ro.product.brand=google
ro.product.name=shamu
ro.product.device=shamu
ro.product.board=shamu
[...]
```

As you can guess, parts of these instructions are specific for every device, but a few of them are quite common. We surely have device model name, brand, codename for product, device and board, and so on.

Some of these common values can be easily edited to obtain interesting behavioral changes in our system. For instance, you have probably noticed the tiny, but perceivable, delay that happens right before the smartphone starts ringing, when you receive a phone call. That delay can be removed by editing just a few lines in the `build.prop` file. Scan the file and look for these two lines:

```
ro.telephony.call_ring.delay=0
ring.delay=0
```

Simply replace whatever value is assigned to them with a nice 0 (zero) and you can say goodbye to the delay.

Ever wondered why you cannot rotate the screen when the phone is displaying the lock screen or the application launcher? No more wondering. Look for these two lines and replace the existing properties with the new one:

```
log.tag.launcher_force_rotate=VERBOSE
lockscreen.rot_override=true
```

Do you want to rotate your device more than 180 degrees? Enable a 270 degree rotation with the following line:

```
windowsmgr.support_rotation_270=true
```

Another UI trick we can achieve with a single line edit is changing the LCD density value. Search for the following line:

```
ro.sf.lcd_density=XXX
```

Replace XXX with the value you want to try. Changing this value will produce a resizing of the system icons and an increase of the screen space: the smaller the value you set, the bigger the amount of free space you get. Unfortunately, there is no exact science here and a little *trial-and-error* is inevitable, so try to experiment with a few values until you find your preferred setup.

Android devices are getting more powerful every day, but, back in the day, the available CPU power was very limited. To guarantee satisfactory performance and user experience, Android used smart tweaks, like the next one:

```
ro.media.enc.jpeg.quality=xxx
```

The previous value alters the rendering quality of JPEG files. Even if it was useful in the past, we can consider it unnecessary on last generation smartphones, and we can safely set it to 100 and enjoy images at 100% of their original quality.

If your smartphone has physical navigation buttons, you can increase screen estate, removing the navigation softkeys at the bottom of the screen by setting the next property as follows:

```
qemu.hw.mainkeys=1
```

If your device has no physical key, you can still remove the softkeys and use gesture to navigate; check out the Google Play Store for gesture apps, like *All in one Gestures*. Continuing on the "screen estate" topic, you can remove the debug mode icon in the system notification bar with the following property:

```
persist.adb.notify=0
```

These last two tweaks refer to networking settings. The first one is as follows:

```
wifi.supplicant_scan_interval=300
```

This line configures how many seconds will be between every automatic Wi-Fi scan. Android performs automatic Wi-Fi scans by default, looking for an open network to connect or just to increase the precision of the navigation system. You can increase or decrease the frequency of these scans, trying to achieve the perfect balance between a higher precision of navigation and a longer battery life. The second networking tweak gives you the opportunity to set a default DNS server:

```
net.dns1=8.8.8.8
net.dns2=8.8.4.4
```

This is extremely useful in countries in which the government filters Internet websites according to their IP addresses. Using the DNS IPs shown in the previous snippet, Google's DNS servers, you will be able to bypass this kind of censorship.

Adding a custom init sequence

Linux legacy is still strong in a few key aspects of the Android architecture. One of the most interesting ones is the possibility to execute custom scripts during initialization time. If you are familiar with Linux systems, you know about the `/etc/init.d` folder. This system folder contains a collection of scripts that can be executed during system startup. To achieve the same behavior on Android, we can use `busybox` and its `run-parts` utility. This utility takes a folder as an argument and executes every script contained in this folder. For instance, the following command will execute every script contained in the `/system/etc/init.d folder`:

```
run-parts /system/etc/init.d
```

To properly copy Linux `init.d` behavior, we want to be able to execute the scripts in a rigorous order. You can achieve this with clever file naming. Just rename your scripts and prepend a number, like in the following example:

```
01settings
02optimizations
```

In the previous example, the `01settings` script will be executed before the `02optinimations` script, and so on. Now that you have a collection of ordered scripts and you know how to execute them one by one, you need to edit the `install-recovery.sh` file we saw in the previous chapters and add the following line:

```
run-parts /system/etc/init.d
```

Advanced Linux kernel modding

When you think about customizing the core of an Android system, you immediately think about customizing the Linux kernel. It manages CPU, sensors, radio, and display, and it's the starting point of every great system customization. As we already saw, modifying the kernel is no easy job, but with the right mindset, knowledge, and toolset, it can be a satisfying experience.

Every embedded system has its own customization possibilities and, when it comes to Android, most of the effort is focused on customizing the following:

- Governors
- I/O schedulers
- CPU overclocking/underclocking

Diving into CPU frequency management

In *Chapter 5*, *Customizing Kernel and Boot Sequence*, we had an overview about governors, how they work, and how you can pick a different one for different scenarios. In this section, you will learn how to customize existing governors and how to add new ones to your systems.

 A *governor*, or CPU frequency manager, describes how the CPU behaves, based on specific environmental factors.

A typical general purpose governor would decrease the number of active cores and their working frequency when the system load is low and push the CPU to full power and full speed when the system is in need of high performance.

A standard Linux kernel provides the following governors:

- **On-demand**: This is the default governor on most of the kernels on the market. It's considered a *balanced* governor because it can guarantee the system to be reactive, quickly increasing the CPU frequency when needed. The truth is that, being so eager to increase the CPU frequency, this governor makes no real evaluation about the CPU power that is actually needed. The on-demand governor does not consider the actual system load; instead it just increases the CPU frequency to the max when it is triggered and then slowly decreases it if not needed. As you can see, this does not work well in a "battery saving" scenario: it is pushing to top speed every time the system thinks it is going to need more power, without a deeper analysis. This approach will surely guarantee a reactive device, but will definitely drain the battery very quickly.

- **Powersave**: This is definitely the most effective way to save battery life, in a way. This governor sets the maximum CPU frequency to the lowest possible value. The battery will surely last *"an eternity"*, but the device will be unusable: a 2 GHz Quad-core CPU can easily go down to 200 MHz, and if it stays there all the time, that's just nonsense.

- **Performance**: This governor behaves as the exact opposite of the *Powersave* one: it sets the minimum CPU frequency to the maximum possible value to achieve maximum performance. Battery-wise, this will drain the battery in no time: a 2 GHz Quad-core running all the time at full power is surely performing well, but the smartphone won't last long.

- **Interactive**: This is a smarter version of the *On-demand* governor. Its goal is to provide a reactive CPU scaling without falling into on-demand pitfalls. The On-demand governor changes the CPU frequency according to preset values, without any specific analysis. The interactive governor, instead, continuously evaluates the system load and adjusts the CPU frequency accordingly, with a more linear CPU scaling curve: definitely a big pro. The whole CPU scaling analysis is not based on raw workload, but is performed according to the requested time. This approach guarantees system fluidity and better performance in a multimedia scenario, because the CPU won't jump up and down in frequency, but will be steady during the whole necessary time, providing a constant framerate when required.

- **Conservative**: This governor is a smoother version of the On-demand governor. Unlike On-demand, the Conservative governor won't push the CPU to the top frequency every single time, but will proceed through a series of CPU frequency steps, according to the CPU load.

- **Userspace**: This is the most customizable and least "automatic" governor. It provides the user with the possibility to manually pick the desired frequency.

Adding a custom CPU frequency governor

If you need a specific CPU behavior, or you simply want to dig deeper into kernel customization, you can create your own CPU governor.

For this task, you will need the kernel source code and to navigate to:

```
<root-source>/drivers/cpufreq
```

This folder contains every governor we saw in the previous section and every possible custom governor you are going to add or that your device manufacturer already added.

Let's create a new governor, creating a .c file in this folder, for example:

```
<root-source>/drivers/cpufreq/cpufreq_mygovernor.c
```

Once you have the file in place, you need to add it to the file mentioned here:

```
<root-source>/drivers/cpufreq/Kconfig
```

We make changes as shown in the following snippet:

```
config CPU_FREQ_GOV_MYGOVERNOR
  tristate "'mygovernor' cpufreq governor"
  depends on CPU_FREQ
  help
  'mygovernor' - my optimized governor!

config CPU_FREQ_DEFAULT_GOV_ MYGOVERNOR
  bool "mygovernor"
  select CPU_FREQ_GOV_MYGOVERNOR
  help
  Use the CPUFreq governor 'mygovernor' as default.
```

Once you are done with the Kconfig, edit the Makefile and add the following line:

```
obj-$(CONFIG_CPU_FREQ_GOV_ MYGOVERNOR) += cpufreq_mygovernor.o
```

As a last step, edit the following file:

```
<root-source>/include/linux/cpufreq.h
```

Around line 400, there is a list of currently available governors, as shown in the following image:

```
x  -  □   esteban@dronix:~/code/embedded_android/msm
                        esteban@dronix: ~/code/embedded_android/msm 108x31
394
395 /* CPUFREQ DEFAULT GOVERNOR */
396 /*
397  * Performance governor is fallback governor if any other gov failed to auto
398  * load due latency restrictions
399  */
400 #ifdef CONFIG_CPU_FREQ_GOV_PERFORMANCE
401 extern struct cpufreq_governor cpufreq_gov_performance;
402 #endif
403 #ifdef CONFIG_CPU_FREQ_DEFAULT_GOV_PERFORMANCE
404 #define CPUFREQ_DEFAULT_GOVERNOR (&cpufreq_gov_performance)
405 #elif defined(CONFIG_CPU_FREQ_DEFAULT_GOV_POWERSAVE)
406 extern struct cpufreq_governor cpufreq_gov_powersave;
407 #define CPUFREQ_DEFAULT_GOVERNOR (&cpufreq_gov_powersave)
408 #elif defined(CONFIG_CPU_FREQ_DEFAULT_GOV_USERSPACE)
409 extern struct cpufreq_governor cpufreq_gov_userspace;
410 #define CPUFREQ_DEFAULT_GOVERNOR (&cpufreq_gov_userspace)
411 #elif defined(CONFIG_CPU_FREQ_DEFAULT_GOV_ONDEMAND)
412 extern struct cpufreq_governor cpufreq_gov_ondemand;
413 #define CPUFREQ_DEFAULT_GOVERNOR (&cpufreq_gov_ondemand)
414 #elif defined(CONFIG_CPU_FREQ_DEFAULT_GOV_CONSERVATIVE)
415 extern struct cpufreq_governor cpufreq_gov_conservative;
416 #define CPUFREQ_DEFAULT_GOVERNOR (&cpufreq_gov_conservative)
417 #elif defined(CONFIG_CPU_FREQ_DEFAULT_GOV_INTERACTIVE)
418 extern struct cpufreq_governor cpufreq_gov_interactive;
419 #define CPUFREQ_DEFAULT_GOVERNOR (&cpufreq_gov_interactive)
420 #endif
421
422
include/linux/cpufreq.h                                          422,1        88%
```

Following the same pattern, let's add your new governor reference, using the following snippet:

```
#elif defined(CONFIG_CPU_FREQ_DEFAULT_GOV_MYGOVERNOR)
extern struct cpufreq_governor cpufreq_gov_mygovernor;
#define CPUFREQ_DEFAULT_GOVERNOR (&amp;cpufreq_gov_mygovernor)
```

Mission completed: your new governor is now available and ready to be integrated in your next kernel build. Try to run `menuconfig` and navigate to the governor screen; you will be able to enable it and set it as the default governor.

Exploring I/O schedulers

I/O schedulers specify how I/O-bound operations must be performed and balanced among CPU cores. Android comes with a default set of I/O schedulers:

- **Noop**: This can be barely considered a scheduler. Practically speaking, it has no effect on the tasks list: it just queues them as they come in.

- **SIO**: This is the first real scheduler. Even if it does no task reordering, it guarantees the smallest possible latency from the moment the task is enqueued and the moment it is performed.

- **CFQ**: This scheduler orders tasks in separated queues, according to specific categories, and assigns an execution time window to every queue. The window size depends on the priority assigned to the tasks involved.

- **BFQ**: This scheduler is similar to the CFQ scheduler, but it uses disk bandwidth windows instead of time windows to group and schedule tasks.

- **Anticipatory**: This scheduler uses prediction techniques to group and schedule tasks, pausing executions for a short time period and waiting for a possible new task to be added to a specific queue.

- **ROW**: This scheduler is based on the *"read over write"* rule: every reading task has priority over writing tasks.

- **Deadline**: This scheduler guarantees termination for the enqueued tasks, trying to avoid "starvation" scenarios. *Starvation* is a well-known concept in computer science and applies to resource management. Imagine that N processes want to use the same shared resource. The shared resource can be used by one process at a time, and processes alternate according to their priority. What is going to happen if a low-priority process is asking for the resource, but the resource never becomes available due to other high-priority processes using it? The low-priority process will wait forever for the resource and never get to enjoy it. In computer science terminology, it will *starve*.

Every available scheduler is stored in the following folder:

```
<root-source>/block
```

Creating an I/O scheduler can be challenging and it's beyond the purpose of this book. What we can do is point you in the right direction and get you curious about the topic.

Looking forward

During the writing of this book, we were lucky enough to have a look at the upcoming Android N. The new version will probably be available at the end of 2016 as a stable release, after a few months of public *developer preview*.

Android N introduces a few interesting features, like the *"Multi-Window"* mode shown in the next image:

At Google, they are very focused on user feedback, and they decided to introduce this feature into the official version after a few months of testing by Samsung. Most of us will recognize the Multi-Windows mode from the already-available Android ROM, by Samsung. In Android N, this will be available for everybody, on every Android device, with full support for both orientations, portrait and landscape, and even the possibility to *resize* the split windows by dragging the "separator line".

According to lots of blog posts, one of the most popular categories for Google Play Store apps is Caller ID filters. With Android N, this feature will be already available as a system feature as for the new "mobile data saving" feature that aims to reduce background data consumption for specific apps.

One of the new UI enhancements that comes with Android N is the possibility to add and remove action icons in the scroll down `quick settings` menu, as shown in the next image:

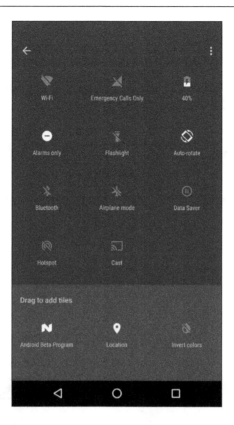

Furthermore, the scroll down `notification` menu comes with a new notification design, that enables richer interactions, with quicker access to common actions, as shown in the next image:

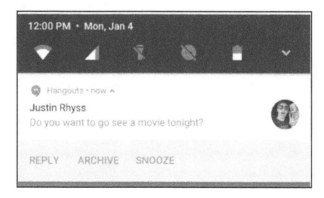

The **Settings** section received a bit of love as well, with the new in-place notifications, like the one shown in the next image, that gives you the opportunity to disable or enable settings without navigating to the specific location:

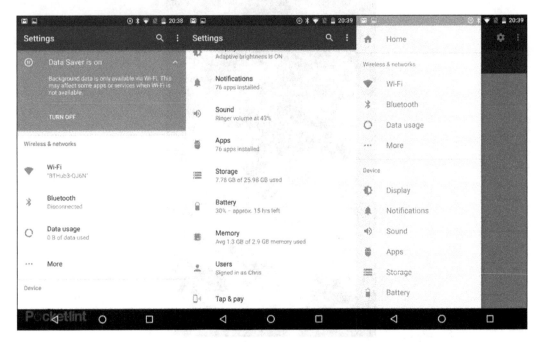

The next image shows, also, the new `Navigation Drawer` that has been added to the `Setting` section, for a quicker navigation to the deeper menu levels:

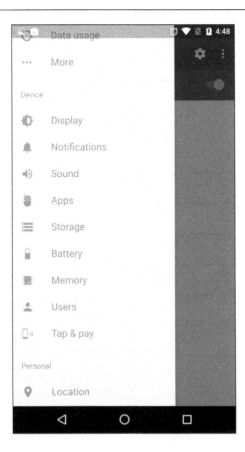

An incredible amount of small fixes will be available in this new version, and lots of improvements are aiming to increase performance and battery life, as the most wanted *doze on the go*, that promises to be a game changer for Android devices.

Summary

In this chapter you learned how to effectively customize Android at different levels, following real-world examples. You now know how to programmatically create a custom ROM from source code, preparing a customized folder structure with every piece in place, ready to be assembled by Android's build system. You also know how to approach the customization task if you have an already-assembled system image, and how to customize and reassemble a binary image.

The next chapter will bring you *outside* the pure smartphone experience and will show you how Android is effectively becoming ubiquitous in our lives: Internet of Things, Android Auto and Android Wear, domotics, and entertainment are just a few of the scenarios in which we can currently find the *green droid*.

8
Beyond the Smartphone

In *Chapter 7, Tailoring Your Personal Android System*, you learned how to add the final personal touch to your custom Android system. You customized both the application layer and the system layer: new menus, new apps, and new daemons.

In this chapter, we are going even further: we are going *outside* the smartphone, connecting to external microcontrollers, sensors, and different devices. We will see how our whole world could be connected and interactive with Android.

You will learn about Android ADK and Arduino, and how Google is filling our lives with Android-oriented devices: from Chromecast devices to Android Auto, from smart watches to Internet of Things.

Meeting Arduino

More than ten years ago, in a bar in a small Italian town, a group of students and researchers created a low-cost microcontroller that would revolutionize the world of DIY (Do It Yourself) — **Arduino**, shown in the next image:

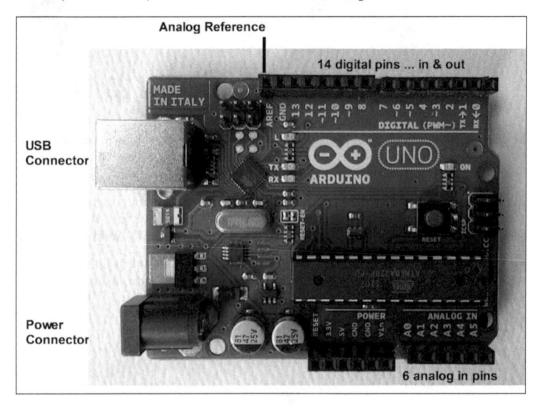

The latest version of Ardunio (or Genuino, for the non-USA market) is called Arduino **UNO**. **Uno** means *one* in Italian and this codename celebrates the first stable version of the IDE (Integrated Development Environment) that comes with the board itself. This board is based on ATmega328P by Atmel and provides a set of controllable input/output pins. It can work as a standalone microcontroller, once it has been properly programmed, and can be used via its USB connection.

The greatest feature of Arduino is its open nature: everything, from the hardware schematics to the development IDE, has been open source since day one. This openness, and the extensible design of the board, allowed manufactures and advanced users to create an infinite number of so-called **shields**:

An Arduino shield is a separate component that can be attached to Arduino to enhance it and to add new features. The previous image shows how Arduino shields can be stacked to create a totally new and customized device. Common examples of Arduino shields are:

- The Ethernet Shield, which gives Arduino the ability to communicate with the outside world via an Internet connection.

- The Proto Shield, which can be used to make a *permanent* version of a prototype that you created with a breadboard.

- The Relay Shield, which enables Arduino to pilot high-voltage circuits. This is crucial for home automation when you need to turn lights or appliances on and off.

- The Display Shield, which gives Arduino a visual way to communicate with the outside world.

Since Arduino came out, it has gained more and more fans and passionate developers, thanks to its easy interface and the extremely flat learning curve. Today, software developers without hardware or electronics knowledge can create projects that live outside their computers and can interact with the external world. To take advantage of these possibilities, in 2012 Google created the Android ADK.

Android ADK

Android Accessory Development Kit is the reference implementation for the Android Open Accessory device. At Google I/O, in 2012 Google provided Android Accessory Development Kits to developers and provided manufacturers with clear specifications for creating their own kit, external accessory devices for Android. One of these certified devices is the Arduino itself, but thanks to the open nature of the whole project, you could build a compatible device yourself.

Unfortunately, Android ADK never really *boomed* among developers. Of course, you can find lots of interesting projects on the web about connecting an Android smartphone to an Arduino, like the one by TCRobotics at `http://blog.bricogeek.com/noticias/arduino/el-adk-de-google-en-un-arduino-uno`. This is surely one of our favorites; it shows the great potential, but also the big sacrifice, of keeping an Android smartphone **wired** to a cable the whole time:

Luckily for us, there are much cooler ways to use Android ADK to play around with sensors and electronics.

Using UDOO as an all-in-one ADK device

As you already know, UDOO can run Android. What you probably don't know is that it comes with an Arduino on it. Yes, both Android and Arduino are on the same board! When you think that you can connect a touchscreen, or even a mouse and keyboard to UDOO, you soon start fantasizing about all those geeky projects of yours becoming reality.

Getting ready

To start playing with Arduino, you just need to set up UDOO and connect the Android part to the SAM3X (Arduino-compatible) part. The following images show an UDOO, as seen from above. On the left, jumper 18 is highlighted. This jumper must be unplugged to enable the SAM3X. On the right, the USB port you are going to connect to is highlighted as well:

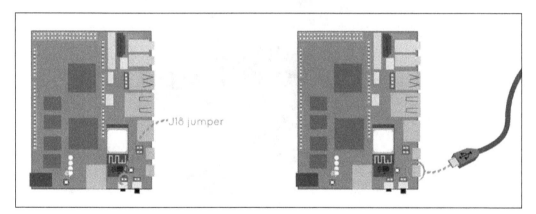

Once the board is ready, you can move to the software part.

Flashing the Arduino board

For this quick example, we are going to command an LED connected to the UDOO. The LED will be connected to input 13 of the UDOO board. Every LED has two pins; the longer one is the anode and has to be connected to input 13, and the shorter one is the cathode and has to be connected to ground, the unnumbered input on the left of input 13:

The electronics setup is in place. Let's download the Arduino IDE from http://www.udoo.org/other-resources/.

The first time you run the Arduino IDE, you will be presented with an empty project file:

This empty Arduino sketch gives you a skeleton structure for our Arduino program:

- A `setup` method that runs once and gets everything in place for the second method

- A `loop` method that keeps on running over and over until the board is turned off

To properly connect and program our Arduino, we need to select the board type and port. From the Arduino IDE Tools menu, select **Board | Arduino Due (Programming Port)**:

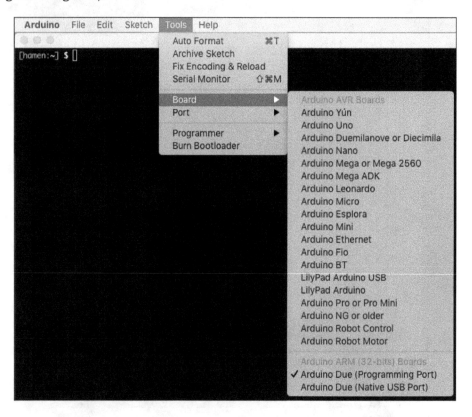

The previous image shows the amount of different Arduino boards that are available on the market nowadays. UDOO is compatible with the Arduino Due, so we are choosing that board model. Once we have selected the proper board, we need to select the **Port** to use to connect to the UDOO:

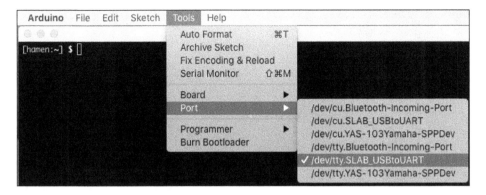

As you can see in the image, the port name could be slightly different on different computers. The previous image shows a common configuration for an Apple MacBook Pro.

Once the IDE has been properly configured, we can start with the source code, as follows:

```
#include "variant.h"
#include <stdio.h>
#include <adk.h>


#define   LED_PIN   13


// Accessory descriptor. It's how Arduino identifies itself to
Android.
char descriptionName[] = "ArduinoADK";
char modelName[] = "UDOO_ADK";              // Arduino Accessory name
(Need to be the same defined in the Android App)
char manufacturerName[] = "Packt";     // Manufacturer (Need to be
the same defined in the Android App)


char versionNumber[] = "1.0";             // version (Need to be
the same defined in the Android App)
char serialNumber[] = "1";
char url[] = "http://www.packtpub.com";     // If there isn't any
compatible app installed, Android suggest to visit this url


USBHost Usb;
ADK adk(&Usb, manufacturerName, modelName, descriptionName,
versionNumber, url, serialNumber);
```

```
#define RCVSIZE 128
uint8_t buf[RCVSIZE];
uint32_t bytesRead = 0;

void setup() {
    Serial.begin(115200);
    pinMode(LED_PIN, OUTPUT);
    delay(500);
    Serial.println("Starting...");
}

void loop() {
    Usb.Task();

    if (adk.isReady()) {
        adk.read(&bytesRead, RCVSIZE, buf);// read data into buf
variable
        if (bytesRead > 0) {
          if (parseCommand(buf[0]) == 1) {// compare received data
            // Received "1" - turn on LED
            digitalWrite(LED_PIN, HIGH);
          } else if (parseCommand(buf[0]) == 0) {
            // Received "0" - turn off LED
            digitalWrite(LED_PIN, LOW);
          }
        }
    } else {
      digitalWrite(LED_PIN , LOW); // turn off light
    }

    delay(10);
}

// the characters sent to Arduino are interpreted as ASCII, we
decrease 48 to return to ASCII range.
uint8_t parseCommand(uint8_t received) {
  return received - 48;
}
```

We can quickly analyze the source code and can find out that:

- We are specifying PIN number 13
- We are specifying the model name, manufacturer name, and version number that will identify our board once we connect it to Android

- We are configuring the serial connection
- We are listening for incoming data on the serial connection and reacting accordingly:
  - turn on the LED if we received 1
  - turn off the LED if we received 0

Once the source code is in place, you can flash it to the Arduino using the IDE **File** | **Upload** menu.

Creating the Android app

The Android app will be super simple: a toggle button to turn the LED ON and OFF. You can create the initial app using the Android Studio wizard, creating an empty `Activity` to get things started. Once the skeleton is in place, you need to add a new dependency to your `build.gradle`:

```
dependencies {
    compile 'me.palazzetti:adktoolkit:0.3.0'
}
```

Emanuele Palazzetti, author of *Getting started with UDOO* by *Packt Publishing*, released a handy Android library, ADK Toolkit (`https://github.com/palazzem/adk-toolkit`), for easier communication between your Android apps and your Android ADK device, and we are going to take full advantage of this library.

You need to add some specific configurations in your Android Manifest. In your `<activity>` tag, add the following lines:

```
<intent-filter>
  <action android:name="android.hardware.usb.action.USB_ACCESSORY_
ATTACHED"/>
</intent-filter>
<meta-data
  android:name="android.hardware.usb.action.USB_ACCESSORY_ATTACHED"
  android:resource="@xml/accessory_filter"/>
```

As you will have noted, the `<meta-data>` tag refers to an XML resource, named `accessory_filter`. Right now, it's missing. Let's create a `accessory_filter.xml` in the `src/res/xml/` folder:

```
<?xml version="1.0" encoding="utf-8"?>
<resources>
  <usb-accessory
    manufacturer="Packt"
    model="UDOO_ADK"
    version="1.0"/>
</resources>
```

This is the exact information we added to the Arduino sketch and will allow Android to properly identify our board.

Setup is over. Let's move on to the UI of our app. Having followed the wizard, you now have a single `Activity` with its own layout; chances are that its name is `main.xml` and it's located in `src/res/layout`. Once you have located the layout, we can add our button:

```
<ToggleButton
  android:id="@+id/toggleButtonLED"
  android:textOn="Turn OFF"
  android:textOff="Turn ON"
  android:layout_width="500dp"
  android:layout_height="200dp"
  android:layout_centerVertical="true"
  android:layout_centerHorizontal="true"
  android:textSize="50sp"
  android:onClick="blinkLED"/>
```

It's pretty straightforward: an ID, a couple of labels, and an `onClick` method to trigger when the button is tapped.

The method referred by the `onClick` will be placed into our `Activity`:

```
public void blinkLED(View v) {
    if (buttonLED.isChecked()) {
        adkManager.write("1");
    } else {
        adkManager.write("0");
    }
}
```

When the button is clicked, we send `1` if it's ON, or `0` if it's OFF. Fair enough, but where do we send this data? What's that `adkManager`?

The `adkManager` module comes with the ADK Toolkit. We create it and set it up in our `Activity`. This is the final result:

```
public class UDOOBlinkLEDActivity extends Activity {

    private ToggleButton buttonLED;
```

```
    private AdkManager adkManager;

    @Override
    public void onCreate(Bundle savedInstanceState) {
        super.onCreate(savedInstanceState);
        setContentView(R.layout.main);
        buttonLED = (ToggleButton) findViewById(R.id.toggleButtonLED);

        adkManager = new AdkManager(this);
        registerReceiver(adkManager.getUsbReceiver(),
adkManager.getDetachedFilter());
    }

    @Override
    public void onResume() {
        super.onResume();
        adkManager.open();
    }

    @Override
    public void onPause() {
        super.onPause();
        adkManager.close();
    }

    public void blinkLED(View v) {
        if (buttonLED.isChecked()) {
            adkManager.write("1");
        } else {
            adkManager.write("0");
        }
    }
}
```

Finally, our app is completed. Just upload it to our UDOO and you will have a huge button to turn your LED ON and OFF:

Exploring the possibilities of the Internet of Things

Knowing that your favorite OS can run on thousands of devices, in hundreds of different customizations, and communicate with any kind of device, both wired or wireless, opens up incredible possibilities.

Android Auto

In 2014, Google presented Android Auto, an innovative project that aims to command an Android system using the controls already available in our cars:

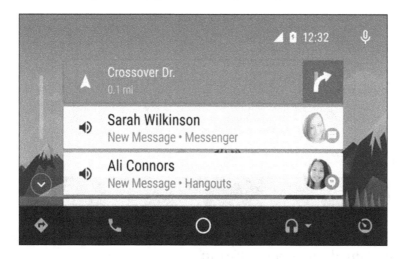

In 2015, the first version of Android Auto was released and the developer community started to really look into it. In 2016, dozens of car manufacturers are going to release models with integrated Android Auto support.

The idea behind Android Auto is to support driving safety and provide users with an alternative way to access their devices when they are driving. To achieve this goal, Google engineers worked with car manufacturers to create a bridge between our Android devices and car dashboards.

Car dashboards and controls represent the top of the user experience and interaction we can possibly have while driving. Everything is placed specifically to be accessible, everything is designed specifically to be easy to use, and everything is created to be effective and powerful, but not distracting.

These constraints forced Google to rethink their popular apps for this new challenge. When you connect your Android smartphone to an Android Auto-ready car, you can enjoy a different OS user interface, tailored for this particular scenario. The next image shows the Google Maps interface for Android Auto:

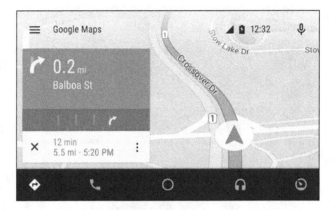

The next image shows the Google Play Music user interface, once we connect our device to an Android Auto-compatible car:

Popular apps such as Google Maps or Google Play Music evolve into a more effective design and take full advantage of the dashboard's bigger screen and wheel controls.

From a developer perspective, Android Auto comes with an obvious question:

Do I need a car to develop and test my apps?

Fortunately, Google provides testing tools for those who want to approach Android Auto: the **Desktop Head Unit** (**DHU**). Available with the Android SDK, the DHU runs on your computer and allows your computer to act as a car dashboard. The following images show how the smartphone switches to Android Auto mode and the UI switches to DHU:

The previous image is an example of how the smartphone display will look once we connect it to the car—it turns black and shows the Android Auto logo. The next image shows how the car dashboard becomes active when we connect the smartphone. The car dashboard turns into the Android Auto user interface and, in this example, shows a few Google Now cards, with traffic and weather information:

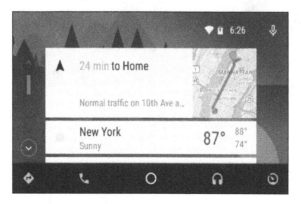

Android Wear

While we wait for Android Auto-enabled cars to invade our lives, we can direct our attention to Android Wear.

In 2014, Google announced a particular version of Android, specifically designed and developed for smart watches. Started as a customization of Android 5.0 Lollipop, Android Wear is currently based on Android 6.0.1 Marshmallow.

Android Wear aims to enhance the way users can interact with the world every day. An Android Wear smart watch connects to an Android smartphone and provides quicker access to notifications, messages, and every possible type of content that can be enjoyed in a better way without interacting with the smartphone itself:

Smart watches like the one in the previous picture provide integrations with dozens of services, such as Google Fit, Endomondo, and IFTTT. They have Bluetooth and Wi-Fi connectivity, GPS, and accelerometers. This huge range of possibilities pushed the Android community to experiment and create solutions for dozens of scenarios.

With the support of Android SDK and the Android community, in the last two years we have seen an increasing number of apps tailored for smart watches — we can turn on our Philips Hue lights with our watch, we can turn off our Google Nest with our watch, and we can know the state of our plants thanks to Parrot Flower Power.

Continuing on this path will take us straight to the next section.

Domotics

We are living in a world where lots of devices, appliances, and "things" that were *disconnected* are now part of a growing ecosystem of interconnected devices. We came from a past where computation could happen only in our computers — we are living in a present where computation happens in our pockets, with our smartphone. We are moving toward a future where computation will happen everywhere: a watch, a car, a drone, a house, a garden, and much more.

We had thermostats that had to be commanded manually and we have intelligent thermostats now, such as Google Nest, that learn from our habits and react accordingly to create a better and more effective user experience:

We had lights that needed a wall switch to be turned ON and OFF and now we have intelligent lights, such as Philips Hue, that can be controlled via smartphone or even smart watch. These lights can turn ON automatically the moment we approach our home, taking advantage of concepts such as geo-fencing. We have light that can interconnect with other devices, such as smart door bells, and can create a visual trigger for hearing-impaired users:

We have plant sensors, such as Parrot Flower Power, that can show a notification on our smartphone and let us know that our plants need water. Knowing that, even if we are thousands of kilometers away from home on some remote beach, enjoying our holidays, we can remotely command a Belkin WeMo Switch to turn on our irrigation system and water our plants.

We have smart refrigerators, such as the Samsung Family Hub, that are connected to the Internet and allow you to actually *see* inside your refrigerator to check whether the orange juice for tomorrow's breakfast is missing. They are becoming so interconnected that the Korean version will be aware of possible discounts for your favorite products and suggests which particular supermarket you have to check to save some money.

We have smart mirrors, such as the one by Hannah Mittelstaedt (`https://github.com/HannahMitt/HomeMirror`), which can be easily created with one of your old Android devices. Give your obsolete tablet a new life and a new purpose. It could give you weather forecast, the latest news, your plants' status, traffic information, or whatever useful information you would like to have while you are brushing your teeth in the morning.

We have smart coffee machines, such as the **Nespresso Prodigio**, that can give us the current status of the water level, coffee capsules remaining, and maintenance necessary. The coffee machines can be controlled remotely, from your couch, and for the first time in our history, the classic joke is not a joke anymore; our Android phone can actually make us a coffee!

Can a green droid entertain you?

Once humanity satisfied every basic need, it started fighting boredom!

Okay, probably that's too much drama, but we are entering the entertaining section, so let's talk about having some fun!

Multimedia

Entertainment is a huge market and Google jumped into it pretty quickly with its Nexus Player and its Chromecast devices:

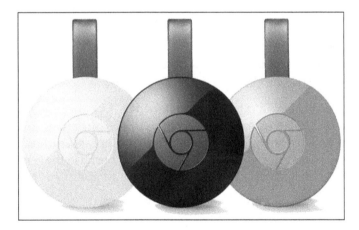

The previous image shows the latest model of Google Chromecast. When Google approached this market, they decided to provide users with a device that was as easy as possible to set up. Google Chromecast has one HDMI connector and a USB power cable; that's it. You connect the HDMI to your TV, connect the power supply, and your TV can now connect to your smart phone.

Your smartphone becomes your remote and, with a few clicks, you can start streaming any multimedia content you want, straight to your TV: your preferred YouTube channels, your preferred movies from Google Play Store, your music from Google Play Music and hundreds of third-party apps can be sources of content.

If you don't like TV and you are a music addict, Google has you covered with Chromecast Audio:

As for the Chromecast, Chromecast Audio is very easy to connect to your Hi-Fi system and it's easy to set up via the Chromecast app you can install on your Android smartphone.

One of the key features is that it has a standalone Wi-Fi connection via your home Wi-Fi system, so that it can be instructed to reproduce your music instead of requiring your phone to stream the music to the Chromecast Audio. You control it using your smartphone, but there is no battery drain, because there is no persistent Wi-Fi or Bluetooth connection between your phone and your Chromecast Audio.

Toys

Nowadays, when we think about Android-powered toys, we can only think about drones!

The first and most popular, the Parrot ARDrone in the previous picture, set the bar and drove the market for quite a while. Over time, lots of commercial alternatives showed up, but, as with the smart mirror, the RC toys community also went full Do-It-Yourself.

During Droidcon Turin 2015 Hackaton, we demonstrated how you could build an RC car, powered by UDOO, controlled via Wi-Fi using an Android device… in 24 hours: `https://www.hackster.io/team-dronix-alter-ego/dronixcar-37b81a?f=1#`:

The RC car was equipped with a video camera, streaming in real time to the smartphone. The smartphone acted as video consumer and remote controller.

The whole project was released as open source, in the classic Android/Linux tradition.

Summary

Our journey is over! It's been quite a rollercoaster, from the history of the operating system to how it can equip devices ready to communicate with the external world. You learned how to retrieve the source code for your devices, how to navigate the source folder tree, and how to create the perfect setup to properly build a vanilla Android system.

You stepped up and started to add customizations to your system, to enrich the user experience, to improve the performance, and to add support for your own hardware. You went deep into the boot sequence's inner structure to customize the system even more. You swam back to the surface to customize the highest part of the architecture pyramid, the user interface, to provide your users with the ultimate customized Android system.

Finally, you saw how easy it is to step away from the Android device itself and find a whole world of devices waiting to communicate and interact, powered by the awesome Android platform.

Our journey is over, but your own has just started! Master what you learned, experiment, try out your ideas, fail, learn more, try again, and finally succeed!

Android is an awesome tool; you can use it to make your craziest ideas become a reality!

Index

H

hardware
 selecting 99, 100
hardware architectures
 about 100
 requisites 100
hexadecimal editor 180
HomeMirror
 reference link 250
host system
 hardware requisites 56
 preparing 55, 56, 130
 software requisites 56, 57
HTC Sense 166, 167
Huawei EMUI 165

I

image
 recreating 73
incremental OTA 193
Init process 147
Internet of Things
 possibilities, exploring 244
I/O schedulers
 anticipatory 225
 BFQ 225
 CFQ 225
 deadline 225
 noop 224
 ROW 225
 SIO 225

J

Java Native Interface (JNI) semantics 10
Just-In-Time compilation 12

K

kernel
 about 147
 binary version, retrieving of 126, 127
 compiling 134
 configuring 131-134

obtaining 125, 126
source code, obtaining 127, 128

L

legacy devices 157
LG Optimus UI
 about 168
 vocal command feature 168
libraries, Android system
 libc 5
 Media Framework 5
 OpenGL 5
 SGL 5
 SQLite 5
 SSL 5
 Surface manager 5
 WebKit 5
Linaro toolchain
 download link 129
Linux kernel 123-125
LOCAL_ variables, Android.mk variables
 LOCAL_CC 78
 LOCAL_CFLAGS 79
 LOCAL_C_INCLUDE 79
 LOCAL_CPP_EXTENSION 79
 LOCAL_CPPFLAGS 79
 LOCAL_CXX 78
 LOCAL_LDFLAGS 79
 LOCAL_MODULE 78
 LOCAL_MODULE_CLASS 78
 LOCAL_MODULE_PATH 78
 LOCAL_MODULE_TAGS 78
 LOCAL_PACKAGE_NAME 78
 LOCAL_PATH 78
 LOCAL_PREBUILT_EXECUTABLES 79
 LOCAL_PREBUILT_LIBS 79
 LOCAL_PREBUILT_PACKAGE 79
 LOCAL_SHARED_LIBRARIES 78
 LOCAL_SRC_FILES 78
logcat 95, 96
logging buffers
 events 95
 radio 95
lunch command 65, 70, 71

S

shared library template 80
shields 232
SoC 101, 102
software requisites, host system
  Java JDK, installing 57, 58
  system dependencies, installing 58, 59
source.android.com
  reference link 53
source code
  about 42-45
  downloading 45
  reference link 42
  working with 46-48
source code tools
  about 37
  Git 38
  Repo 38
standard Linux kernel, governors
  conservative 222
  interactive 222
  on-demand 221
  performance 222
  powersave 222
  userspace 222
SuperSu
  about 177
  reference 177
System-on-chip. *See* SoC
system partitions
  dumping 183-185
system performance enhancement
  about 218
  custom init sequence, adding 220
  system property file, customizing 218, 219

T

TARGET_BUILD_TYPE variable 69
TARGET_BUILD_VARIANT variable 68
TARGET_PREBUILT_KERNEL variable 69
TARGET_PRODUCT variable 67, 68
TARGET_TOOLS_PREFIX variable 69
Team Win Recovery Project (TWRP)
  about 175
  reference 175

toolchain
  obtaining 130
  setting up 129
TouchWiz 164
traces 14

U

UDOO
  Android app, creating 241-244
  Arduino board, flashing 236-240
  used, all-in-one ADK device 235
UDOO family boards 115, 116
UDOO Quad
  about 104, 109
  bootloader, compiling 110
  kernel, building 112
  setup 110
  system image build process, launching 111
  technical specifications 105
  URL, for source code 109

V

variables, Android build system
  buildspec.mk file 69
  lunch command 70, 71
  OUT_DIR variable 69
  TARGET_BUILD_TYPE variable 69
  TARGET_BUILD_VARIANT variable 68
  TARGET_PREBUILT_KERNEL variable 69
  TARGET_PRODUCT variable 67, 68
  TARGET_TOOLS_PREFIX variable 69
versions, Cyanogenmod
  experimental 160
  M Snapshot 160
  nightly 160
  Release Candidate 160
  stable 160

X

Xiaomi MIUI 168, 169

www.ingramcontent.com/pod-product-compliance
Lightning Source LLC
Chambersburg PA
CBHW060526060326
40690CB00017B/3398